Texts, Rocks, and Talk

.

Reclaiming Biblical Christianity to Counterimagine the World

John R. Lanci

A Michael Glazier Book

THE LITURGICAL PRESS
Collegeville, Minnesota

www.litpress.org

A Michael Glazier Book published by The Liturgical Press

Cover design by David Manahan, O.S.B. Photo courtesy of John R. Lanci.

1   2   3   4   5   6   7   8

Library of Congress Cataloging-in-Publication Data

Lanci, John R., 1948–
    Texts, rocks, and talk : reclaiming biblical Christianity to counterimagine the world / John R. Lanci.
        p.   cm.
    "A Michael Glazier book."
    Includes bibliographical references (p.) and index.
    ISBN 0-8146-5883-0 (alk. paper)
    1. Bible—Evidences, authority, etc.—Textbooks.   2. Bible. O.T. Song of Solomon—Evidences, authority, etc.—Textbooks.   3. Bible. N.T. Corinthians, 1st—Evidences, authority, etc.—Textbooks.   I. Title.

BS480.L34   2002
220.6'1—dc21
                                                    2002072900

**For Yvonne Gigliotti and Terri Mackey
and in memory of Marian Bloch Fox**

*There were no formerly heroic times, and there was no formerly pure
generation. There is no one here but us chickens, and so it has always
been: a people busy and powerful, knowledgeable, ambivalent, important,
fearful and self-aware; a people who scheme, promote, deceive, and
conquer; who pray for their loved ones, and long to flee misery and skip
death. It is a weakening and discoloring idea, that rustic people knew God
personally once upon a time—or even knew selflessness or courage or
literature—but that it is too late for us. In fact, the absolute is available
to everyone in every age. There never was a more holy age than ours, and
never a less.*

Annie Dillard,
–For the Time Being

Contents

Introduction

Allow me to begin with a curmudgeonly judgment: there is something very wrong with the way most people are being introduced to Christianity in our time. The fundamental problem with Christianity today is that too many Christians encounter the rules and regulations but miss the best part of what the religion has to offer: an encounter with the living God.

The first Christians didn't come together simply because they liked the value system promulgated by St. Paul and other missionaries. No, the Christian communities that flourished early and lasted through time were those that offered a lively experience of the risen Christ. Christ was not a fond memory; Christ was alive and in their midst when they gathered for prayer. Christ was with them when they rose in the morning and retired at night, in good times and in bad. The first followers of Jesus turned their backs on venerable family traditions, not because Christianity was self-evidently superior to other religions, but because, apparently, the Jesus movement offered an experience of community lived in Christ, an experience of life that was more fulfilling than the life they already possessed.

For the first Christians, the Good News was still good.

As we enter the twenty-first century, what does it mean, this "good news" of Jesus Christ? Adherence to rules? Knee-jerk acceptance of religious authority? Denunciation of sinners? Doing what we're told to avoid hell and go to heaven when we die?

The news these days doesn't look so good.

From the first chapters of Genesis, in which the Creator God walks in the cool of a garden evening, to the books of the New Testament, in which the Word made flesh eats and drinks and talks and knocks Paul off his high horse in a flash of revelatory light, Scripture presents a world in which God and God's Spirit and God's Son cohabit with the human community. It is a world created good and a world, once fallen, that is redeemed. To follow in the steps of Jesus Christ is not at its essence the intellectual acceptance of a set of beliefs, though creeds—recitations of religious truth statements—hold a place of prominence in Christian tradition.

No, at its essence Christianity developed out of a series of human encounters with the divine, and it is sustained today by people who know that God's Spirit moves in every nook and cranny of ordinary human experience. Christians at their best see life as an ongoing conversation (important word!) between God and God's creation. Christians at their best foster an inclusive, generous community dedicated to justice and the right to a full and graced life in this world for everyone, not just believers. At their best, Christians understand that the earth is still a garden, a cherished site of miracles no less impressive than those accomplished by Jesus in ancient Palestine.

Conversation with God. The arena for such a conversation is the believing community in the world today. And the primary means by which that conversation takes place is the Bible.

Hence this book. We need to address the inability on the part of many Christians to experience their God, to encounter the risen Christ in their lives. One way to do this is to address the lack of confidence on the part of many Christians when it comes to reading and interpreting the Bible. I invite you on a journey (another important word!). Our object is a new understanding of the Bible, one that recognizes Scripture as a powerful source of conversation between God and what God created: you and me.

Let the buyer beware: in each section you will not just sit back and passively observe. We are going on a *journey* together. Let me try that again: we are going on a journey *together*. I want to lure you into an experience of the Bible. I'm speaking of the difference between reading an introduction to the Bible in the quiet safety of your room and plunging into the fire of robust and perhaps dangerous encounters with the Bible—dangerous because they may lead you to think about some things you would rather avoid.

Another caveat: many Christian communities recognize not one but three vehicles through which God communicates with people. *Scripture* is the most important of the three sources of divine revelation, but many people find the other two no less valuable, namely, *tradition,* the Church's perpetual reflection on the original Christ-event, and *creation,* that is, our observation of the natural order of things. Our subject will be limited to the first source of revelation, but it would be equally imprudent for the reader to discount or diminish the importance of tradition and creation as parts of the overall journey and conversation of the Christian. If this experiment works the way I intend it to, you will come away from this book with a deeper understanding of the need to interpret sacred texts and greater confidence in your ability to enter into the conversation that these texts provide. You will also, I hope, be motivated to explore the ways that your Christian community (if you have one) can open itself up to the wider divine conversation available in Christian tradition and the created world around us.

The texture of the writing may at first appear unusual or even off-putting to those accustomed to reading books about important subjects. The informality of the prose will sometimes approach the level of slang. I will repeatedly commit the scholarly writer's cardinal sin ("Thou shalt not refer to thyself in the first person!"), elbowing my way onto the page and referring to myself as "I." For the scholarly purist, it gets worse: at the beginning I'll be doing most of the talking, but as the journey continues, the book will increasingly assume the characteristics of a discourse among a group of friends. I've rendered the dialogue as best I can, but I beg the reader's indulgence; I'm trained as a biblical scholar and have no pretensions about my future as a screenwriter or a novelist.

[handwritten margin note: —I like how this is said!]

As for the organization: students sometimes complain that I'm not a very organized teacher, that we set up a nice syllabus but then I allow class discussion to wander off into numerous digressions. That is actually a conscious choice. Sometimes discussion needs to go where it goes if it's to make a difference to the conversation partners. This book will be a bit of a trial for those who prefer clean design and tight organization, for it's grown out of several decades of encounters with students, and I've tried to emulate the rough-and-tumble feel of many of those discussions, which have been personal and quirky, and rarely neat, controlled, or comprehensive.

There is method to this stylistic and organizational madness. As I said earlier, the Bible is an invitation to conversation. If, as I've suggested, many Christians have grown deaf to this ancient and venerable exchange, or never been told that it exists, what better way to introduce them to the Word's communicative potential than by seducing them into reading a book that attempts to model this discourse?

Of course, the archetype of conversation on a long journey is not a new one. It's been the ritual of choice for centuries of pilgrims. As you read this, you might, or might not, consider yourself as a sort of pilgrim, but in any case don't think of yourself as sitting in a classroom. Instead, imagine us as partners on a grand excursion. We'll poke our heads into hot, dry caves in Israel and scan the ruins of an ancient Greco-Roman city. Once or twice we'll shiver in the cold of underheated university libraries in the dead of winter, but we'll also wander through fields of thistles blanched by the Mediterranean sun and quench our thirst at a *taverna* in rural Greece. In addition, we will periodically walk a tightrope over the great abyss of received scholarship and assumed Church positions, both of which will threaten to swallow us up if we aren't careful.

If you are to trust me as your guide and your main conversation partner, you need to know something about my own religious presuppositions. I am a Christian, a Roman Catholic, comfortable in the tradition I've received from my forebears. In what follows I'll be assuming that you, too, believe in God. You may or may not fit well into a Christian community, though I will assume that you are open to such an experience. I do not assume that you are religiously comfortable or a Catholic. My goal is not to convert you to my beliefs; this book isn't a catechism. Think of it as a hard piece of flint against which your mind may spark and your heart catch fire.

If this experiment works and you hang in there to the end, you'll know more about how to study the Bible (and why you should). You might even find yourself pulling together the provisions necessary for further journeys—alone or with others and through fire if necessary—that will move us all a bit closer to new visions of Christian community.

You might even begin to counterimagine your part of the world.

What follows is the result of conversations with many people: Brian Marcotte, Ed Neukrug, Pam Marino, Jane Handshy, Yvonne Gigliotti, Erika Schluntz, Terri Mackey, Marjorie Paul, John Schneider, and Liane Sirois, many of whom read early versions of parts of the text. Yvonne, Marjorie, and Ted Crane lent their names to this project, but the characters who appear here hardly resemble my three friends, except perhaps for a couple of minor idiosyncrasies. A grant from the National Endowment for the Humanities dispatched me to Corinth and Isthmia in 1994 for six weeks of instruction in dirt archaeology under the direction of Timothy Gregory and Richard Rothaus. Stonehill College provided numerous summer grants and a sabbatical; a special blessing upon Stonehill's library staff, particularly Regina Egan, queen of the interlibrary loan division and Wendy Hannawalt, who compiled the index. My friend Bernadette Brooten introduced me to Linda Maloney, editor at The Liturgical Press, who became the wise and patient godmother of this book; her commitment to God and God's people has deepened my own. I owe a debt of gratitude to many fine students at Stonehill College, especially Jenn Borden and Kevin Minoli, who developed the informal style of writing for an earlier collaboration that evolved into the conversational tone found here. Finally, I salute the women and men of the Congregation of Holy Cross, once my sisters and brothers, always my friends. "Resurrection for us is a daily event," their constitutions proclaim. Thirty years ago they invited me on the resurrection road and taught my heart to burn with love.

Chapter One

Why Take It on the Road?

The nervous laughter fades and the five of us settle into the silence of my office on campus. Jeremy stirs after a moment. He is a senior at our college, a criminal justice major, serious, quiet, dark of hair and eyes and mood.

"So," he says, "why are we here?"

The others shift in their seats and look in my direction. I've invited these four people to this meeting because each of them has accosted me in recent weeks with a question or perceptive comment about religion. This is not surprising, since I am a professor in the religious studies department, and I have enjoyed the company of each of them in at least one seminar. As it happens, I'm looking for recruits to embark on the journey I have been mulling over in the back of my mind for several years.

"What kind of journey?" Marjorie asks.

Why do *you* think you're here?

"It has to do with our conversation last week, right?" she says. "I brought the newspaper clipping that I showed you. It still bothers me."

Marj rummages through her backpack and finds the article from the *Boston Globe,* which reads in part:

> Paul Hill, who was sentenced to death for the shotgun slayings of an abortion doctor and his bodyguard, said yesterday that he is worth more to his cause dead and hopes he is executed. . . . Asked if his actions might incite other anti-abortion activists to violence, he replied: "Indubitably."

"This guy is a former minister," she says.

"That's gross," Thad says.

"It gets grosser," Marj says and she returns to the article. "Asked if Jesus Christ would have pulled the trigger, he said: "Absolutely.""

She folds the clipping and puts it back in her notebook. "I came here to ask how anyone who professes to be a Christian could say such a thing."

"I hear you," Thad says. "I was here last week, too, and my question was similar to yours."

"What was it?" she asks.

"Why the hell bother being religious at all?" Thad says. "Spirits? Angels? Heaven and hell? I mean, come on!"

He pauses. "Science and philosophy disproved this stuff centuries ago. What is religion nowadays? What's left?"

He pauses again. "Religion is bigots like Pat Robertson saying God's going to strike Orlando with a major hurricane because an amusement park decides it's OK to hire gays and lesbians."

Jeremy smirks and shakes his head. "It wasn't that," he says. "Pat Robertson condemned the place for hosting 'Gay and Lesbian Day.'"

"Whatever."

"Gay and Lesbian Day?" Jeremy says. "It's supposed to be a family place."

"Homophobia. Right-wing politics. Universal access to guns," Thad says. "This is religion?"

"I agree," Marj says. "Maybe organized religion's time has passed."

Jeremy is not pleased.

"What are you shaking your head about?" Thad asks him. "You told me you were here last week, too, right? Care to tell the folks what you talked about?"

Jeremy pauses but then says, "You know I'm not Catholic. This is a Catholic school. I knew that when I came here, and I don't make any excuses for being here. I was hoping to learn more about another kind of Christianity. I grew up Evangelical and Pentecostal." He passes his hand through his dark, slicked-back hair. "But man, I'm blown away . . . ."

"What does that mean?" Marj asks. He looks over at me for assurance that he can be frank.

"You people are all Catholic and I mean no disrespect," he says. "But are you folks *Christian*? I mean, no one around here seems to know anything about the Bible or how God commanded us to live. Students dress like sluts and studs— sorry." This last is directed to our fourth partner, Yvonne, as well as to me.

"You know what I mean," he continues. "Co-ed dorms. Everyone drinks on the weekends. Hooking up—"

"Hooking up?" Yvonne turns to me. "Back in the old days it was called a 'one-night stand.'"

"People don't think twice about stealing a book or cheating on exams. This"—he raises his voice now—"this is what it means to be Catholic? And then there's the pope and the way Catholics worship him as if he was God."

"We don't worship the pope," Yvonne says, and I know that Jeremy wants to retort "Could've fooled me!" but he won't, since he was raised to respect his elders.

I ask Yvonne to say a bit about my conversation with her. We first encountered each other as part of an introductory course on the New Testament taught over a series of winter evenings a few years ago. She was a bright and highly motivated older student, a woman pursuing her bachelor's degree while working full time and raising a family. We'd met for lunch a few days ago at her request. Her problem was that of a teenager's mom.

"I've been a believing Catholic all my life," she said. "Went to Catholic schools, learned the catechism. I want my kids to be Catholics too," she sighed. "But my daughter Paula refuses to go to church with the rest of us."

She paused. "She asks me why she should go. I don't know what to tell her." Another pause. "It makes me squirm inside that I don't have an answer for her."

Yvonne was back in the office now, doing a bit more squirming. She is not a naturally gregarious woman and was in the awkward position of being old enough to be the mother of the other three students while at the same time functioning as their peer in class and in this conversation.

"Why do *you* go to Mass?" Marj asks her.

She stares into Marj's eyes. "I'm not sure," she says. "I go because I want to, not because I have to. I never had to be forced to go to Mass. I love it. I go to be quiet with God. To think about the week. To pray for my family."

"Why should your daughter go if she doesn't want to?" Thad asks. "If she's a good person, she doesn't have to go to church."

"I don't believe that," Yvonne says and then falters. "But I, well, I'm not a word person. I don't know how to explain what I mean."

I am a word person, and I intervene by handing out an early version of what will become the introduction to this book. They take a few minutes to read it while I listen to a bunch of crows chattering around the dumpster at the edge of the parking lot. It's early spring, but already you can feel heat in the air. It's going to be a very warm summer.

They look up and I invite them, as I have invited you, on a journey of conversation to uncover the power of the Bible.

The Power of the Bible?

Four people with big questions:

- How can a murderer like Paul Hill call himself Christian? Is Christianity today doomed to be associated with right-wing politics and gun-toting fanaticism?
- Has modernity rendered religion obsolete? Has science blown religious truth claims out of the water?

- Where do we discover the authority we need to live a Christian life? Are we to follow the rules and do what we're told? Or do we find the truth within? Do we really need to go to church?
- If we are observant Christians, *why* do we go to church? What does it mean to be a Christian?

A variety of problems for which there are no doubt a variety of possible remedies. Better religious education, more prayer, trained Christian counselors, or perhaps anger management seminars come to mind. As does the Bible.

While it will not of itself disclose one-size-fits-all answers to my friends' questions, I suggest that the Bible offers a way of enlightenment for those who know how to read it. And yet, the power of the Bible to which I refer, the power to guide and transform people's lives, has gone largely unnoticed and untapped by most modern Christians.

Hence my invitation to hit the road.

This road can unleash the power of Scripture to confront us and challenge us, to touch us at the very depths of our souls. That's what Scripture does, or can do, if we let it.

"I guess I need more information," Marj says and brings me back down to earth. "What do you mean by unleashing the power of the Bible?"

I borrow the term from Stanley Hauerwas, whom we will meet along the way. He suggests that the power of biblical texts has remained unleashed in America because people don't know what to make of Scripture. As a result they box both the Bible and its divine source into little, controlled spheres of influence.

"So he thinks—you think—people are ignorant of the Bible?" Marj says.

Yes, but their lack of facility with Scripture transcends the fact that so many Christians don't know how to find Isaiah's haunting prophecies of a just God or are completely unaware of Junia, the female apostle.

"What?" Yvonne says with a start. "There were women apostles?"

At least Paul thought so. Take a look at Romans 16:7 (this means chapter 16, verse 7 of Paul's Letter to the Romans).

Of course, most of us could use more information about the Bible, but information about Holy Scripture is not enough. Even if you know your Bible and can cite it by chapter and verse, you may still be unaware of the nature of the passage you quote. The Bible is a sacred text, not merely a rule book or a flat, straightforward account of historical facts. Sacred texts are not like other texts, but most of us are unaware of their unique character, and therefore we are oblivious to their potential to transform the reader. As a result, Christians drift away from Scripture and, I suggest, from the *experience* that is at the essence of Christianity.

What does it mean for a text to be sacred within the context of a living, believing community? In a communal context sacred texts don't sit bound in a book on a podium next to an altar. When the community comes together, sacred texts are unbound. They talk to us; they invite us into a continuous conversation. In this context, as we shall see, they are living and active, part of a conversation. They are, in fact, the primary way in which God maintains communication with God's people. Our sacred texts are not just something written down two or three thousand years ago. They are timeless; in every age they speak to us in new ways. In other words, Scripture is relational; it sets up and maintains a relationship between the divine and the believing community.

This is the starting point of our adventure: jettison any notion that the Bible is a book on a shelf to which we can go for set answers (flip open the book, find the relevant passage, solve the problem). It's not that easy. No, this sacred book, the Word as a living presence in our midst, is God's ongoing revelation: the Divine continues to make itself manifest and alive in our midst through these texts.

Despite herself, Yvonne has MEGO written all over her face.

"Mego?" she asks.

"My Eyes Glaze Over," Thad supplies.

She sighs. "This does seem a bit overwhelming."

"And a bit abstract," Marj says. "How exactly does one go on this journey of yours if, as I think you're saying, it involves more than just sitting down and learning a bunch of facts about the Bible?"

Think about the Bible not as the subject of a course but as an invitation to an experience.

"An experience," Marj says. "That's still too vague."

I retrieve a notebook from my desk.

Here's what I have in mind. We can access this new experience of the Bible by setting out on a journey comprised of three movements. In the first, which I call "Texts," we will explore the ancient written word, the text of what we call sacred Scripture. Lots of people find the Bible hard to read; they can figure out the words, but they often still don't really know what it *means* for them as they live their daily lives. By the time we're done we will have looked at just that problem. In this first section we'll learn about how the Christian Churches read the text of the Bible. What are some of the tools they use on words written thousands of years ago so that these old texts might have meaning for people today?

From textual analysis we move to "Rocks." Here we will learn about the social and cultural worlds out of which biblical texts arose. We'll wander through the world of ancient Judaism and encounter the might and power of Rome.

"Why call it 'Rocks'?" Thad asks.

Because the study of ancient rubble will provide our entry into the social world of antiquity. Here is where we will experience what misguided people call the "romance of archaeology." Our goal in this section will be to try to place some texts from Scripture within their original context.

We'll go through each of these two movements twice—once with a text from the Hebrew Bible (the Song of Songs) and once with one from the New Testament (Paul's First Letter to the Corinthians).

"We aren't going to study the Gospels?" Yvonne asks. "What about Jesus?"

No, we aren't going to introduce ourselves to a Gospel. The reason is practical: to study a Gospel would put us into a much longer and far more complex journey than the one I have in mind. Consider this a preliminary journey. Before we move into Gospel-land, we have a more basic road to travel.

"So how can it be Bible study if there's no contact with Jesus?" Yvonne asks.

Oh, we'll encounter Jesus. We just won't do it by reading a Gospel. Instead, we'll find him in the last stretch of our journey: "Talk." This is where we bring Texts and Rocks together. Here we will discuss what makes a sacred text sacred and turn the focus of our inquiry to the idea that God has always worked through the lives of ordinary people, calling them into an experience of conversation. How is it that the Bible is a point of conversation between God and humanity? How can I as an individual read the Bible with more confidence and more spiritual profit? But also, how can we as a community hear the Spirit of God at work in our midst?

"And Jesus?" Yvonne doggedly asks.

Jesus? We won't just read about him as we would in the Gospels, my friend. We'll have an opportunity to *meet* him.

Chapter Two

What the Bible Is Not

Right from the start we face a big question: What *is* the Bible? For believers it is the Word of God. But for those of us on this particular journey, even believing Christians, that doesn't really answer the question. *How* is it the Word of God? Where did it come from? How did it come about? Before we get too far down the road, we have to delve into the origins of biblical texts.

Take a look at the opening pages of your Bible, the first two chapters of the book of Genesis. Most of us know the story of God's creation of the world, but few of us have probably read the account in Genesis very closely. Let's do it now. Take a minute or two and read chapters one and two carefully. (Don't even *think* of starting this trip without a Bible close at hand!) As you read, make a note of anything that surprises you.

Welcome back! So, what did you see? Certainly you noticed the central position God plays in the six days of creation and the seventh day of rest. The dome of water, the birds of the air, the plants, the formation of the first man and woman. Did anything surprise you as you read? Did you notice, for instance, that God creates light a few days before producing the sun, the source of all natural earthly light? God, of course, can do whatever God wants to do, but this is a warning that the literalists in our midst may be headed for some trouble.

Did you notice that there are actually *two* creation stories, that God creates the world in chapter one and then does it again in chapter two? And did you observe that people are created differently in each account? In Genesis 1:26-27, God produces all humanity, both male and female, at the same time, while in Genesis 2:18-25 the two genders develop in slightly more elaborate fashion. At first glance it appears that the masculine human unit, a guy named Adam, is created first, while the female, later named Eve, arises from the male almost as an afterthought or a concession on God's part. But first glances can be deceiving. "Adam" here is not a personal name, like Sebastian or Guinevere, but a play on words in the Hebrew; it means "ruddy" or "earth" (as in "the dust of the earth," to which we all return), and it functions in the story's original language as the word for all humankind, not just males. In this situation, is the male created first? Or is the Adam-unit genderless until a part of it is spun off? The details are not clear.

If you managed to let your mind range freely as you read, I'll bet other questions came to mind. How does anyone really know what happened when God created the world? Who would have been there to take notes for posterity? If no one was there—and of course no one was—how did this information get passed down to us? Ancient Jewish and Christian traditions tell us that Moses wrote the Pentateuch, the first five books of the Bible. According to the book of Exodus, Moses had direct access to God, so perhaps God filled him in on a day when they weren't hammering out the Ten Commandments.

But here is the crux of our problem. If Moses got the story directly from God, why are there two creation accounts? And why are they different? And wouldn't God have gotten right the part about the sun being the source of light? Indeed, if you read the rest of the Pentateuch closely (this can be rough riding and will not be part of your homework for this assignment), you will discover numerous inconsistencies and impossibilities. How can we explain them if what we have is a factual account delivered by God to Moses serving as the first reporter assigned to a religion beat?

Yvonne has arrived and overheard us.

"The Spirit of God wrote the book," she says. "God inspired Moses."

But why did God inspire Moses to make mistakes?

Yvonne smiles and shakes her head (Yvonne's smile lights up rooms like God's sun, and as the mother of three daughters, she has shaken that head a lot).

"Don't be silly," Marj says, following Yvonne into the room. "What's most important about the Bible? The details or the deeper meaning?"

Ah, there is the solution to our problem. We only have a difficulty here if we insist that the Genesis story is a literally true and factual account and that it should be read as though it were the front page of the *New York Times*. But do we want to read the Bible in the same way we peruse a newspaper? Is that why people value so highly this set of writings that composes the Bible? Why *do* they read it?

The question of motivation here is very important. You might be reading the Bible right now as part of a college religion course in preparation for a test. The fruit of your labors will be a grade, and you will read the biblical text in somewhat the same way you would read the *Times,* focusing on the surface facts presented and asking the reporter's questions: who, where, when, what, and why? However, if you encounter the Bible as one text among many in a class on great works of literature, or if you read it as a member of a Bible study group at your church, intent on reexamining your religious experience, your goal will be different. Reading the book of Exodus, for instance, you'll want more than a recitation of precisely what happened to a bunch of stiff-necked peasants in the Egyptian desert thousands of years ago. Would your main question be "Did this really happen?" Of course not. You'd be looking for answers of a different sort, such as "What does the flight out of Egypt have to do with my personal current spiritual growth?"

As we saw in the Introduction, to discern the living role that Scripture plays for Christians and their faith communities we have to do more than just determine exactly what happened in days gone by. We need to see if we can understand the meaning of what happened, its significance for communities of God-followers then and now. To do this, we do try to figure out what might have happened historically, but that is only one level of biblical analysis for religious communities, and a surface one at that, for the Bible offers more than information. It offers a way of transformation.

We will investigate the distinction between information and transformation more fully later in our journey, where we will discuss in detail how the Bible functions in the conversation between believers and God. But as we begin our excursion and approach the biblical text as though for the first time, we need to understand something fundamentally important about the language of biblical texts and, indeed, about language in general.

Language Steno and Tensive

Theologians David R. Ord and Robert B. Coote describe two forms of written communication as steno and tensive language. Steno speech is the language of scientists and others who trade in facts and definitions. In this type of text a particular word or phrase stands for one particular thing. We find steno language in newspaper accounts, computer manuals, and traffic regulations, and it needs no interpretation. The S T O P on the red octagonal sign at the corner of your street is not there as an image to be deciphered by motorists. It means, quite simply, what it says: "Come to a complete stop before you move on."

Tensive language, on the other hand, is used in such a way as to create tension; it is the medium of symbol and metaphor. This is the medium of the artist, the poet, the storyteller. A good poem or novel can be read over and over, and each time the reader will discover something new. The tension arises from this fact: the observer cannot quite ever exhaust the material of its possibilities. The fullness of its meaning always just eludes the person beholding it.

For example, take a look again at Genesis. In Genesis 1:27, we read that

> God created humankind in his image,
> in the image of God he created him;
> male and female he created them.

What does it mean for people to have been created in God's image? If this text is written in steno language, it says exactly what it means: we look like God. Conversely, God looks like us. Thus we could draw from this passage a sense that of all creatures on the earth we are the only ones who look like God. But wait! We don't all look alike. Does God look like my grandfather or like my infant goddaughter? Is God male or female? What race or color is God? What about people who are born without the full use of all their limbs? Were they made in the image of God?

Thad steps up to the plate. "This talk about what God looks like," he says, "is beside the point."

Exactly. As far as I know there are no descriptions of precisely what God looks like in the Bible. The images of God that many of us grew up with—the Creator as a robust old man with a big white beard in flowing robes—come from sources other than Scripture. The God of the Bible does make an appearance on occasion to talk to people like Moses and Jesus, but on the whole God is portrayed as unportrayable. Here we would do well to heed the insights of our Muslim sisters and brothers who tell us decisively that we should not conceive of God in human terms. But how, then, are we created in God's image? Go back to the text one more time, reading its words as tensive language. How does Genesis 1–2 portray God?

"God is a creator," Thad says.

Yes. So what? Say more!

"We are made in the image and likeness of an entity that at its very essence creates."

Yes. According to Genesis this is our meaning and our purpose at its essence: to continue the creation that God has begun. Do you see the difference between a surface, steno interpretation (our bodies look like God) and the richer and more involving tensive approach to Genesis, in which we are commissioned to join God in an energetic life of creativity? Every human can identify with such a God. Our elders create a community of wisdom. A child's wonder can rejuvenate for a moment a passerby's troubled soul or coax a purr from a kitten; even an infant can create joy in the heart by flashing a smile as her poppa walks in the door after a difficult day at work.

Tensive language is innately more of a challenge to us, more interesting to us than steno language, for it engages us more deeply. We toss yesterday's paper into the recycling bin, but we save a book of poetry or a favorite novel because even after we've read it we think, well, if I get a chance, I want to take another look at that text; I'm not sure I really got out of it all that I might have.

Although the Bible contains many different genres, or styles of writing, communities of believers have traditionally read it as a series of tensive texts. If we peruse it as though it were composed of steno language, as if it were a weekly newsmagazine or a racing sheet, we miss much of its "tension" and dilute its power. In some ways it would be better to approach the Bible as though we were reading a novel.

My friend Jeremy, he of the serious eyes and dark brow, scowls. "Novels aren't true," he says. "But the Bible is."

Jeremy makes a good point. While we might compare the Bible to a good work of fiction, it is clearly something more. Even the greatest of novels, those of Dostoyevsky, say, or the Lady Murasaki in Japan, have not functioned the way that biblical texts have. We will talk more about this in the third movement of this book, where we will uncover the difference between most texts and sacred Scripture and discuss the nature of truth.

"I was wondering about that," chimes in Thaddeus. "What is truth? Is literal truth the only kind of truth?"

Can you hold onto that until Part Three?

His brow furrows and I know that he'll find it hard to wait for too long, so I suggest we return to Genesis 1–2. Take another look at the passage. If, for the sake of argument, the "truth" of these biblical texts is not a literal, steno truth, our problems concerning the conflicting creation stories, or the pre-solar light, fall away. The author need not get the facts right. But what does that do to our conventional understanding of what is true?

"Perhaps the truth is deeper than the details," Marj says. "Maybe the truth is that God created the world."

Marj is a quick study. The truth is a tensive truth, one that cannot be boxed in and fully comprehended the way we can pin down the facts of a text written in steno language. As we noted earlier, we cannot ever control or assimilate this material completely. We believe the content to be true but we cannot ever really prove it the way we can test a scientific hypothesis and determine its truth. Thus from the start the Bible throws off its shackles and seduces us into a relationship with its contents. As we read the rest of the Bible, we will continue to look back, to reread and rethink and rediscover the "truth" of these chapters. God created the world. That is the truth of the Genesis story.

But there's more. In the text, what is God's attitude toward the created world?

"He sees that it is good," Thad says.

Look at the pattern of each day of creation. Once God rolls up the divine sleeves and gets down to work, separating the waters and allowing the dry land to appear, God manifests a distinct attitude toward what is made. Again and again, in Genesis 1:10, 12, 18, 21, and 25, God looks at what has come into being and sees that it is good. This series of judgments culminates in Genesis 1:31 when, at the end of the sixth day, God looks at all of what now exists and determines that it is "very good." Creation is good, good, good, good, good, and very good. One would have to be very dense to miss the point, the truth of this passage: God created the world, and God created it GOOD. Now don't screw it up.

Which, of course, is what happens in the soap opera of Adam, Eve, and their dysfunctional family in Genesis 3–4, where we discover the Bible's take on the true nature of humanity.

We'll study this question of truth in more detail in the third part of our travels. (By now you are probably getting a bit tired of my way of putting off questions until the third part of this trip, but to study a biblical text means to approach the Bible from a number of different directions at once, something we cannot do on the linear written page. The ways into a biblical text interpenetrate sometimes.) Suffice it to say for now that Christians have traditionally read the Bible as tensive language, the language of poetry and art, at the same time that they have believed the sacred text to be inspired or revealed by God—and, depending on how you define the word, as true.

"The way religious myths are true?" Marjorie asks.

"What?" This is too much for Jeremy. "The Bible is not just a myth," he exclaims with some heat.

Are Bible Stories Mere Myths?

Yvonne moves closer to Jeremy and puts a calming hand on his arm and I attempt to mediate, asking Marj to explain what she means by the "truth" of religious myths.

"Well," she begins, casting a concerned glance at Jeremy, "I'm not talking about what most people think of when they hear the word 'myth.' In our culture, to say that something is a 'myth' is to imply that it's not true. You know," she continues as she turns to me, "as in, 'Oh, it's only a myth that Italian men are great lovers.'"

It is my turn to scowl.

"But," she resumes, "people who study the religions of the world don't mean the same thing."

"How do you know all this?" Yvonne asks.

"I took a course in it," Marj answers. "Anyway, when it comes to the study of religion, myths are stories. The very word comes from the Greek expression for story, doesn't it?"

The Greek word *mythos* means "narrative."

"Myths are the stories a culture tells itself in order to answer the most profound questions we have, the ones that science can't resolve," Marj says. "Where did we come from? Why are we here? What happens when we die?"

Marj is correct. Those who study the phenomenon of religion speak of myth as the filter through which a culture processes its experience of life in the world. Myths, the stories a society tells, help people to apprehend the meaning of life and the core values behind how they live it. Myths are not *historically* true, since they cannot be objectively verified, but they articulate the truth nonetheless.

"You're losing me here," Yvonne says. "I thought truth was truth."

"Yeah," says Jeremy. "You're sounding pretty relativistic to me. Are you saying there is no Truth with a capital T?"

Not at all. Rather, there are different ways of comprehending truth. For example: Yvonne, does your husband Paul love you?

Yvonne blushes. She didn't know participation in our discussion was going to get so personal. But I know that their marriage is rock solid, so I press her.

"Yes," she says, "I know he loves me."

How do you know?

"Well, I just do."

Yes, but how? Can you scientifically verify Paul's love?

She shakes her head. "No. But we do have a history," she says, smiling. "We go way back. Is that what you could call historical verification of the truth of our love?"

Not quite. Yvonne's history with Paul may verify to her satisfaction past love, but how can she say that it is true that Paul loves her this afternoon, or that theirs is true love?

"I just know it's true," she says.

In this case objective verification is not possible, and yet anyone who has been in love knows that even without such verification Yvonne could still be speaking the truth. Lovers, especially those whose feelings have stood the test of time, know love is true even if they cannot explain it or scientifically prove its truth. Do you see how this relates to religious myth?

"No," says Yvonne.

"I think I do," says Thad. "Myths don't even try to answer questions like, 'Did such and such really happen?' Instead, they tell stories that allow people to get in touch with deeper truths, the deeper meanings of their experience."

Marj adds, "Look at what he just said about the truth in Genesis: it's not that God created the world in six of our days, but that God created it good. God at work and God thinking the world is good—that's the truth, even though it contradicts science."

Jeremy has been listening. "OK," he says. "I follow you as far as you go. But the Bible is different from Yvonne's love—no disrespect intended," he nods toward her. "And the Bible is different from other religious truths. It's the real Truth, with the capital T."

I'm not sure that the Bible is of much help when the time comes to discern what a given community identifies as Truth with a capital T. We *will* encounter the most fundamental truth of Christianity, that is, the truth of Jesus Christ, Son of God and savior. But as for the other truth claims of the various Christian denominations, to explore them now would take us very far in a different direction. However, the fact that we cannot now pursue them does not mean that Jeremy's objection and Christian claims to biblical truth are invalid or unimportant. Indeed, they must be addressed by any community seriously attempting to enter into the conversation between God and God's creation.

"Great!" Yvonne says. "So far, I think I know what the Bible is not. But what *is* it?"

Let's take a breather and return to that very question.

For Reflection and Discussion

At the end of most chapters this section will provide questions to allow you to think a bit more about the material we have covered. The questions do not ask you to summarize the chapter; rather, they suggest ways to spring off of what we have discussed into other realms of reflection. You may wish to do this alone, but most of the questions are also designed for group discussion.

1. What image comes into your mind when you hear the word "God?" In your imagination, is God a person? What does this person look like? How does this chapter challenge what you were taught as a child? Do you "buy" it, or not?

2. Later on our journey we will discuss in more detail the nature of "biblical truth." But it is not too soon to begin to ruminate over the Big T. Is the Bible true? What do you think of Marjorie's suggestion that "truth is deeper than the details"? What are the strengths and weaknesses of such an idea?

3. Do you think the world is at its essence good, the way our reading of Genesis 1 suggests? Do you have any ideas about why bad things happen in such a "good" world?

Chapter Three

A Preview of Coming Attractions:
What the Bible Is

In the third chapter of the first book of Samuel, found in the Hebrew Bible, we read the humorous story of Samuel's disrupted slumber. Lying on his bed at night, he hears a voice calling his name. He repeatedly runs to his mentor Eli, asleep nearby, thinking that Eli is calling him. The voice is apparently familiar, but it is not Eli calling. It is God who is calling, God inviting him to a prophet's life.

As far as we can tell, no one in the ancient Mediterranean world ever heard a call in the night to get up, sit down, and write a sacred text. That is not how Scripture came about.

The Bible is not a book; it is many books. It was not written in a few sittings by one person or promulgated by a committee of people; rather, it was composed over a period of a thousand years by a multitude of people who lived in and wrote for specific communities. Whether we study the Jerusalem Temple's greatest hits (that is, the Psalms, most of which were hymns originally developed for worship services) or wonder at the differing stories about the birth of Jesus, we are reading the product of reflection and discussion among particular groups of people.

The Bible, then, did not drop from heaven in some sort of hermetically sealed, celestial plastic bag. Nor did the Holy Spirit perch like a bird on the shoulder of a particularly saintly, solitary writer, whispering holy truths into his ear. No, God worked as the Divine always does and encouraged ordinary people to gather together and struggle over the "big questions," the ones that never seem to get answered and never seem to go away. Where did we come from? Why are we here? Where did the world come from?

What happens when we die? Sex is such a problem sometimes; why are we created male and female anyway? And, of course, the mother of all rumination: What does it all mean?

The Bible can be a noisy companion. Listen closely and you will hear one thousand years of conversation about the meaning of life, one thousand years of people's reflection concerning the big questions. Some of the answers suggested by Scripture are probably a bit too specific for our taste. The stories of the kings of Israel slaughtering their opponents in God's name, well, these tales are part of conversations that don't speak readily to most of us today. But even in its most unpleasant stories, those that theologian Phyllis Trible refers to as "texts of terror," we encounter communities puzzling over their purpose in this world. Their answers may not be ours, but their questions surely are.

The Bible, then, is a record of past conversations, the answers discovered by previous generations. But it is more than that: it is an invitation to your future. As we will discover, to read it is to join in the conversation. This is at the essence of what we call divine revelation. We do not just read these texts as though we were reading a favorite poem, a well-remembered novel, or an operating manual. We, as individuals and as a community, open this book and fall into it. The Bible becomes the place where we encounter God, talk to God. And God talks to us.

"I'm lost," Yvonne sighs. "How does God talk to us through the Bible? I've never heard God talk."

God's talk—we call it revelation—will be the subject of the last movement of our journey. There we shall explore in more detail how this conversation with God is conducted. But we cannot arrive there without traveling through the forest of texts and the dusty fields of ancient rocks, the world out of which the Bible came.

"So for now," Marj says, "how would you describe the Bible?"

The Bible is the written record of the experiences and insights of our ancestors as they struggled to understand who they were, who God was for them, and what life in the world meant. It is an invitation to us to join in an ongoing process of interactive conversation.

"Conversation," Yvonne says. "That sounds easy enough."

Well . . .

"Oh, dear," she sighs.

Perambulating Through the Preliminary Ambiguities

Is it not the case that the big questions that bedeviled our ancestors afflict us as well? Our questions might be general: How are we to live a good and holy life? What are we supposed to believe about God or the Church? Or they might be quite specific: Why did God allow my brother to die in a hit-

and-run accident? Who exactly was Jesus of Nazareth? Should my daughter marry her non-Christian boyfriend? What are we to make of the lesbian couple that just moved in next door?

Many Christians look to their Church leaders for answers to such questions; often those leaders oblige, providing clear answers to difficult questions in the Bible. But for many other people clarity is more elusive. They may respect the authority of the churches and their leaders, but the definitive answers offered, even by those respected for their knowledge and wisdom, do not always ring true. Such searchers may feel a hunger to approach the Bible and read it for themselves. But if they do that, if they try to read the Bible without the authoritative guidance of a pastor or priest, they bump up against a fundamental problem: How do they know what the texts are telling them? How can they know that they are on the right journey of biblical exploration?

The answer is: they can't. Oh, we can be quite sure about some things when it comes to a biblical text. For instance, we can be reasonably certain that the First Letter to the Corinthians dates from the first century and was written for the most part by Paul. But when it comes to questions such as what Paul's intentions were in writing the letter, how the Corinthians received it, or exactly what the author meant in any given passage, we are on shakier ground. When we ask what such an ancient text means for us today, the ground can start to look a lot like quicksand. What are we to do?

The books of the Bible are several thousand years old; they are documents that come from cultures very different from our own. As a result, these texts must be deciphered and decoded.

"Why not toss these texts out," Marj asks, "and come up with some new ones?"

"Or at least add to what we have," Thad says.

That's a good question. Some Christian groups—the Mormons, the Church of Jesus Christ of Latter-Day Saints, comes to mind—have added material to their Sacred Scripture. But religious communities tend to be very conservative about changing their sacred texts in any way. Even changes in translation can be a problem. Once the leaders of the early Christian communities decided in a series of councils what texts they would all consider divinely revealed, they closed the process down.

"But why?" Thad asks.

Because these texts, the ones in our Bible, work the way others don't. Generations of believers have tested them and found them to be inspired by God. They're tried and true.

"But they're also wrong," Marj says as Jeremy winces.

No, not wrong. But they are in need of interpretation. They're tensive texts, remember? Why chuck them into the trash just because their surface information is sometimes problematic?

"How do they work?" Yvonne asks.

That's the point of the journey we're on here.

"And you want us to wait and see," Thad says. "Am I right?"

Well, yes, you are. For now, all I can say is that I think you'll find that the wait was worth it. As I said, we have to decipher and interpret these texts. But when we begin this process, we step off the wide open spaces of self-evident truth and follow a path into a dark and difficult thicket of interpretation. If we want to take the Bible seriously, this path is unavoidable, even for those who claim that the Bible provides simple answers.

Let me give you an example. In the Gospel of Mark, recognized by most people as the earliest Gospel contained in the New Testament, some Pharisees ask Jesus about divorce. He is quite clear that divorce is unacceptable: "What God has joined together, let no one separate (Mark 10:9)." Paul, who wrote his letters several decades before Mark's Gospel was composed, also knows of a saying from the Lord about divorce. Paul rarely makes direct reference to the life or teachings of Jesus, but in 1 Corinthians 7:10 he states explicitly that he received from the Lord a message for the married: Don't separate and don't divorce. So Jesus was against divorce. Period. End of discussion, right?

Not really. Right after Paul says that he has received this warning from the Lord, he freely adapts what has been handed on to him. In 1 Corinthians 7:11 he adds parenthetically that, if a woman does separate from her husband, she should remain single. Then he says that in some cases, particularly those in which a believer is wed to an unbeliever, married Corinthian Christians may indeed permanently separate (for the details, see 1 Corinthians 7:12-16). The author of the Gospel of Matthew, who used Mark as a source, also feels free to modify the received teaching of Jesus. Like Paul, Matthew's Gospel softens Jesus' straightforward declaration and allows for divorce in situations where "unchastity" is involved (Matt 19:9).

Faced with these passages, how do we know what Jesus actually said? Right from the start Christians were playing around with the teachings of Jesus (whatever they were), and given the fact that the New Testament authors themselves apparently felt comfortable tinkering with what Jesus said, how do we know what to do now about divorce? How can we be sure we are on the right path?

Resist the temptation at this point to scramble for an authority figure. Everyone you might turn to has to confront the same problem. Whether they be priests, pastors, world-class biblical scholars, or the pope himself, all the people you might consult are in the same boat: everyone must at some point interpret a biblical text. Indeed, there is literally no such thing as an uninterpreted text. As soon as anyone reads a passage, the mind tries to make sense of the words on the page. And as soon as that happens, the mind making sense is also interpreting.

The question, then, is not what is the definitive meaning of a particular text; rather, it is: what does the text mean for us, here and now, in our particular situation?

The Parameters of Interpretation

"Wait a minute," Jeremy objects. "That means anyone can find anything they want in the Bible."

"Right," Thad agrees. "Remember Paul Hill and Shotgun Jesus."

Well, yes. There is nothing to stop a person from reading the Bible and finding just about anything in it to justify just about any behavior. For centuries Christian churches justified slavery by quoting the Bible, and in our day there is the disturbing case of Hill's avenging savior. But this is actually less of a problem than you might think if you read what is on the page and (this is most important) you do it in conversation with others to test your insight.

"But churches are made up of lots of people," Thad says, "and yet some congregations come up with pretty distorted interpretations of Christianity."

That is true and probably unavoidable. Our goal cannot be to wipe out this possibility, since to do that we would have to ascertain THE meaning of a biblical text.

"But we can't do that," Thad says, "because there is no way to know THE meaning of a text."

Yvonne is looking disoriented. "Aren't we going around in circles?" she asks.

"It does feel as though we are spinning our wheels," Marj says.

We can read and understand a biblical text any way we like. This problem, or challenge, will be the subject of our attention as we travel. For us, conversation is the key, but it will not provide definitive answers to most of our questions. We are learning how to set off on a journey in which the Bible becomes partner to our own traveling conversation. What the Bible cannot be for us is a static book of definitive answers to all the questions of one's life.

I think that before we get very far, we will have to come up with a few guidelines to help us along. Think of what follows as a preview of the sort of adventures we will explore in the chapters ahead.

First of all, remember our goal. *We are not seeking to nail down the one and only valid interpretation of any biblical text; rather, we will try to uncover a range of possible interpretations that do justice to the texts and foster the conversation between God and a specific group of God's people.* At every step we must be careful to ask the right questions, resisting the modern desire merely to learn what "really happened" and focusing instead on questions of meaning, such as: "what could this text be saying to us today?"

On this journey it will be important for us *to read the texts we have as closely and carefully as possible.* It is almost second nature for Christians to read into the Bible things that are not there. For instance, Catholics have a field day with the family of Jesus, composing enormous treatises on the life of the Holy Family while at the same time missing the repeated references to the siblings of the Lord. For their part, many Protestants treat St. Paul as though he were a nineteenth-century systematic theologian instead of a first-century craftsman and Pharisee. Before we can speculate about what a text means, we have to read what it actually says.

Furthermore, we will study the texts within their literary context. If our focus is a story from Deuteronomy or a paragraph from a Pauline letter we will attempt to fit the particular piece into the concerns and purposes of the biblical book as a whole. We will also learn how to interpret the text by comparing it with other Jewish or early Christian literary texts, as well as Gentile and non-Christian texts from similar periods. As you will see, biblical scholars have developed an array of critical methods with which to bring texts into focus for purposes of comparison and interpretation.

We will also learn about the social or cultural worlds that produced the texts we evaluate, while attempting to avoid one of the most common mistakes that interpreters, including many scholars, make: we will not assume that there existed *one* ancient world culture. The Bible contains a millennium's worth of books. Even texts written within a few years of each other come from different cultures; the gospels, for instance, present a world that is largely rural and agrarian, while Paul and his letters are at home in the city.

The eventual goal of all of this analysis, of course, is to understand how a biblical text might become part of the divine conversation. To do this we focus our initial energy on uncovering information about the possible original situation of the text, its author, and its audience. As you can imagine, a certain tension pervades this enterprise: from the start we are aware that we can never recover or know for certain the original circumstances that produced the text. We speculate concerning the original situation not because it will, if discerned, offer us the definitive interpretation; rather, analyzing texts and their contexts with an eye to what might have actually been going on helps us to eliminate many interpretations that might be, as Marj put it, beyond the pale. Thus, for instance, we can lay aside the notion of Shotgun Jesus.

Throughout this enterprise of biblical research, which may at this point seem rather daunting, remember the insights we have already touched upon: the Bible is made up of tensive language ripe for multiple meanings, and our approach to the Bible involves a community of people, not the isolated believer. The journey we are on invites individuals to bring their insights and ideas about tensive, sacred texts to a wider group conversation. We do this to provide some perspective, a check on the more extreme possibilities for biblical interpretation.

The Challenge

So. What is it going to be for you? Will you sit at home by the fire, warm and cozy, and safely read your Bible? In that case, when you hit a perplexing passage you can pull down a reference book from the shelf or call your pastor or teacher and be told what the text means.

Or do you envision your life (and your Bible) as an adventure? Going to school, finding that first job, falling in love, raising children—all these are ports of call on a long and lively voyage. The Bible—and religion—have to keep up. They need legs to walk on and mouths with which to speak, for we travel not as solitaries but in community with family and fellow believers and friends. Our journey is serious, but it is an excursion, too, of light-hearted laughter and the exploration of new things and conversation about the old, just as pilgrimages always are.

The biblical journey is not an easy one, but then religious pilgrimages are not particularly leisurely ventures. The Hebrew Bible depicts God as a driven entity, a stormy divinity absolutely untameable and unstoppable, and the New Testament Jesus, while cut to a more human scale, is a charismatic character given to periodic bouts of prophetic fulmination, and he is always on the move.

The Bible, and the conversation we can have about it and with it, will offer us quite the peregrination.

"Peregrination?" Yvonne asks.

"Trip," Thad says. "It's another word for journey."

But before the Bible can speak, we have to clear our ears so we can hear it and open our eyes so we can see the Bible for what it is, not what we think it should be.

Jeremy looks uncomfortable.

"Are you sure," he says, "that all this isn't just a way to cheapen the Bible? To make it seem just like any other book?"

That is certainly not my intention. Our approach to Scripture will involve an examination of texts composed by real people who lived real human lives, much like our own, lives that they believed were touched by God. Peasant sheepherders wandered into kings' courts as scolding prophets, and fishers and tentmakers roamed the Mediterranean world as Christian apostles. God worked through the ordinary and the mundane. And when God worked through individuals, like the prophets and the first apostles, God did so for the sake of, and in the context of, communities. We will base our interpretation of the Bible on common sense tested by our sisters and brothers in community, for ours will be a preeminently human adventure.

"So," Marjorie says, "you're saying we should relax as we start. That the stakes aren't that high."

Oh, no. The stakes are very high indeed! But this is a journey of discovery, not a mission impossible. The spiritual life is a pilgrimage, not a war zone.

"Chill, then?" suggests Thad.

Wait, at least, until we actually begin the journey before you assume its destination and the problems along the way.

"It's like the Lord would say," Yvonne says. "'Sufficient unto the day are its problems.' Or something like that."

"So let's go already," says Jeremy, a bit on edge.

Indeed, let us proceed. And I know just the place to start!

For Reflection and Further Discussion

1. Have you ever encountered religious explanations for how the Bible is divinely inspired? I was taught about the Holy Spirit sitting like a bird on the shoulders of the evangelists. Do you have any good stories from when you were growing up?

2. Ask a religious person you know and trust to share what he or she believes about divine inspiration. How does that person describe this sort of activity on God's part?

3. Take a few moments alone and make a list of your "big questions" about the meaning of your life.

THE SONG OF SONGS

On the road to Qumran.   Photo: TLP Archives

Chapter Four

Sex on the Page

> Let him kiss me with the kisses of his mouth!
> For your love is better than wine,
>   your anointing oils are fragrant,
> your name is perfume poured out;
>   therefore the maidens love you.
>   —Song of Songs 1:2-3

When I was much younger I set out to read the entire Bible from beginning to end. That was not something I expected to enjoy. It was Lent and reading the Bible seemed an appropriate atonement for a penitential season. I will never forget the day I turned the page and discovered the Song of Songs, which is also called the Song of Solomon or the Canticle of Canticles in some Bibles. Slipped into the Bible between the pessimism of Ecclesiastes ("Vanity of vanities, all is vanity") and the high-minded visions of Isaiah ("Hear, O heavens, and listen, O earth; for the Lord has spoken!") was a book unlike any other in Scripture. I read, with eyebrows raised:

> With great delight I sat in his shadow,
>   and his fruit was sweet to my taste.
> He brought me to the banqueting house,
>   and his intention toward me was love (2:3-4).

And later:

> "Open to me, my sister, my love,
>   my dove, my perfect one;
> for my head is wet with dew,
>   my locks with the drops of the night."

25

I had put off my garment;
   how could I put it on again?
I had bathed my feet;
   how could I soil them?
My beloved thrust his hand into the opening,
   and my inmost being yearned for him (5:2-4).

What was this? And why had I never heard such things when the Bible was read in church? A little homework yielded the discovery that the Song of Solomon is hardly mentioned in the Lectionary, that is, the big book of readings used at many church services. The Song is never read at a Catholic Mass on Sunday and appears only once in the cycle of readings during the week, on December 20, as an alternative reading to a passage from the prophet Zephaniah. You could go to church every Sunday for years and never hear proclaimed a single word from this racy little text.

But what a book! Take a few moments and read it in your Bible. There it sits, shimmering with sexual imagery of astonishing suggestiveness and beauty, never once mentioning the word "God." And yet it is in all the versions of the Bible, Jewish and Christian, without apologies. Indeed, Akiba, one of the wisest and most venerable of the ancient rabbis, who died early in the second century C.E.—

"C.E.?" Yvonne asks.

"It stands for Common Era," Thad says. "People are trying to get away from A.D., *Anno Domini*."

"But why?"

"Well, *Anno Domini* means 'In the year of the Lord,'" Thad says. "But not everyone accepts Jesus as Lord. So instead, we use C.E. to designate the era common to Jews and Christians and B.C.E., not B.C. ('Before Christ'), to indicate 'Before the Common Era.'"

"It still seems to leave everyone else out in the cold," Marj says. "It's not just Jews and Christians who date things this way."

Agreed. But it is a start in the right direction, no?

Marj shrugs in quasi-agreement.

Anyway, back to the rabbi. Akiba once praised the Song of Solomon in language as extravagant as what he found there. Akiba ended a discussion of whether or not the book belonged in the canon of Scripture with the definitive declaration that "the entire age is not so worthy as the day on which the Song of Solomon was given to Israel. For all the Scriptures are holy, but the Song of Solomon is holiest of all."

What?

"You are stately as a palm tree, and your breasts are like its clusters.
I say I will climb the palm tree . . ." (7:7-8).

How could such a startlingly graphic text be considered a part of Sacred Scripture? What were the rabbis thinking?

Return now to the purpose of our journey: to become more familiar and comfortable with the task of biblical interpretation. As we proceed we will rummage around the biblical scholar's toolbox and test out some of the apparatus that interpreters use on texts. Our goal is not to become proficient in the use of all the tools in the box, but to understand how some of them work. That way you will be able to evaluate the quality of the work of other people who use the tools. You may not care to train to be a plumber, but who among us could not benefit from instruction concerning how to stop a leaky faucet? So too with the work of the biblical scholar. You may not have the patience or desire to enroll in a course in Biblical Hebrew or New Testament Greek, but your life journey can benefit from a little more information concerning where the Bible came from. That way you will be able to evaluate the quality of the "work" others (preachers, commentary writers, religion teachers) do with the Bible. You will have more knowledge about how the Bible works in communities of believers, and that will translate into more power over how the Bible affects your own life.

As noted before, we will explore two texts, one from the Hebrew Bible and one from the New Testament. We could examine one of the well-known books of the Bible, like Genesis or Exodus. But I suggest we stick with a smaller text, one that we can do justice to in a brief amount of time; let us leave the creation of the world, the struggles of the patriarchs, and the parting waters of the Exodus event for another day and instead travel more modestly into the world of Akiba's holiest of sacred texts, the Song of Songs.

Besides, it's chock full of sex.

Who wrote this perplexing text? When? How is it structured? What kind of writing is it? What is its purpose? Why is it in the Bible? What does it mean? How have believers interpreted it in the past? How do the churches interpret it now? These are the kinds of questions that will rain down upon us as we walk through the three movements of interpretation—from the words on the page (text) to its original context (rocks) to how communities of believers have appreciated the text (talk).

Translations

At this point Jeremy breaks in. "I don't buy it, all this sex in the Bible," he says. "My Bible doesn't have that stuff in it."

Jeremy hands me an open copy of the King James version of the Bible, perhaps the most popular English translation of Scripture among Protestant groups. He points to a page from the translation of the Song of Songs at 5:4.

"My Bible isn't as graphic as yours is," he says. "Yours translates this verse, 'My beloved thrust his hand into the opening,' and that sounds pretty suggestive. But my translation makes it clear that the image isn't meant to be taken as a sexual one."

That is true. The King James version of Song 5:4 reads: "My beloved put his hand by the hole of the door."

"My translation is more like Jeremy's than like yours," says Yvonne. She is reading from the New Jerusalem Bible, a modern version used primarily by Roman Catholics. Here the text is rendered: "My love thrust his hand through the hole in the door."

We have arrived at the problem, or the adventure, that is biblical translation. The original texts of the Bible were not, of course, written in English. The Jewish Bible was composed predominantly in Hebrew, the New Testament in Greek. If you have ever studied another language you know how difficult it is to produce an accurate translation. You discovered quickly that people don't just speak different languages; they think of, and even conceive of, reality in different ways. This means that there is no completely accurate way to translate a thought from one language to another. Of necessity translation involves a great deal of interpretation. Translators don't just choose words that correspond to each other; instead they attempt to render the original thought behind the words. Take a look at this example from the New Testament.

The text is Romans 16:1-2. Paul's original Letter to the Romans is long gone; only later copies survive, the earliest of which is found on a fragmentary papyrus dating from about 200 C.E. If we had it here, the early text would look something like this:

ΣΥΝΙΣΤΗΜΙΔΕΥΜΙΝΦΟΙΒΗΝΤΗΝΑΔΕΛΦΗΝΗΜΩΝΟΥΣΑΝΚΑΙΔΙ
ΑΚΟΝΟΝΤΗΣΕΚΚΛΗΣΙΑΣΤΗΣΕΝΚΕΓΧΡΕΑΙΣΙΝΑΑΥΤΗΝΠΡΟΣΔΕΞΗ
ΣΘΕΕΝΚΥΡΙΩΑΞΙΩΣΤΩΝΑΓΙΩΝΚΑΙΠΑΡΑΣΤΗΤΕΑΥΤΗΕΝΩΑΝΥΜΩΝ
ΧΡΗΖΗΠΡΑΓΜΑΤΙΚΑΙΓΑΡΑΥΤΗΠΡΟΣΤΑΤΙΣΠΟΛΛΩΝΕΓΕΝ
ΗΘΗΚΑΙΕΜΟΥΑΥΤΟΥ

The letters are Greek but, as you can see, there is no spacing between words, no punctuation, and it is written in uppercase, or capital, letters. Lines end in the middle of words. As far as we can tell, when they received a letter like this, peopleinantiquityhadtoreaditoutloudinordertofigureoutwhatthewordswere, because for them—just as for us—they probably appeared to be a bit of a jumble. The Romans used to tell stories about the great feats of Julius Caesar, and one of the things they found surprising about him was his ability to read silently, without even moving his lips as he did so. Most people apparently had to hear what they were reading to understand it.

Early on in history, copyists took these "uncial" documents, as these uppercase Greek texts are called in the manuscript trade, and turned them into more readable Greek. They divided up the words, and as time went on

The Codex Sinaiticus discovered at Mount Sinai (4th cent. C.E.).   Photo: British Library

scholars supplied some punctuation (not always like ours, though; a semi-colon, for instance, serves in Greek as a question mark, while a sort of floating period signals what we call a semicolon. A comma, you will be happy to know, is still a comma in Greek, and a period a period). Their user-friendly version of the above text looks like this:

Συνίστημι δὲ ὑμῖν Φοίβην τὴν ἀδελφὴν ἡμῶν, οὖσαν καὶ διάκονον τῆς ἐκκλησίας τῆς ἐν Κεγχρεαῖς, ἵνα αὐτὴν προσδέξησθε ἐν κυρίῳ ἀξίως τῶν ἁγίων καὶ παραστῆτε αὐτῇ ἐν ᾧ ἂν ὑμῶν χρῄζῃ πράγματι. καὶ γὰρ αὐτὴ προστάτις πολλῶν ἐγενήθη καὶ ἐμοῦ αὐτου.

This is the text you will find if you consult a Greek New Testament. You might think, "Well, OK. You have the text. Now translate the words." But it's not that simple. For instance, here is the literal translation of what the above Greek passage says in English:

I commend now to you Phoebe the sister of us, being also a servant of those called out the ones in Kenchrea, in order that her you may receive in Lord worthily of the holy ones and you may stand by her in whatever of you she may have need thing. For indeed she one who stands in front of many became and of myself.

Clearly the text cannot just be translated literally; it must be cleaned up and put into readable English. Fine, you say. Do it! Shuffle the words around so they make some sense. Here, of course, is the crux of the problem. Even in translating the Greek into the English gibberish above we have had to make some interpretive judgments. Does Paul really "commend" Phoebe? If we look up the word in a Greek dictionary, we find that it could also mean "to bring together or unite," "to present or introduce," "to demonstrate, show, or bring something out." We are working with a group of words here that all cluster around the notion of putting someone forth or connecting people together. But how do we decide exactly what nuance Paul had in mind? How do we figure out if Paul is patting Phoebe on the back or introducing her to the Romans?

Translation is an art. The choices translators make are choices made in good judgment and with the use of a lot of what we might call "controlled imagination." Translators of biblical texts don't roll the dice or consult Tarot cards; they have a whole collection of techniques to help them choose one definition over another. They consult Greek, Aramaic, and Hebrew dictionaries to determine the full range of possible meanings of the word. Then they examine how the author uses the word elsewhere and how other writers from the same period use it. They look closely at the wider context of the passage, survey how earlier interpreters rendered the word, and then make a decision based on what they have found. The decision, then, is a judgment call based on whatever relevant textual evidence the translators can discover.

Returning to Jeremy's translation of the Song of Songs, we take a close look at the Hebrew original of the text. What my English translation renders as "My beloved thrusts his hand into the opening" appears in the Hebrew as this:

דּוֹדִי שָׁלַח יָדוֹ מִן־הַחֹר

My translation, found in the New Revised Standard Version (NRSV), follows the Hebrew rather closely: "My beloved sends forth/drives his hand into the הַחֹר." This last word, pronounced *khoar*, means "hole," as in a place for people to hide or the hole that lets one lift up the lid of a chest. It also can signify the hole through which one reaches to open a door. However, the Hebrew text just contains that one word and does not specify a hole "in the door." The NRSV economically translates the word as "opening," which, if you check the rest of the passage, includes the possibility of door hole. But the word in Hebrew is ambiguous; with a text this drenched in sexual imagery, it is at least conceivable that the Hebrew is alluding to more than a door hole. Thus none of the translations are wrong, but the ambiguity of the NRSV is closer to the less precise original Hebrew. Since translation is a form of artistic interpretation and not an exact science, you should feel free to consult the version with which you are most comfortable. On this journey, though, we will continue to use the NRSV because we need to stay close to the original texts, and the NRSV is the most literal of the English translations available.

"Fixing" the Text

Whether one is composing a sermon, preparing a lecture, or sitting on the back porch with the Bible in one's lap on a blustery spring morning, the first thing a person attends to is "fixing" the text. By this we don't indicate a need to mend a broken piece of Scripture; rather we mean that the journey of biblical study always involves the selection of, or fixing our focus upon, a particular text. If you are a preacher the text may be designated for you; the lectionary used by many Christians mandates that on any given Sunday certain readings be read and preached. Thus Christians everywhere may be exposed to the same texts on the same day.

We are under no such constraints, and we are choosing our own texts. When we turn to the New Testament we will select a single section of a biblical letter, but for our discussion of the Hebrew Bible we will examine the whole of the Song of Songs.

Done. But for the serious biblical interpreter, choosing which text to read is only the beginning of the process of fixing the text.

As you know, when you read the Bible, the translation that you have in your hands is based for the most part on texts in Hebrew or Greek.

But what you probably don't know is that the Hebrew or Greek text upon which your translation is based never actually existed.

"What?" exclaims the ever-vigilant Jeremy. "Are you saying the Bible never existed?"

No, the Bible is not an imaginary entity. But the Hebrew or Greek text behind your translated Bible is a literary creation. It is actually a composite of many ancient manuscripts that have been culled, collated, and critiqued. We do not today possess the original handwritten version of any book of the Bible. Instead, we have access to hundreds of copies, probably copies of copies of the original manuscripts. Over time, as the copies were modified, the scribes sometimes dozed or lost their place or felt compelled to tidy up what they perceived to be loose ends, and little variations crept into the versions they produced. Those who reproduced the slightly emended copies often didn't catch the errors or changes and instead duplicated them. Eventually, enough alterations crept into the generation of these manuscripts so that no two ancient manuscripts are exactly alike.

"But you're talking about Sacred Scripture," Jeremy objects. "You're saying that Scripture is the product of a bunch of sloppy copyists?"

Some people might say that, but recall my suggestion at the beginning of our journey. Is it not possible that God continued to work through ordinary people even after the texts were first composed?

"In that case," Thad says, "the copyists' errors might have been divinely inspired."

It's possible that scribal errors and corrections were part of the dynamic nature of Scripture, the ongoing process of communication between God and communities of believers. If that is the case, what we have been labeling as "mistakes" might have been corrections appropriate for the communities that first read them.

"I suppose," Yvonne says, "that the Holy Spirit can do whatever it wants."

Surely that is difficult to deny. Meanwhile, in our day it seems appropriate to try to reconstruct what the original authors wrote. Sometimes this is risk-free and easy, since the scribal creativity is obvious or their errors are innocuous, as when a copyist switches the order of two words (this is less of a problem in the ancient languages than in English, for which word order is usually critical). But some texts are irretrievably "corrupt," and we cannot recover with certainty what the author originally wrote. So, for instance, in 1 Corinthians 2:1 we will probably never know if Paul came to the Corinthians proclaiming the "mystery" (τὸ μυστήριον) of God or the "testimony" (τὸ μαρτύριον) of God; the manuscripts are about evenly divided concerning which wording is original, and the context supports either reading.

Once we know what text we want to explore, we need to scrutinize the original language of that passage or book to see how stable or corrupt our

The caves of Qumran overlooking the Dead Sea.   Photo: TLP Archives

text is. To do this for a text from the Hebrew Bible we need to check first what is called the Masoretic text.

"Martoorian. Miss Terion," Yvonne mumbles. "They sound like my daughter's boyfriend's Armenian relatives. And now mass-uh-what?"

Masoretic.

"I don't mean to be rude," she says. "But you're starting to lose me. Are we almost done?"

Almost. Now, the Masoretic text of the Hebrew Bible was created over a period of five hundred years by the rabbis of the early Middle Ages, beginning in the 600s C.E. to address a problem. The texts of the Hebrew Bible were originally written with consonants only. Some of these vowel-free manuscripts have survived among the Dead Sea Scrolls, dating to the third century B.C.E. Readers of Hebrew in antiquity could apparently do without vowels in their texts, just as those fluent in ancient Greek could manage without punctuation marks or breaks between words; but as time passed people needed some help and associations of scholars, or *masoretes,* began to produce manuscripts that included vowel markings and accents to assist in pronunciation. Over thirty Masoretic texts survive, dating from about 800 to 1100 C.E., and one, discovered in Cairo in the 1800s, was so complete that it has served as the basis for all modern versions of the Hebrew Bible. This is the text to which we shall refer shortly.

Now Jeremy is fidgeting. We are almost done. Hold on for just a bit longer.

The other ancient manuscript tradition that we consult for the study of the Hebrew Bible is not even in Hebrew. In the three or four centuries before the Common Era many Jews migrated from ancient Palestine to every corner of the Mediterranean world. In the process they and their children grew up in a wider world that spoke Greek and not Hebrew. The Septuagint (the term comes from the Greek word for "seventy") is the traditional name of the Greek translation of the Hebrew Bible produced in seventy-two days, according to legend, by seventy-two Jewish elders in tents set up on a beach in Alexandria, on the coast of Egypt. This was not the first attempt at Greek translation of the Bible, but it was judged the best and became the standard Greek translation in antiquity. It was also, I should add, the text that many early Christians, including Paul, used as their Sacred Scripture. Thus, as we fix a text from the Hebrew Bible, we want to take a look at the Septuagint as well as the Masoretic Hebrew.

"So how does our text stack up?" Thad asks.

When it comes to the Masoretic and Septuagintal evidence for the Song of Songs, we are in luck. The various Masoretic Hebrew manuscripts of the text show only minor variations. Even the Hebrew of the four fragments of the Song found among the Dead Sea Scrolls at Qumran varies only slightly from the Masoretic text, though the scrolls predate it by hundreds of years. This indicates that the text was copied faithfully over the centuries and remained extremely stable; indeed, as Carmelite priest and scholar Roland Murphy puts it, there is not even any evidence that more than one original manuscript existed. If that is the case, it would be rare indeed for a biblical book. The Greek translation of the Song found in the Septuagint, too, varies from the Hebrew only slightly in its wording; it is actually a very close, almost literal translation into Greek.

The manuscript tradition of the Song of Songs, then, is remarkably free of scribal corruptions, which means, I am happy to report, that we do not have to spend much time comparing Hebrew manuscripts with one another and judging which was the original reading. Instead, we can address the text as we have it and begin to situate it in its ancient location. To do this we will explore the most basic of questions: Who wrote the Song of Songs? And when?

For Reflection and Further Conversation

1. One question to ask at the end of each chapter: Think a moment about your reaction to the material introduced. Did anything surprise you? What was it? Was the surprise pleasant or not?

2. Sit with your translation of the Song of Songs and read through it thoughtfully. Were there any sections that you liked? If so, why did you enjoy them? What parts are perplexing to you?

3. We will shortly commence a detailed exploration of the Song of Songs, but before we begin, do some initial soundings of your own. In particular, can you think of any reasons why this book is in the Bible? Moreover, do you have any idea as to why Rabbi Akiba would characterize the Song of Songs as the holiest of holy books?

4. The differences we find in various translations can sometimes be disconcerting. To accustom yourself to the "adventure of translation," if you are in a group have one person read some sections of the Song of Songs aloud while the rest of you compare your translation with the spoken word. What kinds of differences in translation do you discover?

Chapter Five

Healthy Suspicion:
A Walking Staff for Our Journey

Consider the lilies, how they grow: they neither toil nor spin; yet I tell you,
even Solomon in all his glory was not clothed like one of these (Luke 12:27).

It should be rather simple to discern the author of the Song of Songs. Just look at the first line of the text: "The song of songs, which [is] of Solomon." However, right from the start we must be on our guard with this biblical text, for there are a number of reasons to doubt Solomon's authorship.

This is too much for Jeremy.

"Now we're not supposed to believe the Bible even when it says something as simple as who wrote it?" he asks, shaking his head. "Are you saying it's a forgery?"

Not exactly. We have to keep in mind that the world out of which the Bible came was significantly different from our own. We have many instances from antiquity of people composing a text and then assigning a famous person's name to it as author. Even a person like Plato, the student of Socrates, put words into his mentor's mouth; the followers of Aristotle did the same. This was not understood as dishonest behavior but as an acceptable way to honor someone whom the writer admired. We call this "pseudonymity," the process of creating a new work and attributing it to a revered (and usually dead) forebear. We see the same sort of thing in the New Testament. Virtually no biblical scholars, for instance, believe that St. Paul wrote the letters to Timothy and Titus.

"Oh, dear," sighs Yvonne.

"How do you know this?" Thaddeus asks.

Good question. Let's take a moment to "unpack" this. Paul's letters are a good test case. When attempting to authenticate Pauline authorship we examine the vocabulary and writing style as well as the theological content of the letters in question and compare them with the letters generally agreed to be Paul's. For instance, Paul's undisputed letters contain specific information about how he wanted authority to function in the communities he founded. In this regard he often mentions the leadership of apostles and refers to deacons twelve times. However, only at the beginning of his Letter to the Philippians does he mention bishops (the Greek word is *episkopos*, literally "one who oversees"). Paul's notion of Church order is a model of organizational simplicity, a rather informal gathering of people who share various gifts of the Holy Spirit.

But when we turn to the First Letter to Timothy we see a much more developed and fixed hierarchical church. Deacons are mentioned, but pride of place is given to the *episkopos;* 1 Timothy 3:2-7 is a short treatise on the proper behavior of bishops, who in this text are clearly the supreme authorities in their communities. And only in 1 Timothy and the contemporary Titus do we find reference to presbyters, or elders, the church office from which the priesthood probably evolved. The authority structures of 1 Timothy look very much like those found in the letters of Ignatius of Antioch, a bishop who lived at the beginning of the second century C.E., a half century after Paul's departure from the scene. Thus even though the text of 1 Timothy says that it was composed by Paul, it is extremely unlikely that he wrote it. Rather, it was probably composed a half century after his death by someone who knew his thought, admired it, and wanted to honor him and pass on his wisdom—in the context of more structured Christian communities.

When we turn to the question of the authorship of the Song of Songs we have a more difficult task, since we have no indisputably authentic writings from Solomon with which to compare the style and content of our text. But take a close look at the Song. Solomon appears in the body of the Song of Songs six times, never as the narrator or even as a character involved in the action. Instead, he functions the way he does in the Gospel of Luke, where Jesus prefers the raiment of field lilies to the kind of fabulous wealth that Solomon represented. Both in Luke and in the Song the great king is a symbol of splendor, not a character in the story.

"Granted, he didn't play a part in the Gospel," Thaddeus says. "But he could still have written the Song of Songs, even if it refers to him in the third person."

"Or," Marj adds, "he could have commissioned someone to write the Song, to make him look good."

An excellent guess. Thad and Marj are suitably suspicious about this text and well on their way to forming just what we will need—a hermeneutic of suspicion.

"Whoa," Yvonne interjects, waving a hand. "A Herman what?"

The Virtue of Being Suspicious

A hermeneutic.

"I remember that word from freshman philosophy," Jeremy says, "which class I despised. Hermeneutics has something to do with interpretation, right?"

Here is one instance where doing time in a philosophy class pays off. A hermeneutic is a plan or system for interpretation. The word isn't as important as the concept. Every time we read a text we engage in hermeneutics, or ways of interpreting it, whether we know it or not. In biblical studies, when we speak of a hermeneutic of suspicion we mean that we know we should not do a simple surface reading of what is on the biblical page. Rather, we try to figure out what might lie behind the biblical text, and this helps us to shed light on the original situation out of which the text arose.

The hermeneutic of suspicion was brought to the forefront of biblical scholarship largely through the writings of a feminist scholar of the New Testament, Elisabeth Schüssler Fiorenza. Schüssler Fiorenza has since been joined by a multitude of other feminist scholars (women and men alike; one does not have to be a woman to be a feminist). The allure of a hermeneutic of suspicion for feminists should be obvious to anyone reading the Bible: although then as now the population of the world was roughly fifty percent female, women tend toward invisibility in most ancient texts. Even when women make an appearance, the focus of the authors' attention is almost always on the men in the story.

Female Criticism [handwritten margin note]

A hermeneutic of suspicion comes into play when interpreters suspect that something has been left out of the story or that the text as we have it is not giving us an accurate picture of what happened. They wonder why the text was created the way it was. Why, for instance, do the authors of the Hebrew Bible look back to Abraham as the ancestor of later Judaism while rarely alluding to Sarah, without whose cooperation there would have been no posterity for her husband? Take a look at Genesis 16 and 21, the story of the births of Ishmael and Isaac. The point is that Abram (soon to be Abraham) needs an heir, but he's not the focus of the plot, which centers on a contest of wills between his wife Sarai (soon to be Sarah) and her slave Hagar. Abram has a few walk-ons, but for the most part his role is reactive, not proactive. One begins to suspect that Sarai and perhaps the women active at the time when the Genesis stories were composed were more influential in the founding stories of the Israelites than the texts would indicate.

Suspicions About the Song

"What does Sarah have to do with the Song of Solomon?" Jeremy asks, turning our attention back to the task at hand.

What is important is not Sarah but the suspicions she has engendered. For the biblical scholar, suspicion is a virtue and a valuable support. In our quest to uncover the author and date of the Song we have already exercised a certain level of suspicion, for we have noticed that Solomon functions as a symbol of proverbial wealth in the Song, and this makes it less likely that he is the author or a character in the text. Marj has suggested that he commissioned the text, which is certainly plausible in the context of a Middle Eastern royal court. Let's look a little more closely at the Song, bringing to it a suspicious eye. In the process we will not only delve deeper into the question of authorship but also pursue a date for its composition.

We begin with a foray into philology, the historical and comparative study of language. Among biblical scholars, those who specialize in such study are called philologists. All biblical scholars must be able to navigate the major languages of Greco-Roman antiquity (Hebrew, Greek, and Latin), but philologists are the masters of verbal antiques who untangle with ease obscurities of biblical language while intimidating the rest of us with their control of the most obscure of archaic tongues, like Akkadian, Aramaic, Armenian, Demotic, and Coptic. It is not uncommon for an expert in the Hebrew Bible to acquire a working knowledge of a dozen or more ancient languages before she or he sits down to contemplate a biblical text.

You will be happy to know that your guide is not a philologist by trade or temperament, nor will we be required to summon the experts in proto-Ugaritic to do justice to the Song (though some texts from ancient Egypt loom on the near horizon!). But the study of words and language does offer us clues concerning the date and author of our text.

Recall the first line of the Song, which we rendered "The song of songs, which [is] of Solomon." The Hebrew text is a bit more complicated than it appears in English. For one thing, it is not clear that the text reads "of Solomon." It might also be translated "to Solomon," as in dedicated to him or "concerning Solomon." Moreover, the Hebrew relative word אֲשֶׁר that we translated as "which" is not the form of the relative that is used in the rest of the text.

"My eyes . . . ," Yvonne sighs.

Are glazing over. Yes. Well, simply put, the person who composed the title used a different vocabulary from what we find in the rest of the Song.

"That means the first line, the title, probably had a different author," Thad says.

The title was probably added later.

A close inspection of the place names and vocabulary of the body of the Song of Songs casts further doubt on Solomonic authorship for the text as we have it. Archaeological data indicate that the oasis at En-gedi mentioned in Song 1:14 was not settled before the seventh century B.C.E., three hundred years after the reign of Solomon. Scholars have pointed out that a number of the words for perfumes and spices come from the time of the Exile or just before (sixth century B.C.E.), and several "loan words," terms not native to Hebrew but borrowed from other languages, appear in the text from periods of history many centuries after the time of Solomon. Norman Gottwald and others have shown the influence of Aramaic on the text of the Song, which suggests that it was written in the period after which Aramaic became the common language of the people of Israel. That would place the writing of the text as we have it sometime between 450 and 300 B.C.E., a minimum of five hundred years after the time of the great and wise king.

"Why do you keep saying 'the text as we have it'?" Thad asks.

Good question. Most of the texts in our Bible were not written in one period by one person; any biblical text we possess is the end-stage of a long process of copying and editing. Alas, there is absolutely nothing in the Song of Songs that will allow us to date it conclusively. It is probable that the Song of Songs evolved over centuries and was finally written down as we have it in the fifth century B.C.E. The Song could contain material earlier than the fifth century, but as far as we can guess it was the postexilic sages in Jerusalem who comprehended the value of the text and preserved it.

"So Solomon probably didn't write it?" Marjorie pipes in. She has been off in a corner reading the text closely while we have been playing what the late Marvin Pope called "the dating game" concerning the Song of Songs.

"Good," she says. "I've been thinking about what you said about feminists and being suspicious, and all. I agree. I don't think Solomon wrote this. I think it was composed by a woman."

At this point Jeremy rolls his eyes. "First, despite the fact that the Bible itself says that Solomon wrote the Song, we say he didn't. Now it was written by a woman? Come on . . . ."

Marj holds her ground. "Most of the book is written from the point of view of a woman," she says. "Read it. It sounds like a woman is singing the song."

Jeremy will have none of it. "Male authors write from a woman's point of view all the time."

He's correct, but Marj may be on to something here. A number of commentators, many of whom one would hardly characterize as feminists, have noticed that the female lover's voice dominates the work. As Michael V. Fox observes, "The Song is her song, and there is no scene from which she is absent." For the product of an ancient patriarchal culture, this text presents a striking example of mutuality between the woman and the man. Each experiences the same freedom in love, a gender equality that is unusual for a biblical text; the woman is never referred to as a wife or placed in the context of the birth and rearing of children.

"But that doesn't mean it was written by a woman," Jeremy persists.

Jeremy is once again correct. Even the scholars who entertain the possibility of female authorship for the Song do not claim to have proved conclusively that a woman composed it. We cannot discern with any confidence just who wrote the Song. The text as we have it was written down only after a long period of oral transmission. Someone, probably a later editor, wrote the first line attributing the text to Solomon, perhaps to give the text more of a historical context than it had. It is possible that the editor who did this was relying on the information conveyed in 1 Kings 4:32, which claims that Solomon penned three thousand proverbs and a thousand and five songs.

There is much, then, that we cannot know about our text. "The poetry of the Song," Phyllis Trible writes, "resists calculations and invites imagination." Ours will be a journey into imagination, but first we must sit and study the down-to-earth mechanics of how to evaluate a poetic text.

For Reflection and Further Conversation

1. We discussed the role that suspicion plays as a tool for biblical interpretation. What are the strengths of this approach to the Bible? Can you think of any weaknesses?

2. Does our inability to date or even determine the authorship of a biblical text like the Song of Songs affect its credibility as Sacred Scripture? Why or why not? Suppose you were to encounter some Christians who believe in the literal truth of the Bible as written. What points would you make to try to convince them that we can rest easy even if we don't know the date and author of a text?

3. One interesting way to explore a biblical text, if it contains a story and some characters, is to role-play it. Reread the story of Hagar and Sarai, found in Genesis, chapters 16 and 21. If you are in a group, divide up so that someone becomes each of the characters, including Ishmael. If you are alone, read the story from the point of view of one of the players. Get into your role. How does it feel to be this person in this situation? Does the experience tell you anything new about the text?

Chapter Six

What *Is* This Book?

You're early! Sit with me a while. I'm waiting for our conversation partners, and I for one am still a bit agitated and fixed upon the opinion of Rabbi Akiba concerning the Song of Songs—the holiest of holy books, as he puts it. My curiosity is kindled even more by another quotation from Akiba in which he is supposed to have remarked, "Had not the Torah been given, Canticles would have sufficed to guide the world." In biblical terms, the Torah is the first five books of the Bible. Akiba is effectively equating the Song of Songs with everything in Genesis, the Exodus story, the lives of Moses and the patriarchs. What *is* this book? What did the ancient teachers of Israel see in it that I am missing? If we cannot know when it was written or by whom, can we at least get a sense of its original purpose? What was the situation out of which it came?

Biblical scholars often begin their work with a consideration of the text's purpose or the original intent of the author. Also significant would be any information about the text's original "setting in life," what the Germans call the *Sitz im Leben* (I'd be remiss if I did not expose you to some German on this journey. German scholars have done the most important work in developing the critical techniques we are about to discuss).

Of course, we can't know with certainty the *Sitz im Leben* or the intention of an author who lived thousands of years ago. But that doesn't deter most scholars, who, fired by rampant curiosity about an important source of our common life and culture, are energized by a good challenge. Indeed, a tendency to be curious is probably one of the two most important qualities one can bring to biblical studies. The other, as we shall see, is imagination. Curiosity, then, leads us to speculate and make educated guesses concerning the text's original meaning and purpose. We begin this process by investigating the genre of our text and the possible characteristics of the sources behind it.

The Genre of a Biblical Text

You walk down the street of a small town and see a stranger advancing toward you on the sidewalk. As you pass each other you nod or smile or perhaps say hello, and then you keep going. If the person is indeed a stranger you do not stop and shake hands; you also do not spit, growl, or grunt at the person—not, at least, if you are having a reasonably good day and were raised right. Just about everyone we meet over the age of five seems to know the rules. How do we know what to do?

Each of us has been trained since childhood in what New Testament professor James Bailey calls "well-worn grooves of expectation," which allow everything from chance encounters and social engagements to international commerce and interaction on the Internet to run smoothly. The literature of a culture also develops "well-worn grooves," certain types or styles of writing, each of which we call a literary "genre." Bailey defines genres as "the conventional and repeatable patterns of oral and written speech, which facilitate interaction among people in specific social situations." We encounter novels, poetry, essays, musical comedies, news reports, letters, legends, proverbs, obituaries, and numerous other genres of writing. In each case a reasonably astute reader knows "how to read" these texts. We don't read a fairy tale with the same expectations with which we scan a grocery list or a phonebook. We know that these texts were all written for different reasons.

In biblical studies we have a similar array of genres—gospels, history books, epistles, parables, genealogies, poems, prayers, hymns, apocalyptic visions, prophecies, miracles, folk tales, among many others. Each genre can serve a certain purpose or set of purposes. If we can discern the genre of a text, we can make more of an educated guess concerning its original purpose.

This, of course, is a highly speculative endeavor, since most texts do not arrive with a genre label attached. Moreover, a single biblical text might incorporate sources containing different literary genres. A letter will sometimes include a hymn (see, for example, the paean to Christ in Paul's Letter to the Philippians [2:5-11]), or the ruminations of a prophetic visionary may contain portions of letters, as we find in the second and third chapters of the book of Revelation.

To sort out genres and sources, scholars pick and choose from among a huge array of tools with which to read texts critically: historical criticism, literary criticism, social scientific analysis, rhetorical criticism, tradition criticism, narrative criticism, source criticism, reader response theory, and other critical approaches. In the course of our journey we will have occasion to wield a number of these analytical gadgets. We won't use all of them, though. Some won't apply to the texts we will be exploring; as a result, we will have to content ourselves with sampling the sorts of criticism that biblical scholars cook up for our journey, leaving the rest of the feast for other occasions of textual adventure.

On the road just ahead we will employ two critical approaches. Form criticism explores the pretextual history of a document before it arrived in its present form through analysis of nonwritten, mostly oral, sources. It asks, among other things: Can we discover in our text any evidence of earlier small, possibly oral units? Source criticism seeks to learn if there are any earlier written texts behind the biblical text as we have it.

In this chapter these tools will help us to dig a bit below the surface of the text of the Song of Songs. For a while the going may be a bit slow, but take heart! On the far horizon I see the sands of exotic deserts and what my friend Erika refers to as the jaded romance that is archaeology.

Where to Start: Find the Well-Worn Path

The Bible is a big book. Even the most knowledgeable of exegetes (practitioners of exegesis, the art of interpretation) cannot claim an equally sure footing on every part of the biblical journey. When presented with the task of evaluating a particular text, biblical scholars do not start from scratch. They consult the text in its original language, of course, but they are curious to discover what others before them have discovered about the passage they are studying. They react to and rely on the labors of those who have gone down the road before. In other words, they consult a biblical commentary.

A commentary can be written for the scholar or the beginner. If you are serious about studying the Bible on your own, you should have access at least to a one-volume commentary on the Old and New Testaments. There you will typically find a chapter on each book of the Bible, containing a discussion of the basic questions concerning authorship, dating, the historical situation of the book, its major themes, and, in broad outline, the different approaches that scholars have used when interpreting its possible range of meaning. Such introductory material is often followed by a closer reading of certain sections of the biblical book in question. If you're particularly interested in a text, you can consult a commentary devoted wholly to that single book of the Bible; the introduction is usually much more detailed, and the subsequent analysis explores the technicalities of the language and meaning of the original text.

As we turn to the next stage of our analysis of the Song of Songs we will begin by taking a look at the ruminations of some people who, unlike you or me, have devoted their professional lives to the study of the Song and other related texts. They present us with an assortment of possible genres and sources for their favorite biblical book. Once we have sketched some of the more widely held theories we'll look more closely at the work of these experts and see how they use the critical tools to evaluate each theory concerning the genre of our text.

Any literary analysis is bound to be messy. A text written in tensive language will be full of ambiguous symbols while lacking in helpful hard data for our analysis. A piece of literature reveals itself slowly and never completely; it means many things at the same time. The Song of Songs is such a text. Nevertheless, I cannot resist asking: What was its original situation? Does it resemble any other ancient literature? It is the business of the biblical interpreter to ask questions, and so we roll up our sleeves and prepare to dig.

Before we begin, put this book down and read through the Song once again. As you read, reflect on my questions. What does the Song of Songs look like to you? Read part of it aloud. What does it sound like? Jot down a note or two, and then return here and we'll proceed.

The Song as Drama

That's odd. I thought the Gang of Four would have arrived by now. Anyway. Let's talk about Origen.

Origen of Alexandria was one of the first Christians to commit his thoughts on the Song of Songs to writing. Some time between 240 and 245 C.E. he spent time in Palestine and there composed a commentary on the book. Except for a few brief fragments, his original Greek text has been lost, but some of it has been preserved in Latin translation. Although he refers to the Song as an *epithalamium,* or wedding song, throughout his meditation, Origen assumes that what he is analyzing is best understood as a drama. "It is advisable for us to remind you frequently," he writes, "that this little book is cast in the form of a play." He identifies the major characters as the bride and the bridegroom, with supporting players including the daughters of Jerusalem and the associates or attendants of the groom.

Other later interpreters have followed Origen's lead, but critics whose task it is to locate earlier unwritten sources behind the text cry foul. Perhaps in your reading you have already noticed problems with viewing the Song as a dramatic presentation.

The text does seem at one or two points to set up a dramatic plot that centers on the disappearance of the beloved, who is sought in the city by the woman. But are you able to distinguish a beginning, middle, or end to this story? At least in its current form, it jumps around and defies all attempts to discern any narrative coherence. As Roland Murphy and others have pointed out, interpreters who see the Song as a drama try to rearrange the text as we have it into an earlier form in different order or see fit to add stage directions to clarify what is going on. It's difficult, though, to discern who the main characters are or how many actors inhabit the textual stage. Is it the story of two lovers accompanied by a kind of Greek chorus? If Solomon is a character, as some have proposed, we could have a love triangle here.

"There's no way that the Song of Songs is the script of a play," Jeremy says as the late arrivals enter the room.

"We lost track of the time," Marj says.

"My fault," Thad says. "I told them I needed a jolt of joe to fortify me for the coming storms—"

"And once we were in the cafeteria," Yvonne sighs, "one thing led to another. To frozen yogurt, actually."

"But we used the time wisely," Marj says. "We decided, as Jeremy said, that the Song of Songs is not a drama, no matter what that guy Origen said."

So what is it?

"You tell us," Marj says. "That's why they pay you the big bucks."

Is This a Wedding Song?

My turn to sigh.

Another traditional approach to the Song is to posit its origins in the context of ancient wedding rituals.

"That's what I was thinking," Yvonne says. "My daughter used a passage from the Song of Songs at her wedding. It fit perfectly."

This idea has gained support over the last century by observations of marriage rituals in rural villages in Egypt and Syria, where a type of song that looks a lot like our biblical text is still sung to honor newly married couples. This song, called a *wasf* (Arabic for "description"), features vivid poetic depictions of the bride in particular, comparing different parts of her anatomy to sometimes unlikely aspects of nature, just as we find in the Song of Songs. One *wasf* dating to the early 1800s reads in part:

> Here hast thou thy ornament, O beautiful one! Put it on, let nothing be forgotten!
> Put it on, and live when the coward and the liar are long dead.
> She said: Now shalt thou celebrate me in song, describe me in verse from head to foot!
> I say: O fair one, thine attractions I am never able to relate,
> And only the few will I describe which my eyes permit me to see:
> Her head is like the crystal goblet, her hair like the black night,
> Her nose is like the date of Irak, the edge of the Indian sword;

Zither player from Canaan.   From: *Atlas of the Bible,* Nelson

Her face like the full moon, and heart-breaking are her cheeks.
Her mouth is a little crystal ring, and her teeth rows of pearls. . . .
Her spittle pure virgin honey, and healing for the bite of the viper. . . .
Her neck is like the neck of a roe which drinks out of the fountain of Kanawat.
Her breast like polished marble tables, as ships bring them to Sidon
Thereon like apples of the pomegranate two glittering piles of jewels. . . .

Compare this with the description of the body parts of the bride in the Song of Songs (see 4:1-5; 6:4-7; and 7:1-10), and you will see the allure of the *wasf* as an explanation of the origins of the Song. The connection seems clear and sure. How do the mathematicians conclude their proofs?

"QED," says Thad.

Unfortunately, our situation is not quite so simple.

"Why not?" asks Yvonne. "Can't anything on this journey be simple?"

For one thing, there is a great gulf of time and culture separating Syrians today from the Hebrew poets of antiquity. We cannot presume that a particular custom or literary form would survive unchanged for over 2,500 years, not if it has in the process traveled from one rich religious and social system (Judaism) to another (Islam). And in fact, on close inspection the Arab *wasf* and the Song of Songs manifest substantial differences in imagery and structure. Marvin Pope notes that war songs and a sword dance by the bride are staples of the modern *wasf,* but these martial aspects are completely absent from the Song. The *wasf* genre also makes copious reference to the bride and groom as king and queen; nowhere do we find such imagery in the Song of Songs. Moreover, as Marcia Falk has pointed out, the structure of the modern *wasf* is formal and predictable; it is a catalogue of poetic description, a parade of imagery that processes in order from one end of the body to the other ("Describe me in verse from head to foot," demands the bride in the *wasf* quoted above). We find a suggestion of orderly observation in the three *wasf*-like parts of the Song of Songs, but the overall arrangement of the text is in no way strict.

"The bottom line?" Yvonne asks with a hint of impatience.

The bottom line: despite the evidence of the *wasf* there is little in the biblical text to indicate that a wedding ceremony was its original setting or a wedding song its original genre. The only reference to matrimony is an allusion to Solomon's wedding (see 3:11), and though the woman in the Song is referred to as a bride in two brief sections (4:8-12 and 5:1), we scan the text in vain for the imagery one would expect to find at a traditional wedding: abundant reference to the couple as bride and groom, as well as some (any!) interest in future fertility and the engendering of children. A form-critical approach suggests that behind some sections of the Song may lie the oral poetry of ancient nuptial celebrations, but we cannot assume that this text as we have it originated primarily in the context of the songs sung at weddings. We must look elsewhere for the sources of most of this biblical book.

Did the author or authors rely on earlier *written* sources when composing the Song? To answer this question—

"We need source criticism!" Thad interjects.

The Song as a Fertility Ritual

The Mishnah, a collection of Jewish wisdom and law dating to 200 C.E., depicts the rabbis at one point talking about a festival that takes place in the vineyards of Israel. One of them makes reference to Solomon's wedding in Song 3:11. From this, T. J. Meek suggested in 1924 that the Song, while not to be associated with wedding poetry or the propagation of children, did originate in a wider concern about fertility. Some other scholars have argued that the Song is a remnant of earlier texts composed as part of a fertility cult or sacred marriage ritual. According to this approach the Song contains vestiges of early liturgies or worship services designed to appease the gods.

Jeremy steps in at this point. He has been staring distractedly at a picture of a cuneiform inscription, unknowingly holding it upside down.

"They say that the Song of Songs comes from pagan cults?" he asks. He sees me watching how he holds the book, checks the cover, and turns it right side up. "How would pagan worship get stuck into the Bible? Isn't that blasphemy? Where would Jews have even heard of it?"

This possibility is not as outlandish as it might sound. As a result of archaeological discoveries we know that throughout their history some people in the land of Israel worshiped a variety of gods and goddesses.

"Right," Thad says. "The Gentiles who lived there worshiped their own gods, while the Jews worshiped Yahweh."

Actually, the division was probably not that clean. Statues of other divinities have been found in shrines dedicated to the Jewish God, and the art of early synagogues, which sometimes portrays elaborate renderings of the signs of the zodiac, indicates that at least some Jews were conversant in matters of astrology. It is possible that people of the lower social strata were not always as monotheistic as their religious leaders wanted them to be.

"On this I think you're right," Jeremy concedes. "The prophets chastise people all the time for worshiping other gods."

If some people were hedging their bets and adding other divinities to their devotion to the one God of Israel, echoes of some of their rituals might be able to be detected in the Bible. To find them, though, we would have to have nonbiblical texts to show us the way, and that is what Meek and his successors have tried to provide.

Samuel N. Kramer offers the most recent and thorough treatment of these sources from Mesopotamia (the land between the Tigris and Euphrates rivers, modern-day Iraq). He discusses a body of cuneiform inscriptions concerning the sacred marriage of a god and goddess. The god Dumuzi is the shepherd-king, while his consort is the fertility goddess Inanna, also known as Astarte (among other aliases). Dumuzi represents the land of the Sumerians, and his coupling with Inanna was meant to ensure the fertility of the king and the people's land. The two of them converse seductively in lyric poetical fashion.

The texts date from around 2000 B.C.E., and they were apparently produced as part of annual religious rituals designed to ensure divine blessings on the land. Without divine favor the land would not flourish and the people would starve; to prevent this many (probably most) societies in antiquity developed rites to curry favor with the gods. People gave to the gods so the gods would give back to them.

One can easily see similarities between the Sumerian inscriptions and the Song of Songs. "You have captivated me," declares one Sumerian writer,

> I stand trembling before you.
> Bridegroom, I would be carried off by you to the bedchamber;
> You have captivated me, I stand trembling before you . . .
>   (see Song 1:4; 4:9; 5:2-6; 8:2).
>
> Bridegroom, let me give you of my caresses,
> My precious sweet, I would be laved by honey,
> In the bedchamber, honey-filled . . . (see Song 5:1).
>
> My sister, I would go with you to my garden . . .
> My fair sister, I would go with you to my orchard,
> My sister, I would go with you to my apple tree . . .
>   to my pomegranate tree . . . (see Song 2:1-15; 5:1; 6:2).

"This next part is great," says Marj, who has been reading along over my shoulder. "It ranks right up there with the Song's 'Your nose is like a tower of Lebanon, overlooking Damascus.' Let me read it!" And she does:

> Lettuce is my hair by the water planted,
> Gakkul-lettuce is my hair by the water planted,
> Combed smooth are its tangled coils,
> My nurse had heaped them high.

Clearly, these two pieces of ancient literature share quite a bit of imagery. Courtship between male and female is the theme; love is in the air. In addition to heaped piles of agrarian metaphors and images of gardens and fruit and flocks the two display common motifs of love and desire as well as similar structures (each is composed of dialogue between lovers, interrupted periodically by a chorus of observers and friends). The male in each is referred to as a shepherd, while the woman is called his sister.

Kramer makes a good case for these Sumerian ritual texts of divine marriage as the original source for the Song of Songs. He even suggests that their original concern with the activities of gods may explain why the Song of Songs was included in the canon: even though it had been "purged" of its associations with fertility cults, he suggests, "it still carried with it a hallowed aura of religious traditions that smoothed its way" into the Bible.

Thad leans forward, with an eyebrow raised and a mockingly grave look on his face. "At this point," he says, "you will of course interject that while all of this looks good, you have a problem with it, right?"

Well, yes. Once again we have to ask some serious questions of our Sumerian sources and their modern proponents.

"I figured as much," he says.

For instance, how do we know that the similarities don't originate naturally from the fact that both texts depict the love of a woman and a man? If they both speak of such love, chances are they will share similar themes and motifs, no?

Michael V. Fox raises other questions that I want to outline in a little detail, since he provides an instructive example of a scholar doing source criticism. For starters, he asks: If the Song is based on fertility rituals, why do they lack any hint of myth, ritual, or concern with fertility? There are no prayers in the Song, no divine blessings, indeed, no divinity at all, since God is never mentioned. If, as Kramer suggests, the fertility cult associations were purged in the process of the Song's arrival into the Bible, the purging was complete indeed!

Another aspect of the Sumerian texts that must have been purged is the explicit language. Whereas the Song of Songs renders the couple's amatory exuberance through elegant, veiled allusion, the Sumerian texts often "tell it like it is." I won't share with you any graphic examples (Kramer shows no such scruples!); suffice it to say that the Sumerian descriptions of the private parts of the woman, in particular, leave nothing to the imagination. These are clearly texts focused on fertility.

Why, then, are there no references in the Song of Songs to what Fox calls "universal fertility" and "universal plenitude"? The main characters in the Sumerian literature are gods; thus they are representative figures, and their coupling signals the universal rebirth of nature. At one point the woman/goddess in the throes of love proclaims,

> I poured out plants from my womb,
> I placed plants before him, I poured out plants before him.

In the Song, however, there is no connection between the amorous actions of the lovers and the fertility of the land. When the gardens blossom, they do it without any help from our clearly human protagonists. Fox goes on to note that there is no corroborating evidence to indicate that there were sacred marriage rituals in Israel. Elsewhere such rituals may have involved a reenactment of the divine coupling, possibly involving the king. Such goings-on, Fox

Cuneiform tablet of the Epic of Gilgamesh (c. 650 B.C.E.).   Photo: TLP Archives

notes, "would hardly have escaped the prophets' notice," and yet the prophetic books of the Bible never mention such ritual activity.

Finally there is the question of dates. The Sumerian inscriptions were written over a thousand years before the time of Solomon, and as we have suggested, the Song came about some time after that. Kramer posits a direct line of influence from the Sumerian Dumuzi-Inanna cult through their Mesopotamian successors, the Akkadians, and then down to the Canaanites of Palestine, who bequeathed to the people of Israel an ancient Hebrew fertility liturgy celebrating the reunion and marriage of the sun-god with the mother-goddess.

"What?" Jeremy shouts. "A Hebrew worship service involving a mother-goddess?"

Calm down, friend. There is no evidence for such a service, and thus no evidence to support Kramer's smooth transition from Sumerians to Akkadians to Canaanites, much less to Hebrew tradition. Kramer's argument, which offers a lot of theory but no supportive details, is less than convincing. While it is conceivable that fertility motifs could travel through history, what is missing is hard evidence. Without it, it is difficult to locate our source for the Song in cuneiform texts from Sumeria.

By now Thad is fidgeting, and Yvonne is beginning to glaze over and checks her watch. (Perhaps I should have shared some of the more sexually explicit cuneiform material that I mentioned above.) It's time for a break, but first let's sum up for those who may have nodded off.

One of the primary goals of biblical interpretation is to try to situate the text in its original setting. As we will see in the third part of our journey with the Song (the part we'll call "Talk"), the original *Sitz im Leben* and the intention of the author, if we can recover them, form the basis for our ongoing conversation with and about the Bible.

In their analysis of the original setting of a section of Scripture, scholars employ a number of critical tools to see if they can determine the genre or type of writing of the text they are investigating. We have dabbled with the tools of form and source criticism and explored possible earlier sources, both oral (the *wasfs*) and written (Sumerian inscriptions), but have come up wanting in each case.

We spent a lot of time discussing the *wasf* tradition and the Sumerian inscriptions because the work some scholars have done on them illustrates the difficulties of doing form and source critical analysis. I also wanted you to experience what it is like to investigate and evaluate a number of secondary sources, that is, the work of people writing about original materials. From this we have seen that the labors of even the most reputable of scholars must be read and weighed with care. Just because people succeed in getting their material published does not mean that the rest of us should accept their analysis uncritically. Scholars expect that their readers will challenge their conclusions; most of them (though alas not all) accept such criticism with grace. Actually we have only seen the tip of the scholarly iceberg of theories about the identity of the oral or written sources that may lie behind the Song of Songs. More appear every year. The fun for these people is in the give-and-take of earnest and even heated conversation, and the Song of Songs has been the center of much such debate.

"Wait a minute," Yvonne says. "You're saying people do this sort of thing for fun?"

I nod and Jeremy shakes his head. "Man," he drawls, "there are many different gifts."

It's time for that break.

For Discussion and Reflection

1. After this somewhat involved exploration of form and source criticism the question recurs: Why are we doing all this? Consult again the introductory chapters, and refresh your memory. How would you explain to a skeptical friend why it is important to try to discover the sources behind a biblical text?

2. Spend a few moments contemplating the idea of the ancient fertility cult, its religious context and purpose. Do modern Christians ever mix sex and religion? Does human sexuality have a part to play in our understanding of the sacred? Can you think of any examples of such an interplay of sex and religion?

3. Fertility cults were apparently designed to convince the gods to favor their human subjects with success. Is this sort of thing a part of your own prayer experience? Can you think of any church-wide liturgical celebrations whose purpose is to try to propitiate and convince the Divine to shower blessings upon believers?

Chapter Seven

Love and the Rocks

We have been sojourning in the Near Eastern desert world of fertility cults and Sumerian cuneiform inscriptions, but I trust you are none the worse for wear. However, we still lack an answer to our question: What *is* this text? It's not uncommon for a biblical interpreter to try out one or two critical tools, only to discover that they don't quite complete the job.

"So what else can we do?" Yvonne asks, her resolution to proceed obviously restored.

One traditional way into this text is to examine it as an elegant work of allegory. An allegory is a story or narrative in which the people and events are meant to be understood as symbolizing something else. Texts written in tensive language abound in allegory. So, for instance, Adam and Eve in Genesis are symbols of all humanity, and the garden symbolizes, perhaps, the pristine state of our human consciousness before we give ourselves over to the darker side of human nature, the part that wants control and power.

The Song of Songs has been a playground for advocates of allegory, but let's postpone an examination of this approach. Most of the allegorical study that has been done on the Song dates from a time much later than its composition. Even though the Song lends itself to allegorical interpretation, that does not mean that it was originally intended to be understood this way, and at this point we're still trying to discern information about the original circumstances of the text.

"Can we afford to ignore such an obvious approach?" Marj asks.

Oh, we won't ignore it. I have an idea about the Song's allegorical potential that I want to share later down the road.

"This critical stuff reminds me of working on a jigsaw puzzle," Thad says. "A thousand pieces lie on the table before us, all in different shades of the same color."

I'm puzzled by the structure of the Song. You'll recall that we possess many different critical tools. One that I wish we could haul out of the toolbox is redaction criticism. Its goal is to discern how the writer of a text, or later editors, appropriated sources and stitched them together; in other words, it looks closely at how a text has been edited (or "redacted") into its final structured form. This is the tool of choice for interpreting the gospels, since it is clear that three of them—Matthew, Mark, and Luke—are somehow interconnected. The fun is in guessing the relationship: which one came first and how did the other two adapt and edit it? Redaction criticism can be used with some texts from the Hebrew Bible, particularly those that appear to depend on one another (some of the historical books, for instance). But it's almost impossible to pursue a course of redaction criticism when we have only a single text and no access to any of its original sources, as is the case with the Song of Songs.

"That's too bad," says Thad. "The Song has obviously undergone some stitching together. Look at how it ends."

Thad is correct. The last ten verses of the Song appear to be a catchall of material not easily or clearly related to what has gone before.

"The whole thing looks like a jumble, if you ask me," Yvonne says.

"There's no real beginning or conclusion," Thad says.

Your insights are borne out by the experts, one of whom acknowledges (before he spins his own ideas) that his colleagues have discerned anywhere from seven to forty-four separate units in the Song. Imaginative people use all sorts of literary theories to discover some very imaginative coherencies and connections, most of which make sense.

"But they can't all be right, right?" Yvonne says.

In preparation for this discussion I looked at the work of some of the most respected interpreters of the Song of Songs. I found no consensus concerning its structure. I fear this is one part of the puzzle that will remain unsolved.

"I've been thinking about the possible genres you mentioned earlier," Marjorie remarks from where she is sprawled on a nearby sofa. "Why can't the Song of Songs be just what it looks like—a bunch of poems about the love of a woman and a man, all heaped together?"

Out of frustration eventually may come wisdom. No one doubts that the Song is a poetic text.

"Consensus at last!" Yvonne says.

The problem for us, though—

"Oh, dear," she sighs.

—is that Hebrew poetry is an extremely complex genre to understand, and in many ways it is quite foreign to our sense of the poetic. For instance, there is disagreement among scholars as to whether Hebrew poetry displays anything like what we call meter (remember all those iambic pentameters from English class?). Instead, Francis Landy and others suggest that the poets of the Hebrew Bible focus their attention on alliteration, a great deal of parallel repetition, and what would look to us like wordplay. Moreover, any type of poetry is notoriously difficult to translate from one language to another; since we will not be able to explore the Hebrew original in any detail (no time and, in my case, no talent to speak of!) such a task is beyond the realm of the current quest.

"I see another problem," Thad says.

"You're getting as suspicious as he is," Marj says with a glance in my direction.

"Sure, they had poetry back then," Thad says. "But did they have love poetry?"

"How could they not have had love poetry?" Jeremy asks.

"But was it like ours?" Thad asks him.

"Love is love, right?" Jeremy responds.

Not quite. Thad's question is a valid one. Love isn't exactly always love, at least not the way we understand it.

"Back then love was not love?" Yvonne asks.

That's not what I'm saying. Of course ancient people experienced love of all kinds; we have some of their writings about it. But how they made sense of love, how they articulated their feelings and what those meant to them may have been quite different from the ways in which we express our own feelings and meanings. Before we delve into Marjorie's very promising hunch that the Song of Songs is an anthology of love poetry, we need to talk about the ways in which a society makes sense of love and "constructs" the meaning of everything else of any significance to the daily lives of its people.

"I can tell we'd better get comfortable," Thad says.

Jeremy agrees. "I feel a lecture coming on."

At this point in our journey we move from the examination of texts to focus on their context, which I have designated by the code word "rocks." Marjorie has made an intriguing suggestion: why not determine the genre of the Song of Songs by just looking at what is on the page? It looks like love poetry. Perhaps that is what it is. But we have to be careful.

Somewhere young Thaddeus has picked up a dose of the historian's caution, and that is a good thing to have, since we cannot assume that the people of antiquity shared our customs, our habits, our attachments to certain food or clothes, or even our expressions of love. When reading the Bible many people assume that the world they encounter there is identical to our own. In fact, ancient people understood themselves and their surroundings in ways that would startle and sometimes dismay you.

Before we can evaluate Marj's simple suggestion about the nature of the Song, indeed before we can aspire to read any biblical text well and wisely, we have to explore this reality: cultures pick and choose the meaning they

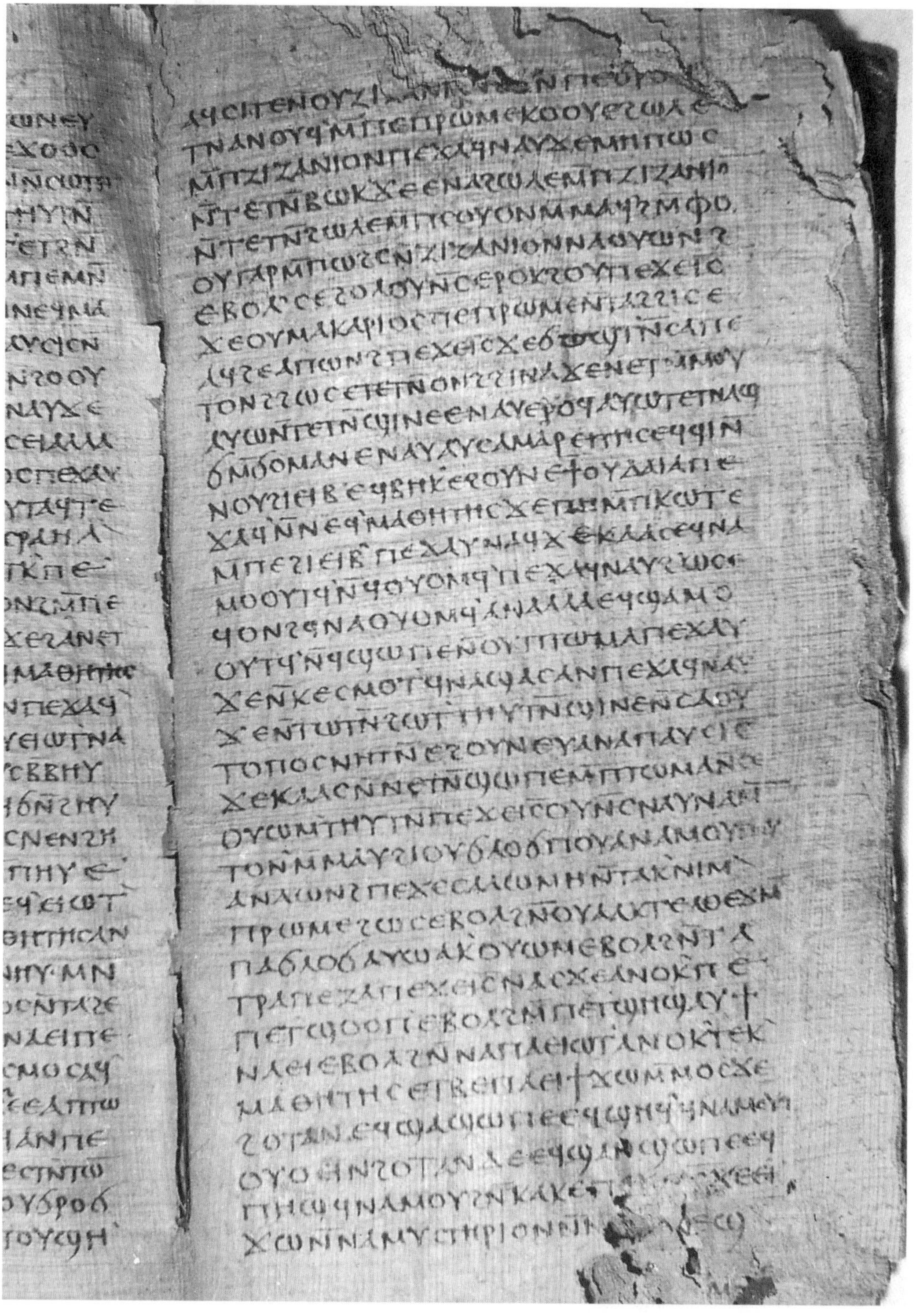

A papyrus document fragment. Photo: TLP Archives

give to people and things. In other words, societies *construct* their reality. To illustrate how this works we will head back into the desert and wander on down to Egypt with two nineteenth-century British archaeologists.

What a Dump!

In 1895 Bernard Grenfell and Arthur Hunt arrived at the Egyptian village of Behnesa, located to the west of the Nile, about 120 miles south of Cairo. They had traveled there to poke around the ruins of the ancient city of Oxyrhynchus (pronounced, as near as we can gather, ox-ee-RINK-us) in a quest for papyrus. The "paper" (we get this word in English from papyrus) of the ancient Egyptians, if buried in the desert sands and left undisturbed, sometimes survives over thousands of years. Grenfell and Hunt had a hunch: Oxyrhynchus had been an important governmental center and thus home to at least a few people wealthy enough to have supported private libraries of papyrus texts. If the archaeologists could find even one such library, they could greatly enhance modern knowledge of the ancient world.

Grenfell and Hunt hit the mother lode in the most unlikely of places. They found no rich family's library. What they discovered was the town's dump. Heaps of ancient rubbish buried in the sand for aeons yielded piles of mostly fragmentary papyrus texts that contained everything from sales receipts, drafts of wills, and petitions for divorce to scraps of lost works of ancient philosophers and playwrights. They even discovered the text of a previously unknown Christian work, the Gospel of Thomas. So many texts emerged from the Oxyrhynchus dump that today, over a hundred years after their discovery, the papyrus documents are still being published for the first time, at the rate of one volume every year or so.

One of the texts discovered at Oxyrhynchus was a letter. It was written "in the 29th year of Caesar"; in other words, it was sent twenty-nine years after Caesar Augustus became the first emperor of Rome. In our calendar this was 1 B.C.E. The text was in pretty good shape, and Grenfell and Hunt published it in the Greek with this translation:

Ilarion to Alis his sister, many greetings
and to my dear Berous and Apollonarion.
Know that I am still even now at Alexandria;
and do not worry if they come back altogether (?),
but I remain at Alexandria.
I urge and entreat you to be careful
of the child, and if I receive a present soon
I will send it up to you.
If (Apollonarion?) bears offspring, if it is a male,
let it be, if a female expose it.
You told Aphrodisias, "Don't forget me."

How can I forget you?
I urge you therefore not to worry.
The 29th year of Caesar, Pauni 23

(Addressed:) Deliver from Ilarion to Alis

Of course we know absolutely nothing about the people involved here—nothing, that is, beyond what the letter tells us. Indeed, we must scrutinize with care even what we see on the page. Ilarion is up north in Alexandria. He writes home to Alis, calling her his "sister." But are they really brother and sister? In ancient Egypt a woman might marry her own brother. Moreover, "brother" or "sister" were terms of endearment used between married people even when they were not blood kin. Thus it is possible—the editors of the text think it probable—that Ilarion is writing to his wife. Who are the other people mentioned—Berous, Apollonarion, and Aphrodisias—and what are their relationships to Ilarion and Alis? There is no way for us to know.

There is something familiar about this letter: Alis is worried about the effects of a prolonged separation on their relationship. She needs to be told that her husband will not forget her while he's in the big city. But Ilarion's tender attention to Alis should not obscure the matter-of-fact way he advises her to deal with the birth of a child. If it is a boy, keep it, but expose it (literally "throw it out") if the newborn is a girl. What he means here is: if a girl is born, take her out to a public place—a square or a well-traveled road—and leave her there to be picked up by the next passerby, who can then legally raise her as a slave.

Ilarion's apparent cruelty here is a warning to us: we should not be duped by what looks familiar to us. Despite his affectionate response to his wife's need for reassurance, his letter is the product of a culture that is fundamentally different from our own. On our journey through the Bible we need to be alert to these differences, how they came about, and how we should handle them as we attempt to converse with people very different from ourselves.

How Can Ilarion's Culture Be So Ignorant?

Any established culture has social norms. People are allowed to do this thing, but no one *ever* does that! Often the rules are unwritten and even unstated, at least in public, but just about everyone knows what they are and most people respect them.

To see this in action you need only take a trip to a suburban shopping mall and watch the people accompanied by small children. Much as the parents may want to browse through a store, they have to devote a great deal of time to training little Carla or Bobby in shopping etiquette. No, we don't talk to strangers. We don't come to a dead stop in the middle of a crowded aisle. And no, you can't walk out of the store with that toy, since we have not paid (and will not pay) for it. Why not? the child's eyes seem to ask. The parent responds, "We just don't," or (my favorite) "That's just not nice."

This socialization process at the mall is part of a culture's attempt to set guidelines and boundaries for the good of all. Sociologists call this *social construction*. A society, they assert, very subtly creates or constructs its own reality, its own set of guidelines concerning what constitutes appropriate behavior. This reality is not always based on logical or even conscious decisions made by the society or its leaders. When we examine some of the "social constructs" of a society we are sometimes at a loss to explain why the people treasure the customs and values that they do.

Why, for instance, do we socially construct appropriate dress the way we do? Jeremy, would you go to class wearing a dress and a string of pearls?

"No way!"

Why not?

"It's unnatural for a man to dress like a woman," he says with some heat.

"What do you mean?" Marj asks him. "Are you males born with a tattoo on your backs that says 'This male-gendered biological unit may not wear dresses and must be restricted to pants'?"

"Well, no," Jeremy admits.

And yet only transvestites and rock stars can wear dresses on any given day and get away with it (though how much a transvestite can get away with in Western culture is debatable). But there are certain times and circumstances in which our socially constructed reality allows a man to wear a dress.

"Right," says Thad. "At Mardi Gras or a Halloween party."

"What about Scottish kilts?" adds Yvonne.

Food is another area in which we can see social construction at work. Those of us in the West who are still carnivores usually do not think twice about eating lamb or veal, even if we realize that we are eating baby sheep and cows when we do it. Why, then, don't we eat puppies?

"Oh," Yvonne moans.

Well, they too are an efficient source of life-sustaining protein, as many societies in Asia have recognized for centuries. Why do so many people in one culture enjoy canine cuisine while the people of another culture are repelled by the idea?

"But the idea of eating puppies is disgusting," Yvonne protests.

Yes it is, to you or to me. But do you see why?

"You mean because we were brought up that way?" Thad suggests.

Precisely. Our relationships are also socially constructed. When a teacher is in a classroom she is somehow different from everyone else in the room. She actually isn't all that different. She might be better educated and a bit older than her students, but she is still just another person. And yet the other people in the room socially agree that she is different, and they grant her a certain authority over them. Why?

"She'll flunk them if they misbehave," Yvonne says.

Yes, because society has given her that power. Social constructions tend to focus on things like food, gender, bodily functions, and power relationships. Most groups of people feel the need to control the behavior of individuals in these areas, but different cultures come up with different behavioral guidelines.

Indeed, the social norms of a single cultural group can change over time. In the United States of the 1950s you did not normally find a mature woman wearing bluejeans in public unless she was working on a ranch or heading for a same-sex club. Today the society no longer attaches a stigma to women wearing pants. Back in the fifties the only people with oddly colored hair were women of a certain age whose touch-ups turned their white coifs a bit blue. Nowadays purple spikes are not all that unusual in certain segments of our society (such as college campuses), and a cross-dresser can be taken seriously as a basketball player.

Worlds in Collision

Jeremy is fidgeting impatiently. Perhaps his feathers are a bit ruffled by the image of him coming to class in pearls.

"What does Dennis Rodman have to do with the Bible?" he asks.

Marjorie jumps in. "I can answer that one," she says. "When we read Scripture we're going to find differences between our own social construction and those of the ancient world."

Jeremy turns to me. "I thought you told me the other day that I shouldn't worry about all this because you will show us that Scripture is timeless?"

Correct. I did say that. As we shall see, Sacred Scripture is understood to be revelational, authoritative, and timeless. But for the mainline churches it is the message of the text—the point that it is trying to communicate—that manifests these characteristics, not all the details of the original circumstances. The Word that calls us into conversation transcends the original *Sitz im Leben*.

For instance, Christians for centuries observed the presence of slaves in the New Testament and noted that St. Paul and others seemed to encourage slaves to remain as they were. From this they concluded that it was morally appropriate to enslave other people. This came about because Christians did not understand the difference between the central message of the text and the social construction out of which the text came. No violence was done to the Word of God when Christians decided that slavery was not part of God's will, even though it was accepted by people in the Bible.

"How do we know what is central to the message?" Marj asks. "I mean, the Bible says a lot about the role of women—you know, we should be submissive to our husbands and all that. That *has* to be part of the ancient social construction, but isn't it part of God's Word as well?"

There is no easy answer to Marj's question.

"Why am I not surprised?" Yvonne mutters.

With respect to this example, some Christians understand what the Bible says about women to be divine revelation, while others do not. Remember, Scripture is an invitation to a conversation within the context of a community. Depending on your community, the discourse may go one way or the other with regard to particular biblical passages. We will explore some of the specifics of how this conversation works in the third part of our trip, the part I label "Talk." But for now here is the bottom line: When reading the Bible, never assume that the world portrayed is identical *in its details* to your own. And if you really want to wrestle with the Word, try to read the text in the context of your own community. In the presence of others we can ask the important questions and discern the ways in which the texts speak from one social construction to people living in another.

Bridging the Gap

Different communities, then, must decide for themselves what parts of the biblical social constructions contain divinely revealed truth and what parts need to be set aside. The mainline Christian churches, the ones that have been around for centuries, begin this process of discernment by gathering as much information as they can about the social context of the original authors. So, for instance—to pick a hot topic for some churches right now—if a Christian community is searching the Scriptures to discover whether or not they should ordain women, they must first go to the text to look for evidence of women's ordination. But then they explore the world out of which the texts came. Were there women in positions of leadership in other religious traditions back then? Do we have any sources outside the Bible that point to female leadership in the Christian communities? If so, how were these women chosen? Did the process look at all like the ordination rituals that have developed over the centuries?

These are the kinds of questions the community asks, but what sources do they turn to in order to find the answers? Traditionally the scholars who were doing the research were trained to read biblical texts with great expertise, and thus when they looked around the ancient world for more information they concentrated on texts. So, for instance, when trying to figure out the social construction of first-century women they turned to the writings of the classical authors, as well as to the Hebrew Bible and Church Fathers.

"But they're all men," Marj says.

And most of them came from social groups that were wealthy, statused, and highly educated. Hence our concern about the Oxyrhynchus dump. Aside from a few garbage dumps like that one, our sources for information about the ancient societies that developed biblical texts were created by the elites, who made up only a small percentage of the people of that society.

We cannot pursue the question of women's ordination here, since that would take us down a very different road. But this discussion—

"Lecture," Thad says. "This lecture . . ."

If we want to describe and analyze an ancient social construction—in this case, the nature of ancient love poetry—we have to look beyond the majority of the literary materials that the ancients left behind. We have to look at the nontextual remains.

"The rocks," says Thaddeus.

Exactly.

For Reflection and Further Conversation

1. Think of some examples of socially constructed beliefs or behavior in your own life.

2. How do you think a wider understanding of social construction might change the way people relate to one another in our society?

3. Is love really a social construction? Is Dennis Rodman?

4. What about societal values? Are they socially constructed? Do you think there are any universally constructed values?

Chapter Eight

Lifestyles of the Dead and Buried: What Archaeology Is and What It Is Not

By the time we disembarked from the bus late each afternoon we were grimy with dust and sweat, thoroughly drained of energy by relentless heat and seemingly pointless work. After a shower we congregated downstairs on the cool patio under sweeping pine trees and talked about the day. Some might wander into town to shop or to sip a coffee or a beer (or two) at one of the *tavernas* in the village square.

At dusk we gathered at the long tables under the pines as the proprietor's son appeared with bottles of homemade retsina, a white resinated wine that tasted as though it had dripped through the piney boughs above our heads. And then the meal would begin: crusty bread, salads of olives and tomatoes and feta cheese, and course after course of sardines, fava beans, roasted potatoes, and (on some days, but not often) bits of lamb or chicken cooked in reddish olive oil. We ate and drank and talked for hours under the stars, and then we climbed up to bed, exhausted by a day's work and half a night of conversation. These were times to remember!

We were on a dig.

"Archaeology in the popular imagination," Brian Fagan observes, "is the stuff of which dreams are made, a world of adventure, intrigue and romance, of golden pharaohs and long-vanished civilizations." The word "romance" appears in the first or second paragraph of every handbook on archaeology in our local library.

In the summer of 1994 I was one of twelve college professors invited to spend six weeks in the village of Old Corinth, a few hours west of Athens.

This quiet field at Isthmia hides the remains of a stadium from which Alexander the Great launched his conquest of the East. Photo by John Lanci

The object of our attention was the ancient sanctuary of Poseidon at Isthmia, about ten kilometers northeast of Corinth. Isthmia was the site of a number of important events in antiquity. Alexander the Great once stood in its stadium and proclaimed his intent to conquer the East, while the emperor Nero visited the holy precincts and participated in the Isthmian games, taking every prize.

It has been a long time since anything like Alexander or Nero hit Isthmia. Our evening meals, with their lush food and even lusher conversation, shimmer in warm memory, but I spent my days in Isthmia wandering around the dirt of something called the "East Field," an area of previously excavated private dwellings. The houses were long gone; all that remained was the outline of their stone foundation walls. Looking across the field from shade of the trees along the modern street above, we saw nothing but sun-seared rubble. Thirty or forty people slaved over this site, and yet I don't recall that in the whole summer we found a single object that would cause a visitor to look twice. One group did find a grave near a beach over at Kenchreae, but even that had been discovered before; the original excavation had apparently gone undocumented and had been forgotten.

People do not become archaeologists in order to jet around the world discovering treasures, à la Indiana Jones. There is little glory and less money to be made in this occupation. The archaeologists I know who have persevered in the field do it because they live in the grip of a passionate curiosity about the world of the people who have gone before us. They recognize, as we did in the last chapter, that we cannot recover that world solely from the written remains of past cultures and that if we limit ourselves to texts we miss most of what happened to most of the people who have preceded us.

Archaeologists do "physical history," studying all the things people have made, including texts. Theirs is a rigorously scientific discipline in which each piece of evidence—a coin, a shard of pottery, or the finger of a marble statue—is examined and described in its surrounding context. The color of the clay potsherd or the stone fragment, the texture of the layer of dirt in which it was found, its relationship to other objects found nearby—all are drawn and recorded in the most minute detail. Hours are spent with whisk brooms and toothbrushes cleaning the earth away, sifting the sand not for emeralds and gold, but for the fragments of an oil lamp with flecks of paint on them. To the untrained eye such detritus is totally worthless, but in the hands of a specialist it might help to identify or date the whole surrounding area.

Archaeology provides interpreters of the Bible with information to supplement what we know from ancient literary material. The information archaeologists uncover rarely sheds direct light on the events or people mentioned in the Bible, but archaeology nonetheless is of enormous importance to biblical studies.

Blessed Rage for Good Order

"So, then, archaeologists explain what's behind the texts," Thaddeus suggests. "They answer the questions we raise as we read the Bible."

Would that this were true!

"It's not?"

While it is true that archaeologists have often helped us situate a biblical text more clearly in its *Sitz im Leben,* they rarely can offer Bible readers unambiguous answers to their questions. And sometimes what they can tell us undermines a community's traditional understanding of a text rather than supporting it.

Exodus, for Example

A famous example of this is the way archaeologists have tinkered with the conventional understanding of the Exodus event in the Hebrew Bible. You know the story: Moses parted the Sea of Reeds (in Exodus it's the Sea of Reeds, not the Red Sea) so the fleeing Israelites could escape the clutches of Pharaoh's army. Even believers have wondered how that could have happened, and a number of theories have circulated of late in the popular press purporting to explain how the sea was parted.

The most frequently cited answer involves a volcano on the island of Santorini, north of Crete, that allegedly exploded and caused tidal waves all along the eastern Mediterranean. The theory goes something like this: the Israelites were trapped by Pharaoh's army in the marshy area of northern Sinai (a sea of reeds) near the Mediterranean. When Santorini exploded, the sea formed towering tidal waves. The water forming this massive surge was drawn from the shore, in a very short time exposing dry (or drier) land over which the Israelites could flee. The tidal waves then crashed to the shore and wiped out the Egyptian army.

"I read about that in *Reader's Digest* once," Yvonne says. "It sounded good to me. But I'm sure you have a problem with it, right?"

Just that there is no evidence for any of it. The volcano at the center of the island of Santorini did erupt quite violently, but it did so several centuries before Moses would have existed. And so far no one has been able to confirm the generation of tidal waves after the blast. Nor has anyone been able to locate archaeological evidence of people wandering in the northern Sinai at the time when people think Moses lived.

"That doesn't mean anything," Jeremy says. "It was a long time ago and they were camping out. How could anyone find anything a couple of thousand years later?"

Certainly the lack of evidence doesn't mean that the Israelites never passed through the Sinai. But archaeologists tend to be wily and suspicious people, devoted to detail, and they do close work. They have discerned traces of the camps of a number of itinerant peoples elsewhere in the Middle East dating back thousands of years. The complete lack of material evidence for the existence of a large band of Israelites wandering through the Sinai wilderness for forty years does throw into question the historicity of the events as portrayed in the book of Exodus.

Jeremy finds it hard to contain himself.

"So the Exodus didn't happen? Fine!" he says, though it is clearly not. "Then how did the Israelites get to the Promised Land?"

Unfortunately, similar problems confront the interpreter of the book of Joshua, which narrates the story of the Israelite conquest of Canaan, the land across the river Jordan promised them by God. Once again archaeology raises doubts concerning what the text says about the conquest, including the famous destruction of the walls of Jericho. It turns out that Jericho and a number of the other cities supposedly conquered by Joshua's army had not been inhabited for centuries before the emergence of Israel. The text of Joshua was probably written in the seventh century B.C.E., about six hundred years after the alleged conquest. As theologians Robert Coote and David Ord put it, "Clearly the writers of Joshua were not entirely familiar with the period they were writing about."

Even if the account in the Bible is not historically accurate, one way or another the Israelites wound up in Israel. Scholars have suggested two other possibilities, each of which has some archaeological evidence to support it.

Social historians refer to the first potential scenario as the infiltration model. In this reconstruction wandering nomads migrated peacefully between the desert and the highlands of Palestine. Archaeologists have found physical testimony to the existence of their settlements, and anthropologists have shown that the movement of such nomads was associated with the need to graze their flocks.

The second scenario also involves the movement of people, this time as a result of a violent revolution. According to this theory (actually there are a number of variations on this idea, too many for us to worry about here), Israel arose as a result of a peasant struggle for liberation from oppression. The revolt might have been fomented by a core group of people who escaped from Egypt, perhaps bringing with them a monotheistic religion and a God called YHWH. Once in the highlands of Palestine, these people didn't conquer their neighbors but united with them to overthrow their masters.

"Let me guess," Thad says. "Their masters were the Egyptians, right? They're the heavies in the Exodus story."

Excavation of the diplomatic archives of Amarna from fourteenth-century B.C.E. Egypt does provide archaeological evidence for Egyptian domination of Palestine at this time. So, yes, it is possible that the writers of Exodus and

Joshua had sources that made mention of the basic core of the story—escape from Egyptian oppression—which they then shaped into the biblical texts we have. Mind you, even this second scenario is highly speculative; the archaeological material renders the revolt model conceivable but proves nothing.

Yvonne looks weary. "I'm beginning to feel like I walked out of Egypt myself," she says. "Why take us through all this archaeology stuff if it's only going to complicate matters for us?"

"Yeah," adds Jeremy. "What good is it if it only confuses people?"

I wanted to postpone questions like this until the third part of our journey, where we will ponder the "why questions" of biblical study. But at this point, with even the long-suffering Yvonne chafing with restlessness, it is time to provide you a preview of what we will discuss in the section of our trip I call "Talk." Here goes.

A(nother) Preview of Coming Attractions

As long as we refuse to reexamine the popular understanding of what the Bible is, that is, an immutable text dictated word for word by God, the field of archaeology cannot support the task of biblical interpretation. The evidence provided by archaeology challenges us to rethink fundamentally the way we read the Bible. Traditionally, people have understood the Bible to be "privileged information." Although it has been generally understood that the books of the Bible came from specific times and places (just as did other texts like the Greek tragedies of Euripides and the Roman historical works of Tacitus), many people have been taught that biblical texts are somehow qualitatively different from other ancient texts: God intervened to see to it that these texts were written in a way that the divine did not act elsewhere.

But what if we delay attributing this special status to biblical texts? What if we look at the Bible as just one of many "artifacts" from the ancient world? (Wait, Jeremy. I'm not going where you think). As believers, we look to the words and lines of these particular artifacts for a manifestation of divine revelation. But what if they were first composed in the same way that other ancient literary texts were generated? What if they were recognized as divinely inspired only after the fact?

Let's take this a bit further. What if the experience of ancient people was very little different from ours with respect to the action of God in their lives? Think for a moment about the people who marched with Moses and their descendants who observed the actions of Jesus of Nazareth. What if these people were not actually given front row seats at the spectacle of God's divine theater? What if they experienced the divine just as we do and had to struggle, just as we do, to discover and interpret the action and will of God?

"I see where you're headed." Jeremy is not happy. "You mean none of it happened the way it says in the Bible, right?"

Not necessarily. What if what happened to them was a lot like what happens to us today? They talked about their experience among themselves and then wrote things down, and as they wrote, they embellished their experiences *in order to make clear the significance and importance of what had happened to them.* As they talked and wrote they discovered that God had been acting in their midst. Think a minute. What would be the implications of such an idea? Do you see where I'm going?

Marjorie jumps in. "I think I do," she says, as she sits upright in her chair. "You *could* be seen as denying supernatural things like miracles, since they happened then in ways that they don't usually happen now. But," she hesitates, "you could also be hinting at just the reverse."

"Whoa," Yvonne interjects. "You're getting like him," she says to Marj and points to me. "And I'm getting lost."

"In other words," Marjorie continues, "what if ancient people lived pretty ordinary lives like we do, but in their very ordinariness they somehow saw God at work?"

"I think I see," says Thad. "The Israelites came to see themselves as a people chosen by God over a long period of time rather than as the result of a single historical event like the Exodus. They looked back on what happened and saw that God had been working with them and through them all along."

Now you have it.

"If that's how it happened," Marjorie continues, "then we are in the same position as the Israelites. We too can look at our lives and see God at work."

And, I add, at work just as powerfully now as back then. There is a danger, you see, in assuming that in ancient times God used to work wonders but now God no longer does so. We start to think that somehow the power of God is a past event, or at least that the people of ancient times had access to it in ways that we do not. On the contrary, the churches have always taught that the power of God consistently works through the believing community. But if we read biblical texts too literally, as though they are written in steno language, we can fall into a trap, thinking that somehow ancient people *knew* what we can only *believe.* It's much more likely that things have not changed all that much when it comes to the working of God.

Does it really detract from the Bible or our faith if we contemplate the possibility that the Israelites had a powerful experience of God but that it didn't happen the way Exodus—or Cecil B. De Mille—said it did, with walls of water on their right and their left? What if, after decades of oppression, they freed themselves of the yoke of Egyptian rule through more workaday methods of resistance and rebellion and only realized later, in their hearts and in conversation among themselves, that their liberation had come about through the active power of God?

I suggest that such thinking adds to, rather than subtracts from, the power of God and the power of Sacred Scripture. This approach encourages us to plunge deeply into the Bible and to engage ourselves in a whole array of reflection and conversation. Instead of encouraging us to *believe* that God parted the Sea of Reeds for the fleeing Israelites, the book of Exodus invites us to *participate* in the Exodus event by discovering the times and the ways that God has freed us and our community from oppression. In other words, Exodus is not a mere chronicle of events that happened a few thousand years ago to people very different from us; rather, it is an invitation, a challenge even, to discover how we are now being liberated by God.

"And how we have oppressed others, too, right?" Thad is now on board. "When I read the text, I can see a part of myself as a good Egyptian soldier, following Pharaoh's orders."

On this particular journey archaeology opens an important door. It invites us to study biblical texts just the way we would scrutinize other ancient texts or coins or column bases or terra cotta pots. Although the discipline of the archaeologist at first seems to kick up dust that obscures our vision, if we're patient, if we hold the evidence of the rocks next to the testimony of our texts, our conversation will be animated and our imagination will be made fertile. And in the conversation and the imagination we will be able to hear when God speaks. We will not just remember earlier exchanges and interactions with God; we will participate in a divine conversation that continues to unfold.

The dynamics of divine and human conversation will engage us more fully later. By now it probably appears to you that we have strayed quite a ways from our discussion of the Song of Songs. However, we're right on track, for in the next chapter we will do what I have just suggested: we will hold the Song in one hand while in the other we observe a very secular text from ancient Egypt. In looking first at the Bible and then at a text provided by the passion of archaeologists we will be able to draw some conclusions concerning the nature of the Song of Songs and hazard some guesses concerning our original questions about it.

For Reflection and Discussion

1. In previous chapters we already began to approach Scripture in the ways suggested above. Let us continue. Read through the story of the Exodus, particularly the call of Moses (Exod 2:23–3:12). Think about your own life. Have you ever had a burning bush experience?

2. Have you ever been liberated by God, as were the Israelites? What were the circumstances? When was it that you "knew" that God had been at work in the experience all along?

3. In this chapter we suggested that one should not read a biblical text as "privileged information." In other words, it is important to look at the Bible as one of many ancient artifacts. Do you approve of such a maneuver? Some very good Christian folks would not. Discuss whether or not you think this is an appropriate way to study the Bible.

Chapter Nine

Making the Heart Forget:
The Love Songs of Ancient Egypt

At this point in our journey we find ourselves once again in Egypt, a land, for our purposes, composed in equal measure of museums and desert ruins. We set out some time ago to see if we could learn something about this strangest of biblical texts, the Song of Songs, trying to figure out how and why a book of such sensual imagery and power was included in the canon of the Hebrew Bible. We explored a number of different scholarly suggestions concerning its purpose and sources but found that none of these quite answered our questions satisfactorily, and in the end Marjorie blurted out in frustration that the text looked like love poetry to her. Why couldn't it just be what it looks like?

We could not answer Marj's question by comparing the Song of Songs to other biblical texts, since no other parts of the Bible bear much resemblance to the Song. It was time to leave the realm of "Texts" and move on to "Rocks," that is, archaeological material that might help us make progress on our journey. Thus we have spent the past few legs of our journey exploring the nature of archaeology and what help it can bring to the study of the Bible.

Now we are prepared to return to Marj's question. Why couldn't the Song of Songs have originated as love poetry that had little or nothing to do with formal religious practice? We agreed that it was possible, but Thad cautioned that we should not assume anything until we confirmed that there was such a genre in antiquity as love poetry. At this point, while you, the reader, were off at work or studying for another class or washing your windows, I sent our pilgrim friends off to do a bit of research. In this chapter we shall see what they discovered on their librarian forays. Their topic was love poetry in antiquity; in particular, I suggested that they try to dig up something on the poetry that the people of ancient Israel might have encountered. They quickly narrowed their topic to the love poetry of ancient Egypt. Let's see what they found.

The Love Poetry of Ancient Egypt

Yvonne begins. "I told them I wanted an easy assignment," she says, gesturing to her fellow researchers. "I'm not a student, after all. So my job was to take notes on the sources."

So what do you have?

"Well, there are four major sources of Egyptian love poetry. The oldest one is called Papyrus Harris 500. It dates to about the year 1300 B.C.E." She flips the page of her notes. "I read that they found the papyrus in a casket in a 'Ramesseum' in Thebes. What's a Ramesseum?"

I am not sure. I suspect it is a tomb or some public monument dedicated to one of the pharaohs named Ramses. I do know that Thebes was a city of great importance for the governing of Egypt in that period.

"The second source is called 'the Cairo Love Songs,'" Yvonne continues.

"This one is cool," Thad interjects.

Yvonne resumes. "It includes two love songs that were found painted on a vase. The vase, of course, was shattered into pieces—thirty-one of them at last count. The vase was, um, 36.5 centimeters high and 43.0 in diameter. I couldn't find out where the vase was from. Maybe it was found in Cairo?"

It is possible. And the date?

"Nineteenth to Twentieth Dynasty."

That would put it close to 1200 B.C.E.

"The third source is called the Turin Papyrus 1966. Its text is unreadable in a lot of places, and it goes back to the Twentieth Dynasty, some time in the 1100s B.C.E." says Yvonne. "I couldn't find any information about where it comes from in Egypt."

This is often a problem with archaeological material. Unless something is as big as a building, ancient remains often have been moved from their place of origin. If the fragment or text does not state explicitly where it is from, we often have to guess.

"Actually," Yvonne says, "the last source I found seems to do just that. It is called the Papyrus Chester Beatty I, and it's the best preserved and most complete text of love poems they've found. And," she adds with a touch of excitement in her voice, "this one tells us where it's from. It seems that this papyrus was one really big scroll, about sixteen and a half feet long. It's a bunch of different texts, like an encon—, an encom—, what's that word?"

Encomium, a series of praises.

"Yeah, that's it," she nods. "Well, the scroll includes a bunch of praises for Pharaoh Ramses V, a short story called 'The Strivings of Horus and Seth,' and three groups of love songs just about completely preserved."

So where is it from?

"The books I looked at it said it definitely comes from Thebes, because at one point the text says"—she finds the quote in her notes—"'It has come to a happy ending in Thebes.'"

That's it?

"Actually, no," she says. "One of the scribes who worked on the scroll signed it. His name was—yikes, I'll spell it: NAKHTSOBK—and he was 'scribe of the Royal Necropolis.'" She puts down her notes. "The book we looked at seemed to think that this proved that the papyrus, at some point at least, found its way to Thebes. But I don't see why."

Yvonne has done some good hunting. The word *necropolis* means, literally, "city of the dead." Think in terms of a large royal cemetery. If the papyrus included an encomium of Ramses V we know that the text dates to the time of his reign, around 1160 B.C.E. We also know that in this period the pharaohs and their families were buried at Thebes. So if the scribe comes from the royal necropolis he—and Yvonne's text—were associated with Thebes.

What we have, then, are four major sources of material. Note that they all come from Egypt and date to within a hundred or so years of each other, from the 1200s to the 1100s B.C.E. Note, too, that most of the archaeological sources are fragmentary; the Chester Beatty papyrus is a rarity in its completeness, while the shattered and reconstructed Cairo vase is more the norm.

The Content and Cultural Context of the Songs

We will compare these poems with the Song of Songs in a bit more detail later, but even as we first dip into these texts the reader of the biblical book is in familiar territory. The texts from Yvonne's sources ache with emotion and beauty:

> [M]y heart is in balance with yours.
> For you I'll do what it wills,
> when I am in your embrace.
> My prayer it is that paints my eyes.
> Seeing you has brightened my eyes.
> I've drawn near to you to see your love,
> O prince of my heart!

We encounter the double entendres to which we have grown accustomed. In one poem a young man observes of his beloved:

The mansion of my sister:
Her entry is in the middle of her house,
her double-doors are open,
her latch-bolt drawn back,
and my sister incensed.
If only I were appointed doorkeeper.

Some motifs of love poetry don't seem to change over time. Do you remember Juliet musing on the larks as she and Romeo awaken after a night of forbidden intimacy? One of her Egyptian forebears, finding herself in a similar position, objects:

The voice of the dove speaks. It says:
"Day has dawned—
when are you going home?"
Stop it, bird!
You're teasing me.

This supple poetry, all of which was found in Papyrus Harris 500, shimmers with evocative beauty. Where could it have come from? What is its cultural context?

Here Thad jumps in with his report.

"The first part of my report, actually," he says with characteristic thoroughness. "I wanted to find out why I had always been taught that the Egyptians were so impersonal and stiff. You know, 'Walk Like an Egyptian.'" He stiffens and mimics the video of the popular song by the Bangles, in which all sorts of people on the street drop what they are doing and imitate the stock two-dimensional figures found in ancient Egyptian tomb paintings.

"I found this book," he continues, coming back to his notes, "by Michael Fox—not the actor—who has put together a theory that sounded pretty good to me. He relates this poetry to what is called 'the Amarna revolution.'"

Here Thad refers to the cultural changes that confronted Egypt rather abruptly during the reign of the pharaoh Akhenaton (1367–1350 B.C.E.).

"Akhenaton was the first monotheist," Jeremy adds. "At least the first one who wasn't a descendant of Abraham."

The Egyptians were polytheists who worshiped the divine in many forms. Akhenaton insisted that all his subjects worship a single deity, Aton, symbolized by the sun's disk. Although our sources are sketchy concerning the theological details, some scholars have suggested that this was indeed an early form of monotheism, the worship of only one God, which, of course, became the centerpiece of the later Israelite religion.

"Akhenaton's religious views have little to do with my report," Thad interrupts. "The Amarna revolution also involved Egyptian art. Much of the artwork of Egypt depicted the life and times of the pharaoh and his court. Akhenaton introduced a more realistic style of portraying the royal family, a manner more natural and private. According to Fox the art of Amarna focused more clearly on the private life of the king rather than just on public occasions. In addition, he says, 'Amarna art idealized the present moment rather than eternity.' That's on page 184," Thad adds. "My English prof told us always to include the exact source when quoting from it."

Akhenaton's focus on the present, I take it, allowed the artists to explore aspects of life on this side of the grave, such as love?

Thad nods. "There was a shift in the artists' interest from the pharaoh's accomplishments in war and statecraft to people's personal emotions," he says. "Egyptian painting at this time depicts more and more people experiencing the pleasures of the senses."

But Akhenaton lived a century or so before the love poems we are perusing were written. And I seem to recall that his influence, and his religion, died with him.

"The religion, yes," says Thad. "When he checked out, the Egyptians reverted to their earlier multiple gods. But according to Fox the pharaoh's impact on Egyptian art, prayers, stories, and (especially) love poems survived and was passed down." Thad pauses. "At least Fox says it is *possible* that the love poetry we're reading was influenced by the Amarna revolution."

Good. Note Thad's hesitancy, which mirrors the caution of scholars such as Fox. When examining sources as old as these we must be careful not to claim too much from so little evidence. It is certainly possible, but not conclusively proven, that the naturalism of Akhenaton's cultural and religious revolution is what spawned the fluid, sensual beauty of the love poetry recovered from the dynasties that succeeded his own.

The Language, Genre, and Purpose of the Poems

Marjorie is up next and explains that she and Jeremy explored the language and possible functions of the texts, along with their genre; even though the texts seemed to be poems, they wanted to know what kind of poetry.

"We have a number of different topics to discuss," she says briskly, as Jeremy sets up an easel with newsprint on it. "For the first part of our presentation I'll talk, and Jeremy will write."

She shuffles through her papers for a moment and then begins. "First, we looked at the language of the poetry," she says, as Jeremy carefully prints "LANGUAGE" at the top of the newsprint page. "The texts were composed in literary Late Egyptian, which was a language written but not spoken. It was taught as a sort of a second language in the schools for scribes. As a result," Marj continues, "scholars suspect that the poems come from the upper classes of Egypt."

"They think this," adds Jeremy, "because of all the talk about scented oils and servants and nice clothes. The poor couldn't afford any of that."

Nor would they have had the time, in all probability, to compose these texts.

Jeremy copies the words "TRANSLATION TROUBLES" on the newsprint as Marjorie continues.

"Translation of these texts is tough, even when the papyrus—or, in the case of the Cairo Love Songs, the vase—can be reconstructed without too many gaps. That is because, among other things, there are so few other texts to compare them with."

Good. We encountered a similar problem when we first approached the Song of Songs, remember? Scholars of any ancient literary source seek out parallels when interpreting textual material.

"We found one person capable of writing about the quality of the Egyptian poetry itself. I think it was Gardiner . . . Yes," Marj says, checking her notes. "He says there is no sustained alliteration or rhyme in the poem, even though scholars have found those techniques in other literary Late Egyptian texts written by the scribes. But even Gardiner draws a blank when it comes to figuring out the meter of the poetry."

Jeremy scrawls "AUTHOR OR AUTHORS?" on his newsprint as Marjorie notes that no one knows who wrote these texts or even if a single author composed any one of the sources we have.

"John Bradley White suggests that the poems are from a bunch of different people and were later loosely united when an editor or editors linked them together based on 'catchwords.'"

Thad looks up from his notebook. "What's a catchword?" he asks. "And do you have a citation?"

"I've got the book right here," Jeremy says. "It's called *A Study of the Language of Love in the Song of Songs and Ancient Egyptian Poetry,* and he talks about catchwords on, um, page 80." Jeremy thumbs to the page. "And he does give an example. The word for 'perfume' appears three times in the collection of poems in Papyrus Harris 500, and he says that even though the poems are probably by different authors the fact that that word appears in each one means that separate poems were linked together. Probably."

"So the ancient editors grouped the poems together if they used similar images?" Thad asks.

I shrug and suggest that such a thing is possible. We have some evidence for a similar collating of materials in the Bible.

"Our friend Michael Fox—not the actor—agrees with White that each source we have might be a collection, an anthology of different texts by different authors," Marj says, adding with an eye to Thad, "on pages 200 to 201. But he suspects that one or more of these texts might be a single, complex poem and not a collection at all."

Yvonne is fidgeting. "Were they religious?" she asks, and as if he had read her mind—or her body language—Jeremy is already printing the words "FUNCTION/PURPOSE" on the newsprint.

"Fox thinks it's unlikely that these poems were written for religious reasons," Marj says. "How does he put it, Jeremy?"

Her partner looks down at the legal pad on the table beside the newsprint stand. "He says the poems hardly mention the gods and are, quote: 'well on the secular side of the border' between secular and religious poetry. Page 234, Thad."

"Thanks."

"Which makes sense," Jeremy adds, "since they're all pagan."

I'm about to object, but Marjorie anticipates me. "I think we need to be careful about calling these poems 'pagan,'" she says.

"But they are!" Jeremy retorts.

"Well, yes, but it seems to me," Marj says, "if we're going to compare the Song and the archaeological evidence we have, we need to show a little respect for both sides."

Jeremy backs down and Marj continues with their presentation.

"Fox says that it's hard to figure out the *Sitz im Leben* (he actually uses that term!) from the poems themselves, and so he sort of sidesteps the question of writing style," she says. "Instead he assumes they're love poetry, or perhaps songs sung by professional banquet singers, and he speculates on the function of love songs in ancient society in general."

"What proof does he have of the existence of such banquet singers?" Thad asks.

"Good question," Marj responds. "He refers to their presence in tomb paintings from about the same time."

I add that this is an example of one important way that archaeologists work: they try to read ancient texts in light of other material evidence, such as paintings, coins, pots, and even architecture.

Marj continues to report on Fox. "He thinks that possibly the poems are courting songs or maybe were sung at weddings," she says. "But he says the problem with this is that no one is sure how Egyptian weddings were celebrated, or if they were celebrated at all. Besides"—she pauses to flip a page in her notebook—"the love songs never refer to the couple being married."

"He wonders if they're magic spells," Marj continues, "but decides they're not, since they don't work the way magic worked back then. I mean," she adds quickly, as she sees Jeremy ready to react, "magic never actually *works,* of course; there's no such thing. But the poems don't have the same *structure* as ancient magical spells."

Jeremy relaxes and she continues. "Fox also wonders if they're funeral songs about love and death, since, as he puts it, 'Egyptians had mortuary festivals the way other people have weddings,' but here too he says no, since the poems hardly ever make a reference to death."

"Which leaves only one possible function," Marjorie says, as Jeremy copies out the words "LET ME ENTERTAIN YOU."

"The titles were her idea," he says as he writes.

"Entertainment. Fox thinks these poems were written to entertain people," Marj says with a note of triumph in her voice. "In other words, the Egyptian love songs are, well, love songs. Pure and simple."

"The evidence?" asks Thad.

Making the Heart Forget

"The evidence is pretty convincing," Marj says. "Even my partner thinks so, right?" Jeremy shrugs his shoulders and nods.

"Probably the most conclusive proof that these poems were created for pure entertainment is the fact that three of the four texts say they were," Marj says.

"Why didn't you say that in the first place?" Yvonne asks her.

"We're doing scholarship," Jeremy says, and he writes the word on a piece of newsprint with a touch of a swagger.

"Where do they say that?" Thad asks Marj, who turns to me, holds up some sheets of paper covered with notes, and asks, "How technical do you want me to get?"

I counsel her to keep it simple, since the next stage of our journey is beckoning.

"Well," she begins, "according to Fox, page 244, three of the collections begin by stating that their purpose is, um, the hieroglyphic word that he reproduces as *shmh ib,* with a little curlicue under the *hs.* Fox says that this means 'entertainment' or 'diversion,' literally, 'making the heart forget.'"

Yvonne smiles. "What a beautiful way to put it."

"He—Fox—suggests that the poems were sung at banquets," Marj says.

"Is there any evidence for such banquets?" asks the increasingly cautious Thad.

"Here is where the archaeology comes in again," Marj says to him. "Murals in tombs from roughly the same period include pictures of some of the same activities and motifs mentioned in the love songs. And," she adds conclusively, "some of the paintings are labeled with the same word as the poems, *shmh ib,* 'entertainment.'"

"What kinds of activities do you mean?" Thad asks.

"One mural urges the viewers to 'divert their hearts' by visiting and enjoying their friends, eating, drinking, listening to good music, even putting on scented oils."

And motifs? I ask.

"Well," Marj says, "I think by that Fox means that there are some similar themes in the tomb paintings and the poems. Like lovers resting in gardens, people dressing up with fine linen or rubbing themselves with oils and perfumes . . ."

"And getting drunk," Jeremy adds. "And having sex."

"One mural shows a man sitting next to his wife," Marj continues. "And she is referred to as 'the beloved of his heart,' the same phrase that is found in some of the poems."

The case looks rather convincing to me. Anything else?

"Not really," Marj says. "Well, maybe just one more point. Between the two love poems in Papyrus Harris 500 the scribes put a song that seems to have functioned as an invitation to party. Fox thinks that this is an indication that the love poems on either side might have been part of the entertainment."

Marj and Jeremy have given us a thorough report on the possible social setting of these Egyptian texts. Now it is time to summarize what our researches have discovered and to ask one last question of the material.

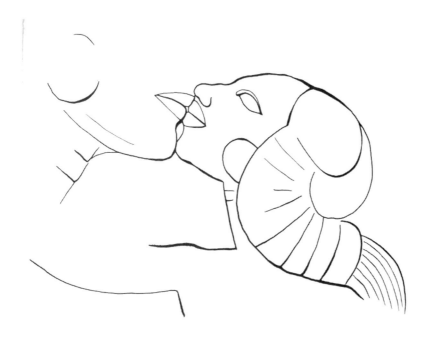

Fragment of limestone relief from Amarna, Egypt (ca. 1340 B.C.E.).

From: *Body Symbolism of the Bible,* Staubli and Schroer

Transmission Problems

"Not so fast," Thad interjects. "As we were doing our research, something was bothering me about all this Egyptian stuff. It has to do with the dates of the love songs."

They date, you will recall, to the 1200s B.C.E., and I think I can see where Thad is going.

"You said before that the Song of Songs couldn't be dated as far back as Solomon but only to a few hundred years after him," Thad says. "Well, I read that Solomon probably reigned in the 900s B.C.E. If the Song was written after that, we're talking about a difference of five or six hundred years between these Egyptian poems and the Song of Songs."

The soul of scholarly caution, Thad has once again put on the brakes for us, and wisely so. We cannot assume that people writing perhaps in the 600s B.C.E. knew about texts that date to the 1200s, especially if the information was limited to a very small number of people in the royal courts and was stored on perishable material like papyrus.

"I looked into this problem," Thad says. "And what I found is the second part of my report." He moves up front to the newsprint and hesitates for a moment. "I'll keep this simple," he says with a crooked smile. "Yvonne looks tired."

She is not alone. Thad plugs on with energy.

"Michael Fox—the scholar not the actor—writes on pages 191 to 193 that there might be as much as a thousand years between the evidence we have of Egyptian love poetry and the writing of the Song of Songs. Now," Thad looks over his glasses at us, "it's possible that the Egyptians continued to write love songs all the way on down to the time of the writing of the Song of Songs but we just haven't found any of them."

"What you mean," Marjorie says, "is that just because we don't have any evidence on paper—or vase—doesn't mean it didn't exist."

"Right," Thad says, and I add that this is always a problem with archaeological material. There might have been a consistent line of poets right down through the hundreds of years from Akhenaton to the Song of Songs; we would then have only a few fragments of the paper or papyrus trail. Nevertheless, the scholar cannot presume that such evidence once existed; rather, we must work with what we have.

"Right," Thad repeats, "and that's what the authors I consulted try to do. They solve the problem of what they call textual 'transmission' by exploring any evidence they can find for interaction between the Egyptians and the people who wrote the Song of Songs. It turns out there was probably a lot of contact between the people of Palestine and the Egyptians. In fact, Roland Murphy, in his commentary on the Song of Songs, page 43, says that Egypt had control over Palestine all through the Bronze Age and that there must have been plenty of opportunities for the Israelites to come into contact with Egyptian love songs all through the 1000s B.C.E."

Ah, yes. I have been doing a little homework of my own. Recall that in our presentation of the archaeological and historical evidence behind the Exodus we found that there is no evidence to support the idea that the Israelites left Egypt proper all at one time in a big crowd. Rather, it's possible that the Israelites in Palestine won their freedom from Egyptians who were the overlords occupying Palestine itself. Murphy and others hypothesize that during this occupation, which lasted for quite some time, a well-developed poetic tradition passed over from Egypt to the people of Israel, who developed it still further, and the result was texts such as the biblical Song of Songs.

Zodiac mosaic at Hammath Tiberias.   Photo: TLP Archives

"That's what Fox thinks, too," Thad says. "He says that at the time when the love songs were written, Egypt ruled the area of Palestine through local Palestinian officials who were trained in Egypt. If they were trained in the schools that scribes went to they could have met people who were writing love songs. That would explain how the Israelites could have been influenced by Egyptian poetry."

Indeed so, and there is some evidence for this sort of transmission elsewhere in the Bible. For instance, biblical scholars have recognized clear connections between Egyptian wisdom literature and the biblical book of Proverbs. If it could happen to one book of the Bible, it could happen to others.

"Also," Thad adds, returning to his notes, "Fox mentions a text from the eleventh century B.C.E. in which an Egyptian woman has a job as a singer of songs in the court of a prince in Byblos, a town in Canaan, which is, I think, just another term for our region of Palestine."

Or close to it.

"And," Thad persists, "Fox makes one more argument. He refers to what he calls the 'tenacity of traditions within a genre.' What he means is that there is evidence for a type of writing being passed from one culture to another over a long period of time. The example he cites is the sonnet, which developed in Europe in the 1300s but got passed down through a bunch of different countries right up to the present."

Thad is eager to share more of his notes, but I suggest to him that it is time to summarize how far we have come in this section of our travels and then break down our camp to move on.

Caution: Doing Archaeological Analysis

Archaeologists, of course, are known for their work with dirt and rubble, with the discovery of building foundations, statues, coins, jewelry, gold, gems, pots, and reliefs carved into marble blocks. However, one of the most significant contributions that archaeologists provide for those working in the field of biblical interpretation is the evidence of ancient texts. We have seen that ancient texts rarely come to us whole; we must learn to be patient with fragmentary material, like the vase that was recovered in over thirty pieces or the papyrus texts riddled with burn holes or partly devoured by ancient worms.

One of the major questions we want answered when confronted with archaeological material is its date, and we harvest a number of clues concerning the dating of our Egyptian texts from a variety of sources: from the language used, from the style of the letters, and from the contents of the texts themselves. While we eagerly pursue the dating game, we remain aware of two abiding concerns: our ancient written sources rarely include information concerning the identity of their authors, and we usually cannot establish the material's point of origin unless the contents of the text tell us where it was written. We cannot assume that any portable evidence from antiquity has been found in the place where it originally belonged.

Nevertheless, presented with a piece of ancient writing, we attempt to discover its *Sitz im Leben,* the social or cultural context in which it was produced. To do this we focus most of our initial attention on the text itself, for it is our primary source. We hunt around for other primary materials, other texts perhaps, or other evidence such as the tomb murals ferreted out by Marjorie and Jeremy. But we also seek out secondary sources, that is, the work done by scholars who have walked the trail before us. Thus we have spent a great deal of time looking at the work of nonactor Michael Fox . . . .

"Can we retire that?" Yvonne asks. "It's getting old."

In other words, we look at what others have written about the primary texts and try to piece together the history and cultural context out of which the ancient material might have come. But we do not accept uncritically the conclusions of other scholars; instead, we keep asking questions, as Thad did when he started wondering about a possible thousand-year gap between the Egyptian love poetry and the Song of Songs. Always we are cautious when drawing conclusions, especially if—as has been our case— we cannot evaluate the secondary sources by reading the primary ones in their own language.

The process by which biblical scholars interpret archaeological material is quite similar to what we have done in this chapter. If we were to go to a national conference of biblical specialists we could sit in on reports just as we have here, although of course the topics would be more technical, and the presentations, if they were any good, would offer some original insight and not just a recitation of what others have already done. The scholar's work is accomplished in collaboration and conversation with others. Such conversations can sometimes generate some heat, but they usually proceed with great caution.

I make a move to go, but Yvonne stops me.

"And our last question?" Yvonne asks.

We look at her, puzzled, while she looks at her watch. "I have to get home real soon," she says. "It's my night to cook. You said that you wanted to do a summary of what we learned, but you always leave us with one more question, right?"

Right. Our perusal of the archaeological and cultural context of the Song of Songs is not quite complete. Before we can move to the next stage of our travels we have to hold the texts of these love poems a bit more closely to

Wall painting from tomb of Sennefer in west Thebes (ca. 1400 B.C.E.).
From: *Body Symbolism of the Bible,* Staubli and Schroer

the text we have in the Bible. Even though they are separated by hundreds of years, it is possible that the Song was influenced by Egyptian texts designed to entertain. You might already be convinced of the connection, but before we can proceed we need to compare the contents of the texts more closely. I promise you, we won't go into too much detail, since to do so would require a knowledge not only of Hebrew but also of late Literary Egyptian, a knowledge that none of us on this journey currently possesses. Still, we can look at the translations and the commentaries a little more carefully to see if the evidence of archaeology—the papyrus texts and the tomb murals, especially—can be strengthened by the literary material of the two sources, Egyptian and biblical.

"That's actually the second part of our report," Jeremy says.

Well, let's get on with it!

For Reflection and Further Conversation

1. After a chapter like this one you might be wondering if all this study is really worth the effort. Take a moment to recall why we are on this leg of the journey. What's the point of spending all this time on Egyptian archaeology?

2. Do you have any favorite love songs? Think of some songs from your misspent youth, or if you are currently experiencing youth, from current recording artists. What similarities can you find between modern love songs and those of the ancient Egyptian or Israelite poets?

3. Have you ever written love poetry? Would you want to try? (Oh, go ahead!) If your heart is not currently romantically engaged, try writing a little poem of love anyway. For your parents? Your cat? For God?

Chapter Ten

The Egyptian Love Songs
and the Song of Songs

Jeremy sits in a corner, paging furiously through a book. "Listen to this stuff," he says, and reads:

> If I am not with you, where will you set your heart?
> If you do not embrace me, where will you go? . . .
> But if you try to touch my thighs and breasts,
> Then you'll be satisfied.
> Because you remember you are hungry,
> would you then leave me? . . .
> Take then my breast:
> for you its gift overflows.

"This is filth," he says. "Pornography. How can anyone compare this with the Bible?"

Marj jumps in. "Listen to this," she says. She opens her Bible and reads:

> How fair and pleasant you are,
>   O loved one, delectable maiden!
> You are stately as a palm tree,
>   and your breasts are like its clusters.
> I say I will climb the palm tree
>   and lay hold of its branches.
> O may your breasts be like clusters of the vine,
>   and the scent of your breath like apples,
> and your kisses like the best wine
>   that goes down smoothly,
>   gliding over lips and teeth.

"Song of Songs, chapter seven, verses six to nine," she says.

Jeremy is undaunted. "But this stuff, this love poetry," he sputters, "it's pagan. It's full of demons and pagan gods." He returns to his text:

> I sail downstream in the ferry by the pull of the current,
> my bundle of reeds in my arms,
> and say to Ptah, lord of truth,
> give me my girl tonight.

"Ptah is a pagan god," he says. "I looked it up in the notes. A pagan god is the lord of truth?"

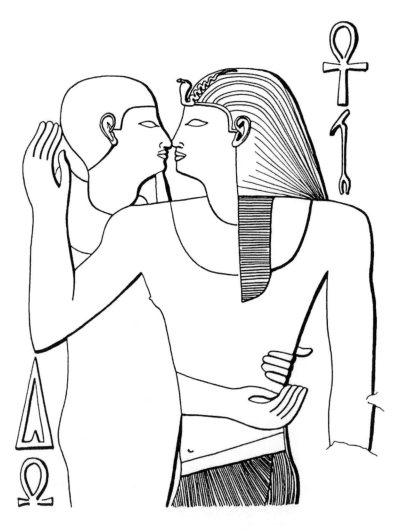

Limestone relief from Karnak, Egypt, reign of Sesostris I (1971–1930 B.C.E.).
From: *Body Symbolism of the Bible,* Staubli and Schroer

Marjorie rises to interrupt him but he cuts her off.

"Listen," he says. "There's more."

> The sea is wine,
> Ptah its reeds,
> Sekhmet its kelp,
> the Dew Goddess its buds,
> Nefertum its lotus flower.
>
> The Golden Goddess rejoices
> and the land grows bright at her beauty.
> For Memphis is a flask of mandrake wine
> placed before the good-looking god.

"See?" Jeremy asks. "The notes say that Sekhmet is a goddess with the head of a lion. Nefertum is a flower god. The Golden Goddess is Hathor, 'the patron goddess of women.'"

He shakes his head. "And at the end, there's idol worship: wine is put on the altar of a pagan god." He puts the book down. "This stuff is crap," he says. "It's worse than crap. It's blasphemy, and to compare it to the Bible is blasphemy too."

Once again we've reached a standoff.

In the past people understood the Bible as a special book, and they enshrined it as the Word of God. But its sacredness has isolated it in some ways from the rest of human life. We are reversing this isolation. The Bible is a potential conversation partner, a vehicle through which God speaks to the human community. If we take the sacred book down off its aloof though sacred shelf, if we put it here on the table along with the other artifacts we have discovered from antiquity, we invite it into our conversation in a way that allows it truly to speak to us in new ways. The Bible is not supposed to be reserved for Sunday worship or the rare pious occasion. The conversation that the Bible provides goes on all day, all week, and in every situation of our lives.

Remember our goal: we want to learn how to interpret the Bible as a vehicle for encounters between God and God's people. We hope to do this precisely by taking the text out of the tabernacle and into the messiness of life. To do this in an orderly fashion, to provide at least some guidelines for our rendezvous with the holy, we explore the *Sitz im Leben,* the original situation of the texts. This is the logical place to begin. And to do that we must uncover the complications, the messiness of life in the world from which the text came.

When we compare the Song of Songs with Egyptian love poetry we aren't cheapening the scriptural text; rather, we are putting it in its place. To speculate about its *Sitz im Leben* is not to denigrate Scripture's sacred nature. Indeed, the goal of our methodology is just the opposite.

The Hebrew Song and the Egyptian Poems

We are closing in on the genre and purpose of the Song of Songs. Marj has suggested that the text is a collection of love poems composed to entertain rather than a work designed for spiritual education. Jeremy has reminded us that the Song is a text considered sacred by many people, and therefore any comparison we make must be accomplished with care and respect. I would add that similar care and respect should be extended to all ancient sources, including the Egyptian poetry. So, when we bring the texts close together, what do we discover?

The first thing biblical scholar Roland Murphy noticed was that each of these texts, the Egyptian and the biblical, is what he calls "humanistic." By this he indicates that they were not designed to function in rituals or intended as instructional religious treatises. As we have already seen, in their initial situation these ancient texts celebrated not divine but human interaction, the relationship of a woman and a man. Murphy envisions each of them as "literary fictions," creations in which the characters drift out of reality and into fantasy. The woman in one of the Egyptian songs conjures herself as everything from her lover's housekeeper to "the mistress of the two lands," a designation for royalty, if not the divine prerogatives of a goddess. Her paramour imagines himself as the doorkeeper of her house, and even her maid and the washer of her clothes. Meanwhile, the bridegroom in the Song of Songs, carried away in a flurry of praise for his beloved, exclaims that a "king" (presumably the bridegroom) is held captive in the locks of her hair (Song 7:5). Elsewhere he is characterized as a shepherd (1:7) and the possessor of a garden (5:1).

In each of the texts the anonymous lovers inhabit a garden of the senses. In the shade of trees groaning with fruit, with the perfume of flowers and spices riding the morning breezes like birds, two people court one another, as Murphy puts it, in an "atmosphere of sensual pleasures: seeing, hearing, touching, smelling, tasting." He and others have pointed out that each set of texts shares certain common literary motifs and themes. Each is filled with praise of the one who is so intensely loved. "One alone is my sister, having no peer," exclaims the young man in the Chester Beatty papyrus, using, we should note, the same form of address ("sister") that we find in the Song of Songs,

> more gracious than all other women. . . .
> Long of neck, white of breast,
>   her hair true lapis lazuli.
> Her arms surpass gold,
>   her fingers are like lotuses.

Limestone relief from temple at Tel-el-Amarna (1377–1358 B.C.E.).

From: *Body Symbolism of the Bible,* Staubli and Schroer

So too are the Song's poems laden with rich imagery and glittering metaphors. "My beloved is all radiant and ruddy," sings the bride,

> His eyes are like doves,
>> beside springs of water,
> bathed in milk,
>> fitly set. . . .
> His arms are rounded gold,
>> set with jewels.
> His body is ivory work,
>> encrusted with sapphires (5:10, 12, 14).

As you can see, some of the imagery, like the golden arms, is identical. When not extolling the beauty of their beloved, the speakers in each set of texts give themselves over to the praise of love itself. "I dwell on your love," the woman sings in one of the Cairo Love Songs,

> Your love is desirable as oil with honey
>> as fine linen to the bodies of noblemen,
> as garments to the bodies of gods,
>> as incense to the nose of the King.

One of the most famous passages in the Song proclaims the power of love as well:

> Set me as a seal upon your heart,
>> as a seal upon your arm;
> for love is strong as death,
>> passion fierce as the grave.
> Its flashes of fire,
>> a raging flame (8:6).

How these people burn with love for one another! Listen to the sighs of the bride in the Song:

> If only you were like a brother to me,
>> who nursed at my mother's breast!
> If I met you outside, I would kiss you
>> and no one would despise me.
> I would lead you and bring you
>> into the house of my mother . . . (8:1-2).

Now compare them with the longings of the Egyptian young man:

> If only I were her Nubian maid,
>> her attendant in secret! . . .
> If only I were the laundryman
>> of my sister's linen garment even for one month!
> I would be strengthened
>> by grasping the clothes that touch her body.

The wish-poems, the *wasf*-like praise songs in honor of the beloved, the elaborate and at times sensuous descriptions of love between "brother" and "sister"—all these motifs are present in each set of ancient texts, Hebrew and Egyptian.

Jeremy has been admirably patient, but now he stirs.

"I'm still suspicious," he says. "Aren't there *any* differences between the Song and the Egyptian stuff?"

Of course there are. Jeremy himself has noticed the presence of Egyptian deities in the love songs; the biblical text never mentions any god. Also, Miriam Lichtheim, editor of ancient Egyptian literary texts, has pointed out that there are no dialogues in the Egyptian poems; even when both man and woman are present, the texts represent interior monologues. This contrasts with the Song of Songs, in which we find an almost antiphonal interplay between the bride and her beloved. Lastly, a number of prominent motifs that grace the Song are absent from the Egyptian material and vice versa. The leitmotif of the bride seeking her beloved in the city, so pronounced in the Song, is nowhere found in the Egyptian love poems, where we find instead the image of the lovers traveling to a rendezvous.

"I'm still not quite convinced," Thad says, adding with a smile, "you did tell us to be suspicious, right?"

Thaddeus is suspicious with good reason. We cannot prove that the Song of Songs was originally love poetry intended to entertain. But elsewhere in the Bible we find circumstantial evidence that suggests we may not be far from the truth. For instance, the fifth chapter of the book of the prophet Isaiah begins this way:

> Let me sing for my beloved
>   my love-song concerning his vineyard:
> My beloved had a vineyard
>   on a very fertile hill.
> He dug it and cleared it of stones,
>   and planted it with choice vines;
> he built a watchtower in the midst of it,
>   and hewed out a wine vat in it;
> he expected it to yield grapes,
>   but it yielded wild grapes (5:1-2).

Sound familiar?

"Isaiah sings to his beloved," Marj says.

"But he's not singing to a woman," Jeremy says. "His beloved is God."

Of course. But scholars suggest that Isaiah's introduction ("Let me sing for my beloved") indicates that love songs like the ones we have examined were composed and performed in Israel in the eighth century B.C.E.

Move on further into the Hebrew Bible, and we encounter our second piece of evidence: Ezekiel 33:31-32. The prophet presents an oracle of the

Lord, who denounces Israel's exiles who come to Ezekiel to listen to him for mere entertainment. "They come to you," the Lord tells his prophet,

> as people come, and they sit before you as my people, and they hear your words, but they will not obey them. For flattery is on their lips, but their heart is set on their gain. To them you are like a singer of love songs, one who has a beautiful voice and plays well on an instrument; they hear what you say but they will not do it.

"These scholars are clever," Thad says. "And they're close readers, too."

Do you see? From this passage we can infer that some people in Israel gathered to listen to love songs as a form of entertainment.

Finally, we have evidence that in antiquity the Song of Songs was itself on occasion valued and experienced as entertainment. One Jewish text from the second century of the Common Era portrays Rabbi Akiba, whom we encountered earlier as a promoter of the Song as Scripture, denouncing people who misuse it. As the *Tosefta Sanhedrin* 12.10 records it,

> Rabbi Akiba says, "Whoever sings the Song of Songs with tremulous voice in a banquet hall and so treats it as a sort of ditty has no share in the world to come."

"I see what you mean," says Thad. "Akiba would have no reason to denounce such a thing if people weren't doing it. Therefore this is a sort of indirect evidence for the origins of the Song of Songs as entertainment."

Almost, but not exactly. The *Tosefta* text is indirect evidence for the fact that some people were *using* the Song as entertainment well into the second century. This says nothing directly about the Song's origins, but it does suggest that the text was associated with love poetry in the minds of some Jews in antiquity.

"That doesn't prove anything," Jeremy says.

True, such an ancient association proves nothing, but it does add one more piece of evidence to the theory that the Song originated as part of a known genre of entertaining love songs.

"Which means," says Marj, "that I was right all along. The Song of Songs is love poetry, pure and simple."

Actually, the most we can say is that Marjorie is *most likely* correct: the genre of the text is love poetry or perhaps lyrics of love songs. It was not composed as Scripture; rather, its original purpose would have been to entertain listeners, perhaps at parties.

Jeremy sits back and shakes his head.

"I hear all this, and if we were not talking about a biblical text I would say it all makes sense. But this"—he picks up his Bible—"this is the Word of God! It's not just any text. It's . . . it's . . ."

"It's more than the words on the page," Yvonne says, finishing Jeremy's thought, and he nods. "It's Sacred Scripture," she continues. "It must mean *more* than what it says."

In their frustration Jeremy and Yvonne point the way to the next stage of our journey. They are exactly correct. Because we meet the Song of Songs in a book of Scripture it does mean more than what it says on the page, at least to the community that believes it to be sacred. We have spent a great deal of time attempting to discover the literary genre and the *Sitz im Leben* of the Song, but our original purpose was not merely to place the text in its original cultural and social setting. We have loftier ambitions than that: we aspire to understand where this text came from so that we can understand how the text speaks to people now. How is it that this text, so full of sexual imagery and human longing, is part of the conversation between God and God's people? Indeed, how does *any* text function as God's revealed word?

"These are the kinds of questions we get answered in the third part of the trip, right?" Thad asks.

I nod and he proclaims, "Onward, then!"

Not so fast. We could move now to the third leg of our journey, but I have two concerns.

"Oh, no," Yvonne sighs.

First, we haven't yet explored some important tools for biblical study. Second, we haven't said more than two or three words about the New Testament.

"So what do you propose?" Jeremy asks. "Do we have to start all over again from the beginning?"

Not at all. You have already appropriated a number of study skills and stretched your imagination in ways that will allow us to make quick progress. We have another world to explore—the world that gave birth to Christianity.

"So we're going back to Israel," Marj says.

Oh, no. We're going to Greece.

For Reflection and Further Discussion

1. What do you think of the notion that the sacred should not be isolated from the mundane affairs of everyday life? Can you think of times when you experienced spiritual realities as a part of the rest of your life?

2. This exercise takes some fortitude: when you're with some people you trust, contrive to toss a Bible on the floor. Be sure it's a good-looking one (you know, leather bound with gold leaf on the edges of the pages). How do you feel when the Bible hits the floor? How do the others respond? If you cannot do this exercise, why not? What do these responses say about people's understanding of what the sacred is all about?

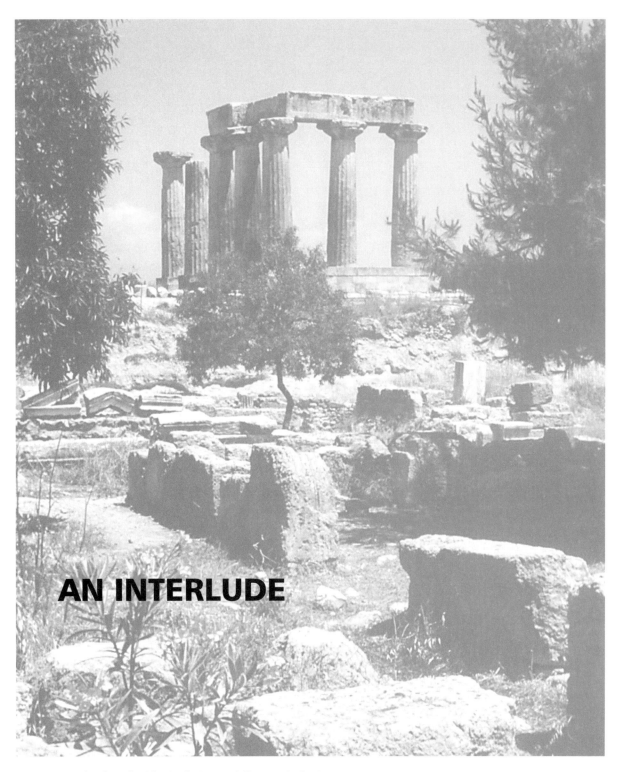

AN INTERLUDE

Temple of Apollo (the "Archaic Temple") at Corinth, Greece. Photo: TLP Archives

Chapter Eleven

An Interlude with Jesus and Christ

A taxi wends its way up from the coast and deposits us in the town square of the village of Old Corinth. This could be any of a thousand Greek villages in the summer: the heat has driven people indoors or under the trees and canopies of the *tavernas* that surround the square. We join them, refreshing ourselves with bottled water and strong Mediterranean coffee. Despite Yvonne's arched eyebrow, Thad has a beer, which is legal here for someone his age. We are here on a pilgrimage; the modern village of Old Corinth surrounds the excavated portion of the ancient city of the Corinthians.

We finish our drinks, wander up the street, and enter the excavation site, passing by the museum so that we can stand on a terrace overlooking the vast space of the Roman-period forum. Presiding over the forum, the modern village, and all that surrounds it is the massive presence of Acrocorinth. A thousand feet high, with craggy limestone cliffs on all sides, the mountain citadel, with its ancient crown of walls, provided citizens with protection from almost three millennia of enemies. Acrocorinth, sacred in antiquity to Helios, the sun-god, shimmers in the heat.

The stone pillars of an archaic Greek temple dominate the excavated civic center of the Roman city. What was once an intricate collection of fountains, statues, altars, and columned buildings now appears to be a scene of utter devastation. We cross the open expanse of the forum, climb a few steps through what was once its monumental entrance, and look up an ancient street running north to Lechaion, one of ancient Corinth's two ports. The highway is still paved in white marble, flanked now on both sides by the ruins of shops, a Roman bath, and an ancient public latrine.

We descend a set of stone stairs into a small enclosure just north of the forum and east of the Lechaion Road. We are standing in the courtyard of the most famous of ancient watering holes, the fountain administered, according to the Greeks, by the nymph-goddess Peirene.

"This place sure is old!" Marjorie whispers. She holds our *Blue Guide* to Greece and notes that Peirene's waters were known to the Greek historian Herodotus, and that Euripides the playwright mentions Peirene a number of times. "In his play about Medea," she says, consulting the guidebook, "he portrays a servant coming upon people relaxing and throwing dice 'where the oldest men are wont to sit beside the hallowed spring of Peirene.'"

"Euripides," Thad says. "That would make this place over twenty-four hundred years old."

Actually, it was already old by the time Euripides wrote about it. Ancient cities were often founded in places that offered a plentiful supply of water. It is possible that Corinth developed as an urban center because of the existence of this water source, perhaps as early as the ninth century B.C.E.

Jeremy has been looking closely at the water system, leaning into one of the arched openings. "Paul could have stood here, in this courtyard," he says as he comes back into the sun.

As we shall see, Paul the missionary sought out big commercial centers for his work, and Corinth in the first century was the largest city in Greece, bigger even than Athens. The Peirene fountain was one of the public spaces most often frequented by the kinds of people Paul appealed to: tradespeople, freedpersons, slaves, and particularly women, those relentless transporters of water in antiquity. So yes, it is quite possible that Paul spent time in this courtyard, and this is a fitting place for us to begin our journey into Christianity and its earliest text, the New Testament.

"Shouldn't the study of Christianity begin with Jesus Christ?" Jeremy asks.

"The man without whom we would not be here," Thad says.

"Yes," Yvonne says. "After all, he is the whole reason I am involved with this project."

So far on our journey we have touched upon a part of the Hebrew Bible, the "Old Testament" of Christians. Now we turn to the "Second" or "New" Testament. We have come to understand that laying down the foundations for the study of a biblical text is not as simple as we learned in catechism school when we were children. When we turn to Jesus and the New Testament, the work is no less arduous. Once again, though, most of our labor will be in tearing down old preconceptions rather than learning complicated new material.

"You had better make one thing clear from the start," Jeremy breaks in. "You aren't going after Jesus, are you? You aren't going to deny the existence of Christ?"

Absolutely not. I assume that you are a believing Christian, as I am. This is not a requirement for participation, of course, but denying the basic beliefs of Christianity is not part of this particular trip. On this journey we explore the *significance* of earlier people and events rather than trying merely to document the details of their existence. Recall that when looking at Exodus, I suggested that if our goal is only to bolster our ability to believe that Moses parted the Sea of Reeds, we miss the deeper power of Sacred Scripture, which invites us not just to belief but to *participation.* So too with Jesus. Will we settle for a discussion and perhaps a lecture designed to strengthen belief in the details of his historical existence? Or is there a way in which we can participate in the experience of his life?

"What about his divinity?" Jeremy persists. "Are you going to deny that?"

Not at all. Calm down, friend, and see if you can follow me here.

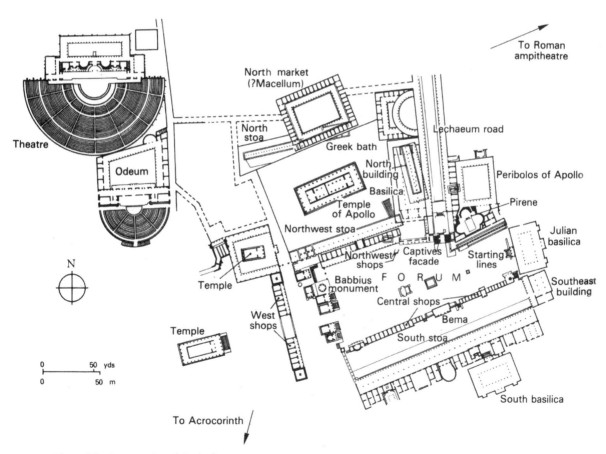

Plan of the Roman city of Corinth.   From: *Illustrated Bible Dictionary,* Tyndale

The Historical Jesus and the Christ of Faith

In the field of biblical studies Jesus is a growth industry just now. At the turn of the millennium, people have questions. Who was he? A Jewish rabbi? A Pharisee? A Cynic preacher? Was he God or just a man? What did he intend by pursuing his ministry and his death? Was he or was he not the founder of Christianity?

Plenty of books dissect these admittedly important questions; I list some of the most intriguing in the endnotes for this chapter. However, our work is going to touch only briefly on these matters. Our task is to learn about the tools of biblical study, tools that will empower you if you decide, once we are done, to return to the question of Jesus in the Scriptures.

The main difficulty we have when attempting to discuss Jesus of Nazareth is a lack of reliable historical source material. The ancient writers upon whom historians rely say virtually nothing about the man. The Roman senator and historian Tacitus, writing in the later part of the first century C.E., notes in passing that Jesus was executed by Pontius Pilate, governor of Judea, during the reign of the emperor Tiberius (*Annals* 15.44).

Suetonius, author of a lively book of imperial biographies, mentions in his life of Claudius a revolt among Jews in the city of Rome, which, he says, was instigated by a *Chrestus.* Modern historians take this to be a reference to *Christus,* the Latin form of Christ ("anointed one"), the title given to Jesus by his earliest followers. If this is true, Suetonius may have preserved an early reference to disruptions in the Roman Jewish community caused by claims that Jesus was the messiah.

Add to these some brief references to Jesus in the work of the Jewish historian Flavius Josephus, and that is about it for information from the first century about Jesus.

"What about the gospels?" Jeremy asks. "They come from the first century."

Herein lies our problem. Jeremy is correct. The gospels of the New Testament were probably written between 70 and 100 C.E. However, they cannot be mined easily or uncritically for historical information about Jesus.

"We studied this in our introduction to religion course," Thaddeus says. "The problem arises because the evangelists, the people who wrote the gospels, didn't intend to record history."

"You mean there is no history in them?" Jeremy asks Thad. "They're all made up?"

"No . . ." Thad responds, hesitating.

"They have some history in them," Marjorie says. "But a lot of the stories are made up."

Whoa, let's slow down a bit here, or we soon may have to restrain Jeremy. Thad, do you recall how the gospels were written?

"I do," he says. "Let's see. Jesus died somewhere around 30 C.E., right?"

Yes. He was executed by Pontius Pilate, who was governor of Judea from 26 to 36 C.E., when he was recalled to Rome because of his extremely harsh style of rule.

"And Mark, the first gospel, was written sometime after 70 C.E.," Thad continues. "That means that for at least forty years the sayings and stories of Jesus were passed around orally. And as they went from one person to the next, they got changed, right?"

We call this a period of oral transmission, a time when the information about Jesus was discussed and "passed around" among the followers of Jesus. It is probably true that during this forty-year period the stories told about Jesus were changed a bit, embellished in order to bring out the significance of Jesus to those who recognized him as the messiah. When the oral traditions were finally written down, most of them probably contained a kernel of historical fact. But here is the important thing to know: the writers, and the communities for which they wrote, were not attempting to preserve an exact history of what happened. Rather, they were attempting to put down as accurately as possible the *significance* that Jesus had for their communities and their lives. For them, what he meant was more important than the historical details about what he did.

The Franciscan writer Leonard Foley illustrates this point quite well. He asks you to imagine that you are a member of a family whose elderly mother recently died. The family is about to gather, and they ask you to sit down and write a tribute to her life. You want to portray her generous hospitality, and so you describe a meal she once served to a host of people, including the pastor, six boy scouts, and a transient person passing through. As you present your memoir, your siblings recall that night but correct some of the details: it was the assistant pastor and four members of your brother's swim team who were at that meal, while your mother entertained the "knight of the road" at a meal with her bridge club. Your brothers and sisters go on to correct numerous other details, and yet when it is time to leave, they heap praise upon you, claiming that you have captured your mother "just the way she really was."

I remember seeing a picture in a catechism depicting the Holy Spirit perched like a dove on the shoulder of one of the evangelists, whispering into his ear the words to write down. But that is surely not the way it happened. You see, the gospel writers were not research scholars or secretaries who took dictation from the Holy Spirit or anyone else. Their job was not to sweat the details but to render on the page *the way Jesus really was.*

"But that means that the gospels are not true!" Jeremy says.

Jeremy is correct only if you equate truth with historical accuracy. If what is true is what can be historically verified, well, then the gospels are indeed not true.

"Then it's not true in the same way the rest of the Bible is not true," Marj says and turns to Jeremy. "Remember when we talked about the 'truth' of the creation story in Genesis?"

"Right," Thad says. "The Bible presents us with tensive truth, not literal truth."

Jeremy is having none of it. "But this is Jesus!"

A question for those who search for historical "truth": Whom do historians write history about?

Jeremy mulls the question, but Thad jumps in. "Dead people," he says. "People from the past."

Correct. Historians sometimes discuss the lives of those still here, but for the most part the goal of the historian is to interpret what has happened in the past. Next question: Do you see why the gospel writers did not want to write history?

Here our interlocutors sit in silence for a few moments. They need a bit of prompting.

Was Jesus dead?

"He was crucified, yes," Yvonne says.

Of course, he died. But did he stay dead?

"Well, no," she says. "He was raised from the dead."

Exactly. You would be astonished at how many of my good Christian students miss this point, the central truth of the New Testament: for the first Christians, Jesus was not a dead man, and when they gathered, their Eucharist was not a celebration of the fond memory of a great teacher or wonderworker. For Christians then and now Jesus is alive, not dead, alive and present in their midst. When the early Christians gathered to do Eucharist, and when they began to record their oral traditions as gospels, they did not focus on the historical past, the details of the life of Jesus of Nazareth. No, they were still encountering Jesus the Christ, who was very much alive for them.

As a result, when we read the gospels we must keep in mind that they are written about two aspects of this man Jesus. They seem to be telling stories about the historical man, Jesus of Nazareth, and indeed, sometimes they are. But the gospels are written from the point of view of people who have experienced the resurrection of Christ; thus they are also discourses about the ongoing power of the risen Christ.

In fact, the major Christian denominations do not understand the gospels as biographies or works primarily designed as historical texts. They caution against such an understanding and encourage believing communities instead to turn to the Scriptures as the source of the Spirit of Christ. The goal of the gospels, as we shall see before our journey is complete, is not to impart *information* but to encourage *transformation*.

"Well, then, what do we know about Jesus the man?" Thad asks.

We know that he was born in humble circumstances somewhere in the Roman region of Palestine and raised as a believing Jew. He seems to have been a follower of John the Baptist, a Jewish prophet in the wilderness who exhorted his listeners to reform their lives. After Herod killed John,

Jesus moved to the forefront of this prophetic movement, preaching, teaching, and performing exorcisms and other healings as part of his ministry. At some point he apparently threatened the powers in control of the region— that is, the Romans and the high-status Jewish families who controlled the Temple—and they had him executed on a cross as a political criminal. A short time later some of his followers had a series of experiences which led them to conclude that Jesus had transcended death at the hands of the Romans, appearing first to Mary Magdalene and later to many of his other associates. These people didn't spend their time documenting the historical deeds of Jesus of Nazareth; they rushed out and proclaimed the risen Christ, the one whom they continued to experience as alive. In the embrace of the powerful reality of their experience, do you really think they worried about historical detail?

On this journey we will walk right around some of the biggest and most difficult (and admittedly most interesting) questions about Jesus: Was he really divine? If so, did he know he was? What about the virgin birth? Was Jesus a virgin? Was he married? Did he walk on water and control the weather? These are not insignificant concerns, but they are beyond the scope of our particular biblical wandering. Ours is a road of experience similar, I believe, to the experience of the first followers of Jesus Christ at the dawn of Christianity.

The Uneasy Rise of Christianity

Powered by these experiences of Jesus still alive and in their midst, his first followers set out to spread the word, and gradually what we call Christianity was born. As with all community movements, the "rise of Christianity" was not an orderly, organized, or orchestrated development. It was, as far as we can tell, a mess. No controlling authorities or validating ministerial licenses restricted the early promulgation of the good news of Christ's resurrection, and a wide variety of "gospels" were preached and written down in the early years. In this period there was no one christology, that is, no one way to understand the nature of Jesus Christ. For some communities he was a wise teacher; others emphasized his miracles. Some saw in Christ a complete freedom from ethical restraint and gave themselves over to sexual profligacy; the members of those groups believed they were already saved in Christ, so it didn't matter what they did with their bodies. Other branches of the early Jesus movement preached a strict asceticism in which self-denial was understood to be the will of God. Some followed the Jewish Torah laws, while others shunned any reference to the Judaism of Jesus.

Several centuries passed before a broad-based sense of what was "orthodox" developed. In the process of the ongoing Christian communal discernment

Christian leaders determined that many texts, including many written gospels, were inappropriate to be preserved as Scripture. Most were discarded, although a few fragments (and one almost complete gospel, attributed to Thomas) remain to remind us that it took quite a long time, and quite a bit of contention, for the complex matrix of early Christian communities to agree to the formation of one Christian Church.

Your Tour Guide Goes on the Defensive

We have in a few paragraphs passed over the enormously complicated process out of which Christianity was born. On this journey we cannot hope to do it justice. Instead, we shall follow as steadily as we can a single movement of early Christian tradition: the mission and ministry of Paul the apostle.

I see a look of disappointment on Yvonne's face. She is too polite to protest, but I know what she is thinking. Why aren't we reading a gospel? If we did that, we could study more closely the mission and ministry of Jesus, a matter of much greater interest to her.

My suggestion that we turn to Paul instead of one of the four gospels is both practical and theological. Practically, we do not have time on this trip to examine an entire gospel. Theologically, it makes sense to study Paul, since of all the "Christianities" that circulated in the first century, Paul's was the one that most powerfully influenced the development of later Christian thought. His letters are the oldest surviving Christian texts of any kind, and they provide us with information about some of the first Christian communities ever to exist.

Jeremy looks pleased with my suggestion, but Marjorie is frowning. "I don't want to read Paul," she says. "He's such a crank. And besides, he's anti-woman."

"I don't know anything about Paul," Yvonne objects, and from the smile on my face as she speaks, she realizes that this is another reason for my choice. "I get it," she says. "Catholics don't know Paul's books, do they?" she asks, as though resigning herself to the administration of a spoonful of distasteful medicine.

By and large, Paul is a mystery to many modern Christians, Catholic and Protestant alike. Even those who think they understand the Pauline letters could use a refresher, since, as Marj inadvertently points out, Paul is greatly misunderstood. (Paul prized the apostolic witness of women and worked shoulder to shoulder with them, Marjorie, as we saw in Romans 16:1-7. Remember?) Misunderstanding Paul is nothing new; his letters have bedeviled Christians from the very beginning, as the New Testament itself testifies: the letters of "our beloved brother

Paul," one writer cautions, contain "some things in them hard to understand" (2 Pet 3:16).

I invite you to keep an open mind about our brother Paul. If you do, you'll discover in his letters—actually, in the one we will discuss—a crack in the door through which we can observe a bit of the world of the first Christians. If we look with care at this text we will glimpse a community grappling with Paul's preaching (and his prickly personality) and encountering Christ in their community twenty or thirty years before the first gospels were written. Our view, of course, will be filtered through Paul's point of view, and he was far from objective in what he wrote. However, it's important to understand Paul's perceptions, both of community and of Christ, since so much of what modern Christians believe comes from the texts he composed.

We sit in the shade of the Peirene fountain courtyard. We'll have plenty of opportunities down the road to discuss the significance and personal experience of Jesus the Christ. Here is my suggestion for now: on this journey let us come to the Lord much the way we might have in the first century. If you lived at that time and became a follower of Jesus, most likely you would not have done so through a personal encounter with the Jewish carpenter from Nazareth. By the time you had heard of him, he would have been gone. No, you would have first encountered not Jesus of Nazareth but Jesus the Christ. The encounter would have happened not in Palestine but in a place like Peirene here in Greece. And it would have happened as the result of conversation with someone like Paul.

Shall we sally forth out of the shade and into the light of a summer afternoon and meet the man?

For Reflection and Further Conversation

1. Review the earlier chapter in which we discussed the tensive nature of biblical texts. Then turn to the gospels and read a single story, a favorite passage or perhaps one chosen at random. Sit with the passage and see if you can discern the "truth" in the text, just as we did when we sat with the creation story in Genesis.

2. What are your earliest memories of Jesus? Your first images of him? If you have time, read the Gospel of Mark straight through as though it were a novella. It won't take long. How does Mark's portrait of Jesus compare with your own? Does this Jesus surprise you at all? Hey, now, be sure to read what is in the text and avoid importing what you "remember" or "think" about Jesus.

FIRST CORINTHIANS

View of the Archaic Temple and Acrocorinth. Photo by Corel

Chapter Twelve

Our Brother Paul

It is now late afternoon, and I am sitting under a canopy of pine trees on the patio outside our hotel in Old Corinth. With my New Testament opened to the third chapter of the letter to the Philippians, I observe Paul as he trots out his credentials. I was circumcised on the eighth day, he writes, a Hebrew, born of the Hebrew tribe of Benjamin, a Pharisee, when it came to righteousness blameless under the law. Elsewhere, in his letter to the Galatians (1:14), he claims that he was one who was more advanced than many others of his own age in his zeal for his ancestral traditions. So zealous was he that he persecuted the first Jewish followers of Jesus, for they claimed that Jesus was the messiah. He tells us that he was very good as a persecutor and only ended that phase of his career when he himself received a revelation from Jesus Christ.

Beyond this and some sketchy logistics concerning his travel plans, we learn very little about the life of Paul from his own writings. He corresponded with people who knew him, so he didn't have to retell his life story. Even in Romans, the one letter we have that he sent to strangers, he says little about himself beyond the fact that he had been, and still was, a Jew. "I myself am an Israelite, a descendant of Abraham," he asserts in Romans 11:1.

The dates of the significant events of his life are obscure. Interpreters generally agree that Paul received his revelation a year or two (or three) after the death of Jesus, whom the Romans crucified sometime between 28 and 33 C.E. His mission probably ended with his death somewhere around 60. Tradition has it that Paul died in Rome, along with Peter, during persecutions instigated by the emperor Nero, but there is no way to verify this.

Paul the Non-Convert

Much of what people think they know about "Paul of Tarsus" derives not from his letters but from the Acts of the Apostles. Only in Acts do we learn that he was a Roman citizen, born in Tarsus (in what is now southern Turkey), and that he studied in Jerusalem at the feet of Gamaliel, a famous Jewish teacher. But this book, Acts, was written by the same person who wrote the Gospel of Luke, at least twenty-five (some suggest forty or forty-five) years after Paul's demise. The author known to us as Luke probably had sources from which to construct his life of Paul, but we should be healthily skeptical about the historical accuracy of his presentation. For example, it's likely that Luke composed Paul's speeches in Acts, for they betray very little knowledge of Paul's own theology.

Paul himself never speaks in detail about his initial encounter with Christ. He had a revelation, he says, and that is as far as he goes (see Gal 1:12). However, the writer of Acts portrays, not once but three times, a much more dramatic encounter on the road to Damascus.

"He gets knocked off his horse," Thad says, "and he's struck blind in the process."

There's no horse in the Acts account, but yes, and according to Luke, Paul has a true conversion away from Judaism and toward Christianity, an experience completed by a "Christian," Ananias, who heals and baptizes him in Antioch (see Acts 9:10-19). But this conflicts with Paul's own account, which, while sketchy on the details, identifies what he experienced as a revelation, not a conversion; moreover, Paul declares emphatically that the process was accomplished without human help. His encounter was with Christ alone (Gal 1:12).

"So," Jeremy interjects, "you're saying that Paul was never knocked off his horse?"

No, not at all. I suggest only that Paul never mentions such an experience. Paul speaks nowhere of a conversion to Christianity, and for a good reason: when Paul accepted Christ there was no such thing as Christianity.

"What are you talking about?" Jeremy asks. "You just said Paul met Christ after his resurrection, not before it."

What I'm getting at is this: in his letters and his theology Paul never repudiates Judaism. He presents his revelatory experience as a deepening of his commitment to his religious heritage.

"So Christ appeared to Paul and told him to be a better Jew," Jeremy says.

I would rather say that Paul's encounter with Christ brought with it an insight, the insight that in Christ, Judaism is fulfilled, not eclipsed. Paul did not view himself as a "Christian," but as a Jew, though one to whom God's plan for the fulfillment of Judaism had been revealed.

He wasn't alone in this position. For several decades those who believed Jesus to be the messiah continued to worship in the Jewish Temple along with all the other Jewish groups. But the author of Acts wrote some years later, after the destruction of the Jerusalem Temple in 70 C.E. and after the Jesus followers separated from the other Jews who survived Jerusalem's devastation. By the time Luke-Acts was composed, the followers of Jesus *were* known as Christians, and they were on their way to forming their own religious practices and beliefs. As a result, Luke portrays Paul's revelation as a full-blown conversion, and that is the story that has caught the imagination of Christians through the centuries.

"I'm not sure I see why this is important to know," Yvonne says.

"I think I do," says Thad. "For two thousand years it's been easier for Christians to forget their connections with Judaism precisely because texts like Acts downplayed that relationship, right?"

Exactly. We can forget that Paul, widely acknowledged as the "first Christian theologian," in fact died a Jew, as did Jesus of Nazareth himself. We do well to restore Paul—and Jesus and Mary his mother—to their Jewish heritage as we exit a century of virulent anti-Semitic fervor.

Paul, the Jewish Apostle

"So Paul wasn't a Christian?" Thad asks.

No, not in the way we understand the term. He was a Jew who believed that Jesus was the messiah. Paul's continued connection to Judaism reminds us that neither Paul nor apparently any other of the first followers of Jesus set out to found a new religion. Just as the Bible was the product of a millennium of development, so too what we now call Christianity developed over a long period of time. Does it really denigrate the Christian religion to observe that it arose in the ancient Mediterranean world in somewhat the same way that other religious traditions did—gradually over time, through the thoughtful reflection and courageous action of many individuals and groups?

"So how is Christianity the result of divine revelation?" Jeremy asks. "You make it sound like the product of a committee."

I'm not saying that Christianity is not a revealed religion, that is, a religion founded on divine revelation. I am suggesting, though, that Christianity developed over a longer period of time than most people think. It didn't appear in a flurry of miracles in one brief moment in time; instead, it was guided by the daily activities (and the daily miracles) of the Spirit of God. Would the gradual work of the Holy Spirit result in a religion any less legitimate than one fashioned in a single dramatic burst of activity? Isn't that the way God works in our lives—a little at a time? Why do we need to believe that God works all that differently now than when Jesus was here?

"OK, let's move on," Yvonne says, a little anxious. "I'll think about this later."

Although Paul did not give up on Judaism to found a new religious system, the Jews he encountered regularly gave up on him. He notes in one of his letters that he was in danger from his own people, and "five times received from the Jews forty lashes minus one" (2 Cor 11:24). However, Paul managed to aggravate and alienate even his fellow missionaries. He and Peter did not get along, and he was abandoned by his close colleague and mentor Barnabas (see Gal 2:11-14). In response, Paul struck out on his own to territories where the gospel had not yet been preached.

"So what was his problem?" Yvonne asks. "Why'd he have so much trouble getting along with other people?"

In addition to manifesting a fundamentally contentious personality, Paul had to deal with the uniqueness of his message. You see, Paul preached a gospel that was somewhat different from the gospel preached by other early Jewish followers of Jesus. For him, as for them, Judaism found its fulfillment in Jesus the messiah. But for Paul the fulfillment of Judaism involved the incorporation of Gentiles, non-Jews. Other followers of Jesus probably sought out Gentile converts as well, but Paul's take on all of this was different in one significant way: Jesus was not only the fulfillment of Judaism, he was also the fulfillment of the Jewish Law.

"I don't see the difference," Yvonne says and continues to fidget.

According to Paul, Jewish Law had completed its purpose with the coming of Jesus. Thus the Law no longer applied. Paul taught that Gentiles attracted to his brand of Christ-fulfilled Judaism did not have to follow Jewish dietary laws and, most important for half of the potential audience, did not have to be circumcised in order to participate in the covenant. Other followers of Jesus were loath to accept such ideas, and this probably led Paul to contemplate the first of his missionary journeys. He took for himself the goal of preaching not to Jews but to Gentiles and left the land of Israel, heading north to Asia Minor (modern Turkey), Greece, and the wider Hellenistic world.

Thad intervenes. "Why *didn't* Paul just start a new religion?" he asks. "That way he could have spared himself all the punishment he took at the hands of his own people."

A good question, but almost impossible to answer since we cannot get into the mind of the apostle. Perhaps he knew the dismal track record for wholly new religions in his world, which distrusted the new and venerated the old. It's also possible that he didn't think he had enough time to start something new.

"Did he think he was going to die?" Yvonne asks.

In a way. Paul was convinced that Jesus would be returning very, very soon and that "this age" would come to an end. "The appointed time has grown short," he writes in 1 Corinthians 7:29; "the Lord is at hand" (Phil 4:5). In this context Paul's major goal was to get out the word rather than set up lasting institutions. It was only later that the religious system we call Christianity coalesced into being.

"So Paul thought the world was going to end," Yvonne says.

The world as he knew it, yes.

"But he was wrong," she says. "The world didn't end."

"Paul couldn't be wrong," Jeremy says, and I can feel a spat coming on.

It's true that many Christians through the ages have thought that Paul—and even Jesus—believed that the world would end during, or shortly after, their lifetime. However, John L. White and other Pauline scholars have suggested that a close reading of the texts, including those we cited above, indicates that it was the current *age* that Paul preached was ending. If that was the case Paul was at least theologically correct, no?

Paul's Experience of God in Christ

Jeremy is still pondering Paul's experience on the Damascus road. "If he wasn't knocked off his horse, and he never knew the earthly Jesus," he asks, "what *was* his experience of Christ?"

Aside from a reference to the Lord's Supper and a couple of times when he alludes to a teaching that he says he received from the Lord, Paul is not concerned with the historical life of Jesus. Instead, for him all is Christ. Christ is the wisdom revealed from God. Christ is the Lord of creation. Christ is the vehicle through which the Spirit of God dwells in believers. Take a look at the first chapter of any Pauline letter. The First Letter to the Corinthians is a good example: Paul proclaims the name of Christ seventeen times in the first chapter alone.

"*Christ* is Paul's mantra," Thad says.

Yes, and his master. Paul characterizes himself as a *slave* of Christ (Rom 1:1), as Christ's *prisoner* (Phlm 1). Paul is owned by Christ, captivated by him. But the bond between them is even stronger than that. Jeremy, you still have the book opened. Read Romans 5:6.

"'For while we were still weak, at the right time Christ died for the ungodly,'" he reads, adding, "now you and I are on the same wavelength. This is what it's all about, Christianity. Christ died for our sins."

Yes, Paul believes that to be the case, and he argues the case well. The remainder of Romans 5 is a well-developed piece of theology in which Paul contrasts the sin of Adam with the reversal of that sin available through Christ. But don't make the mistake of understanding Paul as a theologian writing about spiritual things that we are supposed to take on faith. Again and again Paul exhorts his listeners to be as he is, to do what he has done, and Paul himself does not have mere faith in Christ. No, his relationship to Christ is a matter of *experience,* not mere belief.

"Mere belief?" Jeremy repeats, incredulous that I would utter such a phrase.

Paul's connection to Christ is not rooted in his beliefs about Christ's historical life or Christ's teachings or even Christ's divine nature. Paul is rooted in the experience of Christ. Recover yourself, Jeremy, and read to us from Galatians 2:19-20. Here Paul writes about Christ's crucifixion, a topic of supreme importance in Paul's theology.

"'For through the law I have died to the law, so that I might live to God,'" Jeremy begins. "'I have been crucified with Christ; and it is no longer I who live, but it is Christ who lives in me.'"

Paul is not talking here about belief alone. He is articulating an experience of union with Christ that is so powerful, so real, that the boundary between Paul and Christ has melted away.

"He sounds like a mystic here," Thad remarks. "There's a sense of complete union with Christ."

"It sounds as though he's in love," Marj adds.

At times, yes, he does appear to be in complete and loving thrall of Christ. Take a look at Romans 8, for instance. To my mind this is one of the most eloquent articulations of Paul's understanding of Christ. If you had the time or inclination to read only a single passage from Paul, this would be the one. On and on he goes, writing of the freedom we can find in Christ, freedom from the oppression of our old ways, freedom from the power of eventual death itself. It is a passage of great hope: for those who love God, he says, all things work together for good. But Paul is not naïve; he understands suffering, and not just his own or even ours. All creation, he says, has been groaning like a woman in long and difficult labor. But in the face of suffering, Paul envisions new creation. Not only we but all creation will be set free from decay and death, since

> if God is for us, who is against us? He who did not withhold his own Son, but gave him up for all of us, will he not with him also give us everything else? Who will bring any charge against God's elect?

Yvonne uncharacteristically jumps in at this point. "Let me read this part," she says as we turn to Romans 8:35. "I don't know a lot about Paul, but I know this passage.

"'Who will separate us from the love of Christ?'" she begins. "'Will hardship, or distress, or persecution, or famine, or nakedness, or peril, or sword?'"

"'No,'" Marj interrupts and continues the passage, "'in all these things we are more than conquerors through him who loved us.' This is the passage I was thinking of when I said that Paul seemed to talk about Christ as though he were a lover. Listen to this: 'For I am convinced that neither death, nor life, nor angels, nor rulers, nor things present, nor things to come, nor powers, nor height, nor depth, nor anything else in all creation, will be able to separate us from the love of God in Christ Jesus our Lord.'"

She closes the book with a flourish. "That kind of writing can only be the product of someone head over heels in love," she says.

Marj is right. Perhaps the best way to enter into the thought of prickly Paul is to recognize that everything he writes is done in the context of a profound love—

"No," Marj interrupts, "it's done in the context of Paul being *in* love with Christ."

Jeremy shakes his head. "I didn't think this was possible," he says to Marj. "You and me agreeing on something in the Bible."

I am comfortable with Marj's correction, as long as we keep in mind two things. First, remember that as a first-century Pharisaic Jew, Paul gave his deepest love and commitment to God. For Paul, Christ is the vehicle of Paul's transformation; God is the object of his worship.

"I thought Christ was God," Yvonne says.

Not in the letters of Paul. The notion of the triune God developed (in Christian terms, "was revealed") over time; the roots of the Trinity can be found in the Bible, but several centuries passed before it reached its fullest expression.

The second thing to keep in mind is that Paul's love for Christ is love in the most mature and deepest sense. When we are infatuated with another person we can focus on the other and on the relationship, and the rest of the world disappears. This never happened for Paul. His love for Christ infuses his entire life with love, for it reveals to him that the risen Christ, his beloved, is to be found in other people and, as we shall see, in the community of believers when they gather together.

Marj is also right when she notes that Paul seems to manifest an almost mystical union with Christ. But this experience did not cause him to close in on himself and leave the rest of human society behind. Just the opposite: Paul's experience of Christ impelled him out of himself and into the world. He was not just a slave of Christ; he was an apostle, and as such his mission was to share this love of God in and through Christ with the whole, wide, Gentile world.

Paul, Missionary to the World

Whether or not he was from Tarsus, Paul was a Jew at home in the wider Gentile world. Like many of the Jews of his age, he wrote and conversed comfortably in Greek. We know nothing about Paul's formal education, but he was capable of presenting skilled rhetorical arguments, and his letters indicate that he was familiar with the thought of at least some Hellenistic schools of philosophy. Of course, as a Jew he didn't have much good to say about the nature of Gentile religions, but he was apparently not overly concerned about his followers interacting with nonbelievers (see 1 Corinthians 7:12-15, for instance, where he counsels believers to remain united with their nonbelieving spouses).

Paul does not try to separate the followers of Jesus from the world around them. As he tells the Corinthians, his goal is not to encourage them to dissociate from their nonbelieving fellow citizens, since to do that they would have to leave the world altogether (1 Cor 5:10). Such a leave-taking is not what he has in mind, for, as we shall see, he wants the community to sit in the middle of the world as a lure to bring Christ to all the people of the world.

Although we know few of the particulars of his life as a missionary, we do get a sure sense of how Paul went about his work. He did not wander the Roman world by himself, single-handedly converting Gentiles to Christianity. He traveled with associates he could trust, like Timothy and Sosthenes, the latter of whom appears at the beginning of 1 Corinthians perhaps as a coauthor. When they arrived at a new location—usually a large town, like the capital of a Roman province—they would seek out the followers of Jesus who already resided there. Earning his keep as a craftsman, Paul would preach and encourage the local believers to bond together. From the central city where he resided, he would then found congregations in other areas nearby. Once he was satisfied that the local communities were strong enough to do without him, he and his associates would move on to another provincial capital and begin again.

Letters provided Paul with a means of keeping in touch with the communities he organized or founded. Except for Romans, each of the letters that has survived was addressed to a congregation brought into being by Paul. In his letters he continued to teach, to encourage, and to challenge believers to remain faithful to the vision of faith in Christ that he presented to them. Paul's was, as New Testament scholar Helmut Koester has put it, "a well-planned, large-scale organization" supported and preserved by the contact he was able to maintain through his letters.

In the next few chapters we will spend some time with Paul at Corinth. Why Corinth and not, say, Ephesus, Philippi, Thessaloniki, or the towns of Galatia? Paul visited all these, but I think that his correspondence with the Corinthians offers us the best possibilities on this trip through biblical study. For one thing, we have undisputed writings from Paul to Corinth, whereas the letter to the Ephesians and 2 Thessalonians may have been written by his followers after he died. The Corinthian correspondence comes from Paul, and while this is going to cause Yvonne grief further down the road . . .

"What does that mean?" she asks.

Complications, my friend. In some ways this road won't be any less complex than was our journey through Song of Songs.

As I was saying, even though the letters come from Paul and not the Corinthians themselves, they offer the careful and suspicious observer access to what it must have been like to be a follower of Jesus within twenty or thirty years after his death. In addition, these letters have been particularly significant to later Christians. Paul's Corinthian reflections on everything from the proper attitude toward sex (hands off!) to the appropriate female attire at worship (hats on!) have shaped the way generations of our forebearers have lived out their own experiences of Christian life and community. And last, in contrast to the hometowns of most of the other people Paul wrote, the city of Corinth that Paul visited still exists, albeit in ruins. We can visit it; thus we can expand our biblical trek into the world of archaeology and explore the relationship between a particular biblical text and a specific ancient location.

"So, we're here!" Thad says. "Let's get started."

Not so fast. First, I want to tell you a story from my early years. It's about a conversation I had when I was a graduate student.

"But we're in Corinth!" he exclaims with the exuberance of a young man revving up for a night on the town. "I mean no disrespect," he continues, "but this is Greece!"

And you wouldn't be here if I hadn't had that conversation.

For Reflection and Further Discussion

1. We spoke of the reality that Jesus and his family and friends were all Jewish. Why, do you think, has this been largely overlooked by later Christians? Why has anti-Semitism been such an important factor in the development of Christianity and the history of the West?

2. This question comes verbatim from this chapter: Would the gradual work of the Holy Spirit result in a religion any less legitimate than one fashioned in a single dramatic burst of activity? Isn't that the way God works in our lives—a little at a time? Why do we need to believe that God works all that differently now than when Jesus was here?

3. Although he doesn't offer many details, Paul's initial "revelation" of Christ profoundly changed his life. Look back on your own life. Have you had any revelatory moments, times when the meaning of an important situation, a relationship, or even life itself was made clear? Perhaps such an experience was not what you are comfortable identifying as religious; what was it like?

Chapter Thirteen

We Raise an Eyebrow in Surprise: Paul, the Corinthians, and a Letter

I was sitting in a cramped office in the old section of the library at Harvard Divinity School, fidgeting as one of my mentors read my latest attempt to come up with a topic for my dissertation. Around the room were scattered binders of papers, envelopes, letters, slides, and books—books everywhere, books in different languages, books lined up on dark, heavy, wooden shelves. I watched a particle of dust float quietly in the soft afternoon light and felt a sense of dread.

My professor looked up from the page and shook his head.

"This still isn't very good," he said, with feeling. That is not actually what he said; when sufficiently frustrated, he sometimes muttered expletives that I cannot reproduce here.

He was frustrated. We were going nowhere, and I was beginning to think that I would never get out of graduate school. He grabbed the worn Greek New Testament that accompanied him everywhere and began flipping through the pages. I hauled my own copy out of my backpack and waited.

He was studying the beginning of 1 Corinthians, the letter of Paul I had halfheartedly told him I wanted to explore.

"Look at this," he said, and I could feel the excitement rise in his voice. This man had spent fifty years poring over these texts, and he could still get worked up about them.

He translated the Greek of 1 Corinthians 1:26: "Not many of you are wise according to the flesh, not many powerful, not many well-born."

"Why do you think," my mentor asked, "that Paul begins this letter, a letter devoted to the religious claims of the Corinthians—why does Paul at the start refer to *social* categories, not religious or spiritual ones?"

Acrocorinth looms over every part of the city including the Odeion, an ancient lecture hall.
Photo by John Lanci

I looked at him and then back at the text.

"That is very unusual for Paul," he continued. "Only at Corinth does Paul introduce his theological reflection by discussing social status. Only at Corinth! Why?" He looked at me from behind his desk and said nothing more. As it turned out, I wrote my doctoral dissertation on a different topic, but I have been thinking ever since about that biblical verse and the question my mentor asked that day. Why only with the Corinthians does Paul raise the question of social status? What might that tell us about the community there, who they were and how they came to believe in Christ? What we discover about them—could it tell us anything about how *we* could follow the Lord?

The ancients had a saying that went: "The voyage to Corinth is not meant for everyone." The journey we have before us, also a voyage to Corinth, may get a little rough in the next chapter or two.

Don't worry, Yvonne (she has just let out a great sigh and now she is frowning). You can stop us at any point and ask a question. If you persevere you will observe how some New Testament scholars go about their business, and I will finally have the opportunity to wrestle with a text that, well, still gets me worked up.

Who Were These Corinthians?

As with virtually every aspect Paul's life, we are unsure exactly when he arrived at Corinth or how long he stayed. Acts 18:1-18 suggests a lengthy sojourn, which seems reasonable considering how influential Corinth was to the eastern part of the Roman Empire and, presumably, how significant a Corinthian community of Christians might be for the future of the movement. As noted above, people from all over the empire passed through the region of Corinthian influence, and it would have been a smart strategic move for Paul to found a strong community in such a place. It is safe to assume that Paul lived among the Corinthians for a goodly amount of time, a year or so, and that he worked among them at his trade (he was a leatherworker or tentmaker) to earn his keep.

Who were these people, the Corinthians attracted to Paul and his message? Their letters to Paul have been lost; thus we have to turn to Paul himself for information. In doing this we exercise some care. Paul wrote to Corinth after he had left the city, and he wasn't always pleased with the ways the community there was growing and developing. The relationship between Paul and the Corinthians was not as rocky as his relations with the Jesus followers of Galatia, whom he denounces as fools (have a look at Galatians 1:6 and 3:1). But he and the Corinthians did not always see eye to eye. This is apparent from his repeated attempts to justify his authority (see 1 Corinthians 4 and 9, as well as 2 Corinthians 10–12), which include

The Archaic Temple, Corinth's most famous ruin.   Photo by John Lanci

occasional bursts of sarcastic temper (1 Cor 4:8-13 and 14:36). His letters to Corinth were written as part of a process of conversation, instruction, encouragement, and outright argument.

So who were these people? The evidence from Paul includes 1 and 2 Corinthians, as well as the last chapter of his letter to the Romans. Romans 16 appears to be a letter of recommendation for Phoebe, a *diakonos* ("deacon" or "minister") from Cenchreae, one of the two ports serving Corinth. In that chapter Paul mentions a number of other people with Corinthian connections (Erastus, Prisca, Aquila), so we can be confident in assuming that this section of Romans tells us something about Corinth's community.

What do we know? Well, the leadership of the Corinthian Christians was a mixed crowd of men (Stephanas, Fortunatus, Achaicus) and women (Phoebe, Junia, and perhaps Chloe).

"What about their social status in Corinth?" Thad asks.

We can gather from what Paul writes in 1 Corinthians 7 that the Corinthian followers of Jesus included both women and men, married and single, slave and free (and, as we shall see, *freed*). From 1 Corinthians 12:2, in which Paul reminds his correspondents of their former situation, we infer that the Corinthians were Gentiles, which makes sense since Paul proclaims himself as an apostle to the Gentiles; however, we can suspect that there were some Jews or Jewish sympathizers in the crowd as well, since he makes easy reference to Jewish customs in his arguments.

These are among the first tasks for the biblical interpreter: discerning the author and the audience. We'll explore the social situation of Paul's correspondents in greater detail shortly. Before we do that I'd like to turn our attention once again to the text we will be examining.

Text-Critical Issues?

We will proceed a bit differently with 1 Corinthians than we did earlier with the Song of Songs, which we examined as a whole. This time, while looking first at the text as a whole, we will zero in on one small part of it: 1 Corinthians 1:26. We will ask some of the same questions that we did when journeying with the Hebrew Bible, but many of our answers will be less tentative, for we know a lot more about the literary and social situation of Paul's genuine letters than we do about Solomon's alleged song.

Recall the preliminary questions concerning authorship, intended audience, date, place of composition, genre, and purpose of the text. Some of these we have already tackled: the text was written to some Jesus-followers in Corinth in the middle of the first century C.E. We are not sure where it was written, though scholars follow early tradition and suggest that it was composed and sent from Ephesus, a major city in Asia Minor (modern Turkey).

No one doubts that Paul wrote the text we call 1 Corinthians, since the letter shares with his others a distinctive voice and style in the particular ways he uses certain words. But some people do wonder if he wrote it in the form we have it. By ancient standards (as well as modern), this is a very long letter for a person to have written at one time, even if, as we think, he dictated it. Many scholars believe that some of the other Pauline letters we have in the New Testament are actually composites, that is, they are cut-and-paste jobs, not single letters. For instance, 2 Corinthians, another very long letter, looks suspiciously like a bunch of different Pauline letters that have been stitched together by a later editor. A careful reading of the letter indicates abrupt changes in tone and content. What we call 2 Corinthians is probably fragments of a number of genuine letters of Paul all combined into one, with some bridging words to hold the different parts together.

A number of scholars suggest that 1 Corinthians is also a collection of shorter letters knitted together into one treatise. However, no one can seem to agree on how to subdivide the text. Throughout the letter Paul seems to be dealing with the same circumstances and, as we shall shortly see, writing with the same main purpose in mind. It is certainly *possible* that the text we call 1 Corinthians was originally a variety of different Pauline letters cleverly combined by a later editor. Indeed, an excellent case can be made that one or two passages were added later and may not even be by Paul. But for the most part there is nothing to prevent us from assuming that Paul wrote 1 Corinthians as we have it.

Now, when we first approach a New Testament text the questions we ask are similar to those we asked with respect to the Song of Songs. First, are there any text-critical problems? In other words, do the earliest versions of the Greek text all agree on the wording of our text, or are there significant differences?

As it was with our text from the Hebrew Bible, so too here: we have no original manuscripts of the writings of the New Testament. The letters that Paul and his scribes first created probably crumbled to dust within a century of his death. Did you ever leave a newspaper in the front seat of a parked car on a summer afternoon? It turns yellow in the space of a few hours, since newsprint is not meant to last. Books, on the other hand, survive a lot longer, since the paper used is of higher quality. In antiquity an important document might be scratched on parchment made from the leathery skin of animals, or perhaps carved in stone. But for the most part ancient letters were written on more flimsy material, like papyrus, which usually decomposed rather quickly.

Paul's followers probably did save most of his letters, and when these began to deteriorate the early Christians probably copied them, just as the Jewish scribes copied and preserved their Hebrew texts. As time passed they copied the copies. Then as now, the people who did the job gave themselves to their work with varying degrees of skill and motivation. Some of the copies were probably fair and accurate reproductions of the originals. But virtually no one, then or now, could be expected to copy a long manuscript right down to the last jot and dot without committing a single error. Remember, the world is teeming with error, and so too are some of the ancient manuscripts.

Many early manuscripts of the books of the Christian Bible survive, but the gradual process of copying resulted in discrepancies between the surviving copies. Biblical scholars who feel particularly attracted to the study of the Greek language and Greek manuscripts have devoted their lives to sorting out the different manuscripts, comparing them and attempting to reconcile them when there are differences in the details. The result is composites, texts in Greek that are modern people's best guesses at what the originals looked like.

Most of us would probably find such a task—the sorting out of the minute differences between Greek manuscripts—to be an effective rendition of hell on earth, but this job is extremely important for the study of the Bible. The object of our current adventure—an explanation for the social status terminology Paul uses in 1 Corinthians 1:26—does not present many text-critical problems; the variations among the earliest manuscripts are minor.

"We're in luck!" Thad says.

Another text-critical question we ask at the beginning of our Corinthian journey involves interpolations into the text. Was the text a part of the original letter, or was it added later, either by Paul or by a later editor? We luck out again. Our passage does not present any problems on this front. It appears in all the manuscripts, and it appears in the same place in all of them. Thus it was probably not slipped in, or interpolated, by a later author.

The next question: Is there a detectable written source behind the passage?

"You mean it's time for source criticism," Thad interjects.

Right. Is it likely that Paul borrowed it from some other context in another text?

"If he did, we need to know that," Thad says. "We can learn about how Paul used the words here if we see how they were originally used."

Correct. We know that Paul elsewhere in his letters occasionally uses written sources. We have an elegant and theologically important example in the second chapter of his letter to the Philippians. Paul is encouraging his correspondents to be united and to "do nothing from selfish ambition" (2:3). In this context, in verse 6, he subtly digresses from the situation at hand to a disquisition on the nature of Jesus Christ, "who, though he was in the form of God," did not put much stock in being like God. At this point Paul switches to a previously composed source, probably an early hymn to or about a redeemer figure like Christ. Paul adapts it here to fit into his argument.

Returning to 1 Corinthians 1:26, again we come up blank, at least when we haul out the tools of source criticism. The three significant words he uses here—which we translate as *wise, powerful,* and *well-born*—sometimes appear together elsewhere. Paul may have been influenced by similar terminology, for instance, in his Bible (see Jer 9:23). But as we shall see, this section of the letter was probably composed by Paul himself as part of the argument he was making.

"How about form criticism, then?" Thad asks.

Remember our discussion of the Song of Songs? The goals of form criticism are to discover the form of the original units of tradition behind a biblical text and to see if we can discover how the oral form of the tradition took the shape of the text we have. We do the same sort of work in New Testament exegesis, particularly with reference to the gospels, which are chock-full of reshaped oral tradition. We can find oral forms of tradition behind sections of the Pauline letters as well; indeed, some sections of our letter do have oral sources behind them. In 1 Corinthians 1:11 we can discern clearly such a source behind the letter as a whole: Paul acknowledges that he is responding to information from "Chloe's people." But as we will shortly see, our particular verse is placed within part of the letter that is composed by Paul, apparently without previous sources.

"We are 0 for 2," Jeremy mumbles.

True, neither source nor form criticism offers much help.

"What about the words themselves?" Marjorie asks. "People who study literature spend a lot of their effort scrutinizing individual words, like the words of a poem. Are any of the Greek words Paul uses unusual or weird for him?"

Recall that this is exactly what caused my mentor to raise an eyebrow. We may have something here that will unlock the gate to the next place we need to go. Turn back to chapter one of the letter. After some preliminaries, in 1 Corinthians 1:18 Paul plunges into a discussion of wisdom, power, and Christ. A focus on Christ is certainly not unusual. He characterizes Christ as the power of God and the wisdom of God. Paul identifies the cross of Christ as the power of God, which he contrasts with the wisdom of the wise and the wisdom of this world.

Nothing that Paul asserts here is in any way unusual for him. Christ is to be the source of spiritual wisdom and power for his followers. But observe what he says in 1:26. "Consider your own call," he says. He reminds them that not many of them are wise, which fits in with what he has just been writing. But then he continues, noting that not many of them are powerful or well-born either. Power and especially the status of one's family were prominent markings of ancient social position, not of one's spiritual situation. When he refers to them as well-born, the Greek word he uses is *eugenēs,* the only time he uses the word in his letters.

"So it's weird," Thad says.

Well, yes, it is unusual, at least for Paul. While he sometimes acknowledges the social status of his audience, only in the Corinthian correspondence does he focus so clearly on status concerns. This is the kind of anomaly that causes the twitching-eyebrow reaction for scholars.

So. We have fixed the text, but this passage is quite different from the Song of Songs. We know the identity of the author and roughly when it was written. And we know the genre: it is a letter. The critical apparatus that we used on the Song of Songs is so far of limited value to us. But the box contains other tools for us to try out.

Let us gather in the shade of the pine trees on the patio of our rooms in Old Corinth in the late afternoon. Bring your Bibles, roll up your sleeves, and let's get to work.

My Baby, She Wrote Me a Letter

"The fact that this is a letter should make it easier to figure out than the Song of Songs was," Yvonne says, hopefully glancing down at the first page of 1 Corinthians in her Bible.

In some ways, yes. But reading this letter is not as straightforward as you might think.

"Right," Jeremy says. "Paul didn't write letters the way we do. His letters are different. They're formal. They're Scripture!"

Well, yes, they are now. But that's not how they started. Paul the letter writer and missionary was not a systematic theologian. He wrote real letters to real people, not literary or theological treatises. As you can easily discern if you read all the Pauline epistles one after another, Paul addresses problems and situations that have arisen in particular congregations. If he tells us anything about how he understands the imminent end of the current age, for instance, he doesn't do it as a freestanding discourse on eschatology (end-of-the-world theology). Rather, we get his thoughts on the subject as part of a conversation because some of his correspondents (in the case of eschatology, the Thessalonians) are worried about the end of the world as they know it. If no one in Thessaloniki had been troubled about the fate of their recently deceased relatives and friends, Paul might never have recorded his thoughts on the matter. If the Galatians had not been confused about the role of Jewish Law in their congregation and had not begun to accept a different spin on circumcision we might not have gotten quite the picture we have of Paul's view of Jewish Law. Even Paul's letter to the Romans, a community he had not founded, seems to have been written at least in part to address problems he had heard they were having.

Because Paul wrote letters addressing specific situations in specific places we have to employ some care in reading them. Otherwise we will repeat the most common mistake that people make when reading a Pauline epistle, which is to assume that when we read his letters we are getting an accurate and objective picture of what was "really going on."

"That would be a steno reading, right?" Thad asks.

Yes, but that's not what I was getting at.

"I know," Marj says. "Paul's letters are only half of the conversation. We get this perspective, but who's to say he's objective in the way he sees things?"

"There you go again," Jeremy says, "putting down the authority of Scripture."

But I don't think that's what Marjorie intends. We will treat 1 Corinthians as a sacred text, one that must be interpreted as tensive language. After all, we want to try to understand and appreciate the first Christian conversations and appreciate what they can teach us about our own potential for dialogue with and about God. But to do this we need to sit for a minute or two and reflect on the nature of a letter, any letter, including the ones Paul wrote (remember, he wrote these texts as real letters, with no intention of creating Sacred Scripture).

You know how letters work, how one-sided they are. You're home visiting your parents, and while there you explore the attic. Maybe they've asked you to help them clean it in preparation for the inevitable move to smaller quarters that so many of our folks have to make. While upstairs you open a small tin box and discover a cache of old letters bound with string. You proceed to have a Madison County experience.

"A what?" Thad asks.

"The Bridges of Madison County," Yvonne tells him.

"Terrible movie," Jeremy says. "All about adultery."

"Worse book," Marjorie says. "All about bad writing."

Back to the attic. On the yellowed envelopes you see the name of your great-grandmother Lillian. You open one and discover that it is a love letter from someone named Alphonse. Who is Alphonse? Your great-grandfather's name was Henry. You bring the letters downstairs and show them to your mother, who doesn't recall seeing them before and, in fact, knows very little about her grandmother, whom she never met. She produces a diary kept by her great-aunt; this is the only source of information from the period that she has ever seen. The letters are not dated, but the postmark on one envelope is clear: New York City, 1916. Wait. Your great-grandmother was still married to Henry at that point, at least according to the diary. You *thought* the marriage was a happy one, but now here you find these letters indicating that Lillian had an admirer on the side, unbeknownst to her husband. You read through the diary's entries for 1915 to 1918, and while Henry is evident there, no Alphonse appears. Lillian led a secret life.

But do you know that? How do you know that Henry didn't know about Alphonse? You don't. Anything you will ever know about Lillian and Alphonse will have to be reconstructed from the letters in the tin box. Oh, you will be able to piece together some things—where they went, what they did. But love letters are very vague about details. After all, why should Alphonse inform his audience? The woman he's writing to was close to him in some way, so we can presume that she shared his experiences and he didn't have to recount most of them in any detail. We can get a glimmer from his letters how Alphonse felt about your great-grandmother, but even here we cannot push it too far. Do the letters indicate how he felt or how he wanted Lillian to *think* he felt? Note that modification: even with his letters in hand you'll never know what Alphonse was really thinking and feeling; you will only know what he put down on paper to share with Lillian. Was he in love? Was he some scoundrel wooing your great-grandmother for her meager fortune? Had he been enticed by a secretly bored housewife? Much as you may speculate, much as the possibilities intrigue you, you can never know the truth of what really happened.

So too with Paul and his correspondents. We possess Paul's letters, and as a result we have some access to his way of thinking. But there is a lot that we don't know and shouldn't presume that we do know. The people to whom he wrote had shared certain experiences with him, and so he spares them—and, unfortunately, us as well—the details. Thus we are often in the dark concerning the situation he is addressing, though his correspondents most probably were not. We don't know what was going on in Paul's mind when he wrote his letters; we only know what he wrote. Paul, like Alphonse, may have had any number of motives for writing. And, most importantly, we have no access to what his correspondents wrote back or thought about what they received from him. Reading Paul's letters, like reading the love letters of Alphonse of New York, is eavesdropping on one side of a conversation.

To interpret our passage we need to try to reconstruct as much as we can of the whole conversation associated with this biblical letter. Why did Paul write to these people? What was their situation? What were their concerns? As we wrestle with these questions we will make further progress on our journey. As we observe the first believers reflecting on what it is to follow Christ we cannot help but learn more about how *we* might follow Christ too, right?

Thaddeus agrees. "But," he adds, "this is going to be very different from the work we did on the Song of Songs."

Yes. In this case we know who the author was, who his correspondents were, and approximately when the letters were written. We'll have the chance to look at some new techniques for reading biblical texts, and we will face some new challenges.

For Reflection and Further Discussion

1. I suspect it's time for the "so what question." Go back and quickly review this chapter. Then locate two or three points of contact between what it presents and some aspects of the reality you live. In other words, does this material offer any facts or ideas that might make a difference in your life? Can you take any of the tools or "interpretive moves" that scholars use on biblical texts and apply them to other, perhaps nonreligious aspects of life?

Chapter Fourteen

The Rhetoric of a Text

One day while rummaging through the bowels of Harvard's massive Widener Library, I came across an edition of Greek texts from ancient Egypt. They had been found under the stairway of a house in Karanis, a town in the northeastern section of the Fayum, an area of life-supporting oases west of the Nile. The text that caught my eye was a letter. Some time during the first quarter of the second century of the Common Era a soldier named Terentianus, who was living in or near Alexandria, wrote to his father:

> Claudius Terentianus to his lord and father, Claudius Tiberianus, very many greetings. Before all else I pray that you are well and prospering, which is my desire. I myself am also well, making obeisance on your behalf daily before the lord Sarapis [a major Egyptian deity] and the gods who share his temple.

> I want you to know, father, that I have received a basket from Achillas. [Such baskets were vehicles for a sort of informal parcel post.] Similarly, another basket was given to me by the soldier . . . and from the father of Julius a small basket and my small baskets and a sword-sheath. He sent word to me about a woman; on receipt of my consent, he would try to buy one for me.

> Already two years ago I wanted to take a woman into my house, but I did not allow myself nor am I now permitting myself to take someone apart from your approval, and you will not hear otherwise from me about this matter. If it is the case somehow that the woman I bring down should be one who, for my sake, would be more kindly disposed to you and have more consideration for you than for me, it works out that I do you a favor rather than that I am a cause of blame by you. For this reason, lacking your approval, until today no woman has entered my house. You yourself know, for another thing, that I have driven away your difficulties (causes of consternation); whatever woman you approve is the one that I also want . . . . Greet all those from the Caesareion, each by name.

139

Terentianus concludes with good wishes for some specific people and a few practical requests. Because he is a soldier in a Roman legion stationed far away he cannot be present to his family, and so he sends a letter home. He begins with wishes for good health and promises his father prayer for his well-being, albeit a prayer to Sarapis, a god quite different from our own. Terentianus treats his father Tiberianus with deference, and from the beginning of the letter places himself in a position subservient to his dad.

Terentianus does this, as would you or I, for a reason: he wants something. He begins with a small matter but subtly moves to his main point.

"I'll say," Marj interjects. "He wants to buy a woman."

Well, yes. He tries with great care to convince his father that it is time for him to be partnered, sketching for Tiberianus the benefits that he himself would enjoy if his son had a pleasing woman around the house while gently reminding him of faithful past service ("I have driven away your difficulties"). He closes the body of the letter with a final statement of acquiescence, assuring his father that "whatever woman you approve is the one I also want."

Alien though the letter is in some of its details (most of us don't buy our lifepartners any more!), we can recognize Terentianus's dispatch to his father as a letter that is also an attempt to persuade its recipient to take some action. When we speak of the "rhetoric of a text" we're not talking about "mere rhetoric," the kind of flourish someone uses in a speech just to sound good or to entertain. Instead, by rhetoric we mean the strategy writers use to make their points and convince their audiences to think or act in certain ways.

As you can probably imagine, biblical texts such as the letters of Paul are full of rhetorical content. But just about any biblical writing can employ rhetoric since, as we have suggested, the purpose of such texts goes beyond the reportage of the facts. Thus when we read the Bible we must be aware that the author of the text has a purpose for writing it. To uncover what that purpose might be is one of the most important goals of biblical interpretation.

At this point Yvonne looks a bit forlorn.

"I can't do this stuff," she says. "How do I know how to interpret the intentions of someone who has been dead for two thousand years?"

Actually, we don't try to ferret out the author's inner thoughts. Yvonne is right; these people are unavailable for consultation, and we have no access to what they were thinking. All we have is the text, so we try to figure out the purpose of the text we have rather than the mind of the author we don't have.

"I don't see much difference between the author and the text," she says.

Ah, but this is a critical distinction. Take a look back at the letter from the Roman soldier Terentianus. Can you discern his purpose from that text?

Thad nods. "He wants permission to marry, if you can call what he wants 'marriage.'"

Yes. But why? Why does he want to marry? Look at the text.

"He doesn't really tell us," Jeremy observes. "He just says he wants to."

Exactly. We can see his purpose rather clearly: he wants to convince his father to let him marry. But his inner thoughts and the reasons behind his writing to his father are not clear. We only have as much of his thinking as Terentianus chooses to share with us.

"So he might be hiding something," Yvonne says.

"Of course he is!" Thad responds with a sly smile. "He's writing to his father."

"So what does this have to do with the Bible?" Jeremy asks.

"Wait," Marjorie interrupts. "I think I get it. When Paul writes the Corinthians or the Galatians, he's writing just the way any of us would. He doesn't necessarily tell the people to whom he writes all of what he's thinking or why he says what he says."

Thus we can look at the text and figure out what his purpose probably was, but we cannot really know. We have to stick with the text. There is a difference between the text and its author.

"But that means we might be wrong," says Thad.

It is true that we might be misjudging the original intention behind a biblical text, since we cannot ask the author for a clarification. But remember what we said 'way back in chapter two about steno and tensive language. The letters of Paul look a lot like a soldier's plea to his dad, and when he wrote them they were just that—letters. However, Paul's letters are now considered Sacred Scripture, and we read them differently than his original audience did. No matter what the original intention of the author, if we read these texts as though they are composed in tensive language, the language of Scripture, there may be a number of possible deeper meanings to them.

"But then why spend any time at all worrying about Paul's original purpose?" Marj asks. "Just go for the deeper meaning."

"I have a feeling that would be a lot easier," Yvonne says. "And we could spend a lot less time in libraries."

Marjorie's is an excellent question.

"But you want to dodge it, right?" Thad says.

No, but I do want to delay it.

"OK," Thad says. "For now, let's get back to your point."

"Which is?" Yvonne asks.

"We can't just read what's on the page," Thad says. "But we also can't just get into Paul's head to know what he meant."

"So where do we turn now?" Jeremy asks.

Reading a Pauline Letter

Remember our goal: to learn about how biblical scholars interpret Scripture so that later we can suggest how the rest of us can do it.

"Uh-oh," says Yvonne. "I see a pattern here."

"Me, too," Thad says. "When you invite us to reflect on why we started this adventure in the first place there is some heavy lifting on the horizon."

"Here it comes," says Marj.

Calm down now, and recall Alphonse's letters and the difficulty we had figuring out what really happened in the lives of two (possibly) clandestine lovers. We are going to have some of the same challenges with 1 Corinthians.

To put it bluntly: Paul wrote his letters to tell his correspondents how he thought they should behave as followers of Jesus, and he did this out of a concern, so he says, for their own good. So in a Pauline letter we're getting Paul's view of things and his rhetorical response to what he thinks is going on. He is trying to move his audience in the direction he wants them to go.

According to analysts of ancient rhetoric Paul and the authors of other texts that became part of the Bible were not just setting down historical facts but were responding to situations as they saw them. Rhetorical analysis is particularly important in reading the letters of Paul because, whether or not they convinced his intended audiences, Paul's arguments eventually won the day: his letters, written to particular audiences at Corinth or Philippi, became Christian Scripture, while the responses of his correspondents were not preserved. As a result, people today often make the assumption that a Pauline letter reveals to us the actual historical situation in which he and his audience lived. In reality these letters describe the situation *as Paul saw it,* which may have been a very different thing from how it really was or how his correspondents would have perceived things.

"So," Yvonne breaks in, "let me get this straight. Back in the attic we have Alphonse's letters but none of Lillian's. He could have made the whole thing up. The affair between them, I mean."

"Or maybe they did have a relationship," Marjorie suggests, "but Lillian saw it differently than Alphonse did."

In either case—that of Lillian and Alphonse or the Corinthians and Paul—we have to be careful not to assume that the letter writer is an objective observer and unbiased narrator of a situation. Paul's letters contribute mightily to our effort to learn about the first Christians, of course, but they represent only one side of an ancient process of conversation that Paul did everything he could, through the use of persuasive speech, or rhetoric, to steer in the direction he thought it should go.

"Are you saying that Paul was some sort of literary scholar?" Jeremy asks.

We know next to nothing about Paul's educational background. Biblical scholars generally agree, however, that he was a skilled letter writer who, even if he lacked an extensive formal education, was well versed in the use of rhetorical persuasion. We should not, then, approach a Pauline letter as if it were a learned treatise composed according to classical rhetorical theory, but neither should we forget that Paul knew how to compose a compelling argument. He was capable of stirring eloquence and the skillful manipulation of imagery, and he frequently marshaled persuasive arguments to make his point.

"Sort of like a politician," says Thad.

Very much like a politician. Or a pastor on Sunday morning. Now, if we examine his rhetorical approach we will have a better understanding of how he made his argument, and a better chance of reconstructing the other side of the discussion.

"Why do we need to do that?" Marj asks.

That is an integral part of the journey of the biblical interpreter: not only do we try to guess what the author of the biblical text is trying to say but we also attempt to listen to the hidden voice of the audience—in this case the reaction of Paul's correspondents.

"Yes," Marj persists. "But why?"

Well, if we understand Paul's letters as rhetorical texts we are accepting them not just as ancient artifacts or as sacred texts set in stone with one meaning for all people at all times. Instead, we see them as the product of a conversation between Paul and his audience and, by extension, as part of the ongoing conversation between God and God's people. And we offer proof of my thesis.

"What was that again?" Marj asks.

"Yeah," says Jeremy. "Refresh our memory."

My thesis is that ever since the beginning the Spirit of God has lived among and worked with real people in the concrete circumstances of their real, ordinary lives. If we examine how the Corinthians and Paul experienced the Spirit of God inhabiting their lives we might be able to learn more about how God is dwelling with us today.

What we are going to do now is picture 1 Corinthians both as a letter and as a persuasive argument that Paul makes in an attempt to influence the behavior of his audience, the Corinthians. If we can locate his purpose—the goal of his rhetoric—we might understand a bit better what it was like to live among the first Christians. We might come to understand how and why this text—a letter, after all, written by some guy two thousand years ago—became Sacred Scripture and an invitation to the divine conversation for all later Christians.

"So that's why we can't just go to the deeper meaning?" Marj asks.

Yes, it is. The exegetical journey involves a bit of a balancing act. If we look at a text merely as the product of an ancient culture, that is, if we focus only on the reconstruction of the original circumstances of its composition, we limit or ignore its ability to function as sacred texts do, and it won't reveal God's end of the conversation today. But if we ignore the original situation of the text, its author and audience, and play with the many possible "deeper meanings" that our imagination might concoct, we cut ourselves off from thousands of years of insightful conversation and inter-action between the human community and God. We have to study the origins of this text, dry though such effort may be, so that we can surely anchor our own experience of the text as part of that conversation.

"But why not just let God speak to us today through the Scriptures?" Yvonne asks.

"Actually," Marj says, "why use these texts at all?"

"See?" Thad interrupts and gestures toward me. "That's his point. If we don't stay close to the text, what's to prevent us from finding any 'deeper meaning' that we want?"

I can feel the energy that has built up begin to dissipate in the ensuing silence. We are all thinking the same thing, which Marjorie puts into words.

"And then we are Paul Hill," she says, "finding Shotgun Jesus in the New Testament gospels."

"I need a break before I do any more of this heavy thinking," Yvonne says.

At this point let's all put this book down, stretch, and pick up Paul's First Letter to the Corinthians for a quick perusal.

The Stated Purpose of First Corinthians

Are you all settled?

Think of this section as an example of what rhetorical critics do rather than as a skill you have to acquire. The Christian community needs people who can do this but, as with each of the technical aspects of our journey, not everyone in the community needs to be an expert at the different critical approaches. Does this help?

"I'm fine," Yvonne says. "Bring it on!"

To be faithful to rhetorical criticism we should be doing a detailed analysis of the entire letter. But for the sake of brevity we won't be doing much rhetorical spadework beyond the opening sections of the letter.

My conversation partners don't look overly reassured, but we move on.

Now, a Greek letter usually opens with greetings that set the stage for what follows, often referring to a common base of interest between the sender and receiver of the letter. Recall how Terentianus the Egyptian soldier buttered up his father before he got up the courage to ask his permission to marry. When the preliminaries were over, the writer moved to the body of the letter, that is, what he really wanted to talk about.

"Yeah," says Thad as he flips back to the Egyptian's letter. "It's clever the way he goes from a prayer to Sarapis to 'I got a basket from the father of Julius, in which there just happens to be a letter about a woman.'"

In Greek letters the transition from opening greetings to the real topic was commonly signaled by a set phrase, such as "I appeal to you" or "I want you to know," followed by the main purpose of the writer. We see the same sort of things in modern letters. A while back I got a rejection letter in response to a query I sent about this manuscript. As they always do, the publisher's assistant greeted me with good cheer but quickly dropped the bomb in a brief, unadorned sentence. Then the rest of the letter softened the blow, soothing my ego with assurances that the quality of my writing and the self-evident importance of the endeavor had little to do with their decision; rather, it was a problem of too many worthy manuscripts and too few resources, etc., etc., etc.

In his letter Paul greets the Corinthians with compliments (he calls them "sanctified in Christ") and a hearty wish for grace and peace (1:1-3). He thanks God for the witness of their great virtue, piety, and faith in Christ, and then, at verse 10, he gets down to business. "I appeal to you, brothers and sisters," he says, using the standard formula,

> by the name of our Lord Jesus Christ, that all of you be in agreement and that there be no divisions among you, but that you be united in the same mind and the same purpose.

Here we have an expression of concern as well as a succinct summary of the stated purpose of the entire letter: Paul perceives among the Corinthians dissension that must cease.

When we approach the letter as a piece of rhetoric, 1 Corinthians 1:10 stands out for the same reason. Ancient rhetoricians followed certain conventions. A rhetorical argument began with an *exordium,* a sort of opening exhortation which, like a letter's opening thanksgiving, sought to catch the audience's attention and interest, establish esteem between the rhetor and the audience, and preview the points to be raised. Paul accomplishes this in 1 Corinthians 1:4-9.

After the *exordium* came the statement of the thesis that was to be argued. It could be quite short, such as an appeal for an action the rhetor wanted the audience to do. Verse 10, calling for unity and the absence of dissension or factions, is the thesis statement.

Thus, whether we look at 1 Corinthians as a letter or as a sustained rhetorical argument, we discover the same stated purpose for the letter's composition: Paul appeals to the Corinthians to modify their behavior so that there may be no dissension among them and that they be united (literally "be fitted together") in the same mind. Paul claims at the beginning of his argument, then, that dissension among the Corinthians is what has caused him to write the letter.

There. End of rhetorical analysis, at least for now. How's that?

Thaddeus looks a bit worn out. "Where's all of this going?" he asks.

We have examined the preliminaries—authorship, audience, genre, and the general context. A brief dose of rhetorical theory has helped us to locate the probable purpose of the letter. Now it is time to look at the specific text we have chosen.

"The one with the weird, uh, unusual words," Thad says.

You could put it that way.

For Reflection and Further Discussion

1. Think of the letters or perhaps the e-mail messages you receive from friends and relatives but also from companies or groups seeking to interest you in their products or services. Take a look at one of these letters and see if you can apply what we have discussed about rhetoric to this modern "genre" of text.

2. Return to 1 Corinthians as a whole. Even before we move on to it, can you discern some of the possible causes of the dissension that Paul argues against? Make a list of "stress points" you see in the text.

Chapter Fifteen

What Kind of Fool Is God?

It's late afternoon and I am enjoying some solitude and a glass of retsina at a Greek *taverna* situated along the south side of the Corinth canal. As I sit here our fellow pilgrims are probably winding down after a full day. They spent the morning at Isthmia, shadowing archaeologists as they excavated a field of ruins next to the great sanctuary of Poseidon. It was their idea, not mine, and from what I heard after lunch, one day of dirt archaeology was quite enough, thank you. The temperature reached one hundred degrees by noon, and there is little shade in a place where trees have been removed to protect the artifacts. Lunch consisted of quickly compiled slabs of salami and hard cheese on tough Greek white bread brought up from the village, a soft drink, and a cookie.

I, meanwhile, have been luxuriating here, near an architectural wonder of another sort. First attempted almost two millennia ago by Nero but completed only in the nineteenth century, a dramatic canal cuts through the isthmus of Corinth from the Saronic Gulf in the east to the Gulf of Corinth in the west. I say dramatic because it was carved straight through hundreds of vertical feet of rock. Positioned as I am at the east end of the canal, I see a giant V-shaped wedge chiseled out of the rock, an unnatural gorge of stratified, clean-cut canyon walls sloping down to a ribbon of water about sixty feet wide at the surface. An impressive sight, even without the retsina.

Of course, you and I aren't about to spend much time lounging in the afternoon sun by the sea. Remember when I sat in my mentor's office at Harvard and he burst forth with excitement over Paul's use of three words in 1 Corinthians 1:26? That happened as he and I were doing a preliminary scan of the first part of the letter, seeking out anything that looked odd or interesting. That is how biblical interpretation (exegesis) begins. I propose that we return to the first chapter of 1 Corinthians and take an even closer look than we have so far. I'll point out the kinds of questions a modern

A taverna by the Corinth canal with view of the high bridge.   Photo by John Lanci

reader might ask of the text. At this point all we'll do is raise some questions; feel free to jot down your own as we go in case I miss one or two (as I cannot help but do). Now, go and get your Bible, and let's take a look. You do the English and I'll struggle with the Greek.

Is God a Fool?

The first thing I notice is that, as we saw before, Paul begins his letter in typical epistolary and rhetorical fashion. He sets out his credentials, identifying himself as *klētos,* ("one who has been *called*") and "apostle." He engages his audience's attention and shows his good will to them, praising them by identifying them as "called," just as he was. He continues his praise, identifying the Corinthians as holy, people enriched in "speech and knowledge of every kind . . . not lacking in any spiritual gift" (1:5, 7). Furthermore, he addresses the Corinthians as a community—an *ekklēsia*—which, while existing in Corinth, is called to holiness within a wider context, "together with all those who in every place call on the name of our Lord Jesus Christ, both their Lord and ours" (1:2).

The forms of many of the Greek verbs at the beginning of 1 Corinthians suggest something that may be significant. (Yvonne is not present here to get all edgy at the thought of Greek, so indulge me as I take advantage of her absence and bathe you with a bit of it). Paul writes that the Corinthians have *been* made holy (*hēgiasmenois,* 1:2), have *been* enriched (*eploutisthēte,* 1:5), have *been* confirmed (*ebebaiothē,* 1:6), and they have *been* called (*epikaloumenios,* 1:2; *eklēthēte,* 1:9). Both in Greek and in English this is the passive voice, and I suspect that in a very subtle way Paul uses these passive verbs to emphasize that the Corinthians are in the passive position: they are acted upon by God rather than being in control themselves.

At this point it is not clear that any of this is significant, but we press on.

As I said above, from Paul's opening words we learn that he understands his audience to be holy people who are rich in knowledge and possess every spiritual gift ("not lacking in any spiritual gift," 1:7). Nothing Paul says here points to his having a problem with what people in Corinth are preaching about God and the gospel. But Paul doesn't go on forever with his praise in 1 Corinthians. As we saw in the last chapter, he identifies his problem in 1:10: there are dissensions *(schismata)* among the Corinthians. The word that he uses here is odd; a quick check of my concordance to the Greek New Testament indicates that *schismata* never appears in another Pauline letter, but it pops up three times in 1 Corinthians (1:10, 11:18, and 12:25). This uniqueness suggests that it may offer a clue to understanding the letter, and we'll have to come back to it, especially because I'm already wondering about Paul's perspective here. Is there really dissension at Corinth, or is it something he *thinks* exists there? Hmmm.

Back to the text. Next, a number of personal names catch the eye, particularly Chloe, Apollos, and Cephas, and although I recognize Cephas as the Aramaic form of Peter no other ancient source that I know of places Peter in Corinth, and I want to know more about the others, since it looks as though the text connects at least Cephas and Apollos with the dissension Paul perceives at Corinth. Can we sort out this network of friends (and possibly adversaries) almost two millennia after the fact?

I wonder, too, about Paul's concern with wisdom in this chapter. He seems to distrust it. In 1 Corinthians 1:17 how could it be that if Paul preached "with eloquent wisdom" he might empty the cross of its power? Wouldn't Paul *need* eloquence to pitch to his listeners a theology of the cross? How the power of the cross might be lessened by preaching well about it is not self-evident to me. Moreover, it's not very often that Paul writes about the "word of the cross" or its power. Why does he do so here?

Virtually all the commentators on 1 Corinthians agree that at 1 Corinthians 1:18 Paul shifts from his introductory remarks to the first of his "proofs," that is, the first section in which he attempts to address his major concern (in the jargon of rhetoric, his thesis). This first section of proofs will last until 1 Corinthians 4:21, and in it Paul attempts to convince his correspondents that they are indeed in trouble because of the dissension he has heard about. Beginning with 1 Corinthians 5 he will spend most of his time answering questions that some Corinthians have asked him. Our particular journey won't allow us to pick our way through the entire letter; we'll focus only on a few sections of this first proof.

At 1 Corinthians 1:18 the pivotal words that link the introduction to the first proof are "cross" and "wisdom." Paul moves from a reference to his own avoidance of eloquent wisdom in verse 17 to a text from the prophet Isaiah that portrays God as one who "will destroy the wisdom of the wise." What does Paul mean by "the wisdom of the wise" or, as he puts it in verse 20, "the wisdom of the world"? Is wisdom a topic he brings up in his other letters?

Our writer then asserts that the word of the cross *is* the power of God, and again I wonder how often he makes this claim. If it is rare for him, this statement, coming so close to the beginning of his first proof, might be of critical importance to our understanding of his arguments throughout the letter.

So far, wisdom and power may be key concepts to keep an eye on.

And then there are the Jews and Greeks of 1:22. What are the "signs" that Jews of Paul's time might be seeking? Is the "wisdom" of the Greeks that he mentions the ruminations of the Greek philosophical schools? And note that once again Paul contrasts the striving of these people with the cross, here "Christ crucified," which he now labels clearly in 1:24 as "Christ the power of God and the wisdom of God" and "God's foolishness."

God's foolishness? In what way might God be a fool?

An Odd and Interesting Bridge

By now we've reached our verse, 1:26. And by now you'll have noticed that I ask a lot of questions about Paul's use of words—their meanings, the frequency of Paul's use of them, and their possible relationships to one another. Some themes or concerns appear in many of his letters, but recall that Paul was a situational writer—he wrote to specific groups about specific problems or questions. Therefore if we find that he employs any words or introduces some ideas or flags a problem only in 1 Corinthians, that may mean that something unique was going on at Corinth, and we may be able to guess what it was. Why is that important? Well, those are the kinds of clues that we use to help us get behind the letter to see if we can reconstruct a little bit of the historical situation of some of the first Christians. All this, of course, is tentative, but it might be helpful to us to know as much as possible about the lives, the beliefs, and the struggles of our first ancestors in the faith.

Ah, our friends have returned to continue the conversation.

"Not yet," Jeremy says. "There's an oil tanker coming. We want to watch the bridge," and they saunter over to the canal. I join them. You see, when a ship arrives at the east end of the canal, the bridge doesn't go up; it goes down, submerging itself completely and sitting at the bottom of the canal, twenty-five feet below, as the barge or ocean-liner-sized cruise ship floats over it. Once the boat is clear, the bridge rises to the surface, a fish or two flopping on its drenched wooden boards, which quickly dry in the Greek sun. The gates go up, and pedestrians and vehicles resume their journey.

Not to be missed.

The Naïve Readers Arrive

"Wow!" Marjorie says as we return from the canal. "A bridge *under* troubled waters."

Yvonne rolls her eyes and sits down at my table with a sigh, not even bothering to wipe the omnipresent dust from her chair.

"You sure were right about the 'romance of archaeology,'" she says.

Did you find anything?

"Dirt," she responds. "Lots of dirt."

Any interesting finds? Did you see any stratification?

"No coins or anything," Jeremy says. "Just different colored dirt. In a hole inside a trench."

A hole? That might be significant—a post for a building or a burning pit perhaps.

Thaddeus arrives and pulls up a chair. "Jeez," he says, and stretches arms that are sunburned and already aching from heavy lifting. Wheelbarrow duty, no doubt.

"Did you know," he says, "that normal people *pay* archaeologists to do that all day?"

And they do it for weeks on end. What about the excavation house and the library? Any luck there?

"That was about as exciting as standing in the trench all morning," Yvonne says.

"But," Marj adds, "the Naïve Readers Brigade did do its homework. Over lunch we read through chapter one of the letter, pooled our observations and questions, and found a couple of commentaries that can help us."

Thaddeus pulls some books out of his backpack and I review for them the main points of our own ruminations: We noticed Paul's praise for his correspondents and that there was no ready evidence from chapter one that Paul had a problem with someone preaching an alternative gospel. However, he clearly was worried about what he identified as division, and we wondered why he used the word *schismata,* unusual for him, to characterize it. We discovered an emphasis on God as the one who acts, while Paul seemed to characterize the Corinthians as reactors. We wondered about the significance of the people he names, like Chloe, Apollos, and Cephas. We paused at the references to Jewish sign-seeking and the Greeks' quest for wisdom and, in general, pondered the whole question of the cross, the word of the cross and its power, and the way Paul seems to fix upon Christ as "crucified." And then there was the question of God being a fool.

"We overlapped a bit with your questions," Marj says. "Our big topics were, um . . . ." She glances at Yvonne, who pulls a small notebook from her bag.

"I was the stenographer," Yvonne says, rifling through the pages. "Yes, here we are. We spent some time reading about factions in Corinth," she says. "That would be the same as your . . . what did you call it? Stigmata?"

Schismata.

"Yeah, well we found out some stuff about that," she says. "And we spent a lot of time reading about wisdom."

"And gnosticism," Thad interrupts. "That was really neat."

"Really weird, you mean," Jeremy says.

"We didn't do much with the cross," Marj says. "But we did take a closer look at the leaders mentioned, like Apollos and Cephas. And," she adds, "I found a book that talks a bit about some of the women of Corinth, like Chloe."

She draws a book out of her sack and puts it on the table as though stock-piling ammo for a battle to come. I read the title: *Rhetoric and Ethic: The Politics of Biblical Studies,* by my first Bible teacher, Elisabeth Schüssler Fiorenza.

How did you get these books out of the excavation house, anyway? It isn't exactly a lending library.

"That Dr. Gregory is such a charming man," Yvonne says of the excavation's director. "And generous. We told him we'd bring them right back after we met with you."

The charming, middle-aged Albanian waiter arrives, flashes a smile directed particularly at Yvonne, and takes the new arrivals' drink orders.

"Did you see how he looked at her?" Jeremy says as the waiter turns and crosses the patio to the *taverna* building.

We kick back, enjoy the afternoon breeze off the Saronic Gulf, and prepare for a session of exegesis.

Does it get any better than this?

Factions at Corinth?

We take out our Bibles and turn to the first chapter of 1 Corinthians (why don't you join us?).

Thad begins. "I was reading 1 Corinthians 1:11-13, where Paul identifies factions at Corinth. Some people 'belong' to Paul, others to Apollos or Cephas or even to Christ."

He looks over at the stack of commentaries on the table. "You would think, looking at this passage, that Paul is talking about groups of believers headed by different leaders."

"Almost like slogans for political parties," Marj says.

"And yet," Thad resumes, "we couldn't find any commentaries that agreed that there were different parties among the Corinthian Christians."

No theories at all about factions at Corinth?

"Oh, yeah," Thad says. "We found all kinds of theories."

Here Jeremy pulls out his notebook. "They let me do most of the commentary work, I think because I'm the only one who had ever heard of a commentary before we started this gig," he says as he checks his notes. "Your scholar friends write about all kinds of oldtime faction theories. Some of these theories said the factions were caused by wandering preachers or by Judaizers—"

"What's that?" Yvonne asks.

"Darned if I know," Jeremy says.

They were followers of Jesus who believed that Gentile converts had to follow some parts of the Jewish Law. You find Paul debating their views in his letter to the Galatians.

Jeremy picks up where he left off, though you can tell that his heart is still not in this sort of scholarly approach to Holy Scripture. "Some think the factions were local Corinthians called 'the strong' or even Thad's gnostics."

And yet you say you couldn't find any support for these theories in the more recent commentaries. Why not?

"Well," Thad says, "for one thing, there's no evidence from the ancient world for party slogans like 'I belong to Apollos.' And there's another problem: these parties or factions, or whatever they are, never get mentioned again in 1 Corinthians."

That is correct. The letter is addressed to the community as a whole, and Paul shows no knowledge of distinct groups with different theological belief systems or worship practices, though it's pretty clear there were divisions of opinion on a number of issues within the community. I was wondering if the word that Paul uses for "dissension"—*schismata*—might be of some help. I'm thinking of a study by Johannes Munck. Did you notice any references to it?

Four blank stares. Time to earn my keep.

Munck did a close study of the words Paul uses to signify the dissension he perceives, both *schismata* and also *erides* (the latter is found in 1:11 and is a word Paul uses to denote "quarreling"). Munck's conclusion was that they do not indicate some sort of fully developed factional dispute, but they do point to something that can be just as bad for communal morale: verbal bickering.

"It would seem to me that if there were actual factions," Thad says, "we'd be able to say something—from the text, mind you—about the content of their differences."

Commentators have certainly attempted this kind of reconstruction. The First Letter to the Corinthians has been combed and tweaked and prodded. But no consensus has ever developed, and where theories abound historical likelihood is not to be found.

"He's rhyming," Yvonne says, and she signals our attentive Albanian waiter. *"Por favor,"* she says to him with a smile. "Another glass of retsina for our teacher, yes?"

Marj leans over to Yvonne. *"Por favor?"*

"Whatever," Yvonne says, saluting the afternoon sun with her own empty wine glass, and it's time for us to move on.

Apollos, Cephas, Paul, Christ . . . and Chloe?

We aren't done with this question of factions.

"But you're beginning to lose me again," Yvonne says.

"This is getting kind of complicated," Marj says.

Krister Stendahl, Lutheran bishop emeritus and one of the grand old men of New Testament studies, once wrote that "pedantry is the chief sin of exegetes."

"Pedantry?" Yvonne asks.

Pedantry: an overemphasis on book learning or technical expertise. According to Stendahl this vice develops both from the theologian's passionate spiritual faith and from what he calls "theological greed." Many scholars approach biblical texts with great respect but with a greedy desire to prove them to be more complex theologically than they really are. Stendahl says the reasoning goes like this: "If it is the word of God, it has to be at least as deep as I can be, and then some."

This particular bishop is capable of a fine, dry wit, and he uses it, both in writing and in person, to counsel clear-headedness when approaching a sacred text. Use a "light touch," he says, and a minimalist approach. Then you'll have a better shot at reading the text you actually have before you.

Let's try to stick with Stendahl's minimalist approach and cling to what we see in the text.

The first section of 1 Corinthians is a thicket of intertwined themes and images, and this notion of dissension is caught in the middle of them. If we aren't dealing here with factions, I wonder if it would help to look at the people Paul names in this section of the letter. What did you find?

"Cephas was Peter, right?" Jeremy asks, and I nod in assent. The Aramaic *Cephas* and the Greek *Petros* both translate along the lines of the word "rock" in English. We see them connected explicitly in the story of the call of Simon in the Gospel of John (1:40-42).

"Some of the commentaries say that Peter might have been in Corinth," Jeremy says.

"And didn't you tell us, Jeremy," Thad interjects, "that they associate the hypothetical Judaizers in Corinth with Cephas?"

"Yes, they do," he says. "But I don't see why."

This theory may come from the fact that Peter and Paul went head to head on the issue of Jewish Law earlier in their careers when they encountered each other in Antioch. The letter to the Galatians indicates that people preaching a stricter approach to the Law than Paul thought necessary had wandered into Galatia and were interfering with his missionary work. In defending his own version of the gospel Paul tells the story in Galatians 2:11-14 of how he confronted Cephas—pretty much called him a hypocrite to his face—because he thought that Cephas was wrong to make Gentile converts follow Jewish dietary laws.

"I take it there was no love lost between Peter and Paul," Marj says.

No, there surely was not. Since Cephas is mentioned in 1 Corinthians it's possible that his interpretation of both the gospel and Jewish Law was known at Corinth; he might even have visited the city. But there's no evidence from the letter to help us determine the nature of Peter's influence, since adherence to Jewish Law is not an issue in this letter.

"What about 2 Corinthians?" Jeremy asks. "Paul seems to be fighting your Judaizers there, right?"

"We were looking at that," Thad says. "In 2 Corinthians 11 Paul talks about other apostles, 'super-apostles' in my translation. Look at how he defends himself," he continues as he opens his book to the passage. "He puts his *Jewish* credentials up against theirs."

"Yeah," says Jeremy, and he takes the Bible from Thad and quotes 2 Corinthians 11:22: "'Are they Hebrews? So am I. Are they Israelites? So am I. Are they descendants of Abraham? So am I.'"

He gives the book back to Thad. "See?" he says, "He's talking about these super-apostles who preach a different gospel, and they're Jewish, just like Cephas was in Galatians."

Good point. It's possible that 2 Corinthians provides testimony that Cephas was at Corinth.

"But . . ." Thad says.

Well, there are reasons why I haven't made reference to 2 Corinthians in our discussions. First of all, most interpreters agree that it's really not one letter but a composite of at least two or even as many as five of Paul's letters. The sequence of these stitched-together letters is impossible to pin down, and it's even harder to relate them chronologically to 1 Corinthians. Also, as Jeremy pointed out, in 2 Corinthians Paul is opposing what he sees as another gospel (see 2 Cor 11:1-4), but there's no such gospel evident in 1 Corinthians. Thus we need to keep a bit of space between the two extant Corinthian letters, although it can't hurt to keep our ears open for issues that appear in both letters. That being the case, I suggest that we return to the minimalist road: let's try as hard as we can to avoid reading into one text what we find in another.

"Man, your scholar friends really know how to spin a tale when it comes to Apollos," Jeremy says. "I spent half the afternoon trying to figure out where some of those guys get their information."

"All we really know about him comes from the New Testament," Marj says.

"He was Jewish and came from Alexandria," Yvonne says, reading from her notes. "In Egypt."

"He was 'eloquent and mighty in the Scriptures,'" Jeremy says, quoting his King James Bible. "Acts 18:24-28 tells us that he was instructed in the Lord's way but also says that he only knew the baptism of John the Baptist and he needed more training. He got that from Priscilla and Aquila at Ephesus. After he got retooled he went to Achaia—Greece, right?—and he became a powerful preacher there."

Right on all counts.

"I've got a question," Marj declares. "Even some of the commentaries that agree with you on this point seem to imply that Apollos and Paul were in some sort of conflict. But, naïve reader that I am, I don't see it. If Paul and Apollos aren't bickering about how to read Scripture, what could they be fighting about? Why do the commentators think they're fighting at all?"

"Probably because Paul's always so feisty," Yvonne says. "He has to be fighting with somebody."

Thad flips through his text. "Perhaps it's because of 1 Corinthians 16:12, where Paul writes that Apollos has resisted Paul's strong suggestion that Apollos go to Corinth for a visit."

One could indeed argue that he is a bit irritated with Apollos here.

"But if Paul disagreed with Apollos or they were rivals, wouldn't he want to keep him away from the Corinthians?" Jeremy asks.

"Right," Marj says, "and there's something else." She draws herself up straight in her chair, and her brows indicate that she is focusing her thoughts. "Try this: If Acts can be believed, and Apollos got a theological fine-tuning from Priscilla and Aquila, and if we know from Paul's letters that they were his good friends, wouldn't it make sense that the brand of Christianity that Apollos preached was compatible with Paul's?"

"Sounds good to me," Yvonne says.

I am about to jump in here when Thad beats me to it.

"You may indeed be right," he says. "But even if Apollos personally is in agreement with Paul, it's still possible that some of the Corinthians who were taught by Apollos could have been rivals of the people Paul taught or even of Paul himself."

They look to me. I take a deep breath, but we are distracted by a large cruise ship emerging from the canal, its decks lined with tourists high above our heads. I'm thinking: Can you believe these allegedly naïve readers are so engrossed in all this? Don't miss the significance of what our friends are doing here. They have sifted through both the biblical text and the ideas of later commentators. Oh, they have not come up with *the* correct interpretation. Nor have they demonstrated that the scholarly interpreters are all wrong. But they are wrestling with a text in their own context, bringing their own intuitions and insight to our *taverna* table talk. In this way they have wandered to the threshold of the third part of our journey, "Talk."

We have to wrap this up soon or we'll miss the bus back to our lodgings in Old Corinth. I return to the fray.

It's very possible that Apollos and Paul were missionary and theological allies but that some of their followers were not. The problem is that if we look just at 1 Corinthians we can't point to any group of followers espousing the thought of Apollos in opposition to Paul's. It surely looks as though there was some friction between different Jesus followers at Corinth but, as we have seen, the presence of organized, theologically distinct parties is a tough case to prove.

"So, what do we have then?" Jeremy asks.

Again I suggest we take a minimalist approach to the text and to Apollos. Rather than worry too much about him I suggest we salute his memory and retire him from our discussion for the time being with the reasoned judgment of Raymond Collins, who characterizes him as "a well-known, almost legendary figure in the early Christian movement" about whom we can say little more with certainty.

I make a move to flag down our waiter for the check, but Marj stops me.

"Wait!" she says. "What about Chloe?"

Yikes! I forgot about Chloe! What do we know about her?

"Not much," Thad says. "She's only mentioned once in the Bible, in 1 Corinthians 1:11. Paul says 'her people' have told him about the quarreling at Corinth."

"The commentators seem to think that Chloe was a wealthy woman," Marj says, "at least rich enough to have servants or slaves to send to Paul with their report."

"But didn't they say that no one's even sure she was a Christian?" Yvonne asks.

"Right," Thad says. "Members of her household might have been converts, while she wasn't."

"What?" Jeremy looks up.

"Well," says Marj, "it's possible that her servants were Christians, while she was oblivious to the whole Jesus thing."

A lot of speculation here, no?

"A lot of wine," mumbles Jeremy, as he sips from his soft drink.

Marj picks up a book. "Your friend Elisabeth Schüssler Fiorenza has some interesting things to say about this chapter of 1 Corinthians," she says. "She agrees that there were no parties. But her argument is different. She claims that commentators who try to supply the absent details—about who these people were and what the parties were like—are missing a fundamental point."

I'll bet I know what it is: they're all making the same assumption, right?

"Yep," Marj says. "They all assume that Paul's account of what is going on in Corinth is identical with what actually is happening there. They've forgotten that he knew how to use rhetoric, and he might well have been reading the situation wrong."

"Wrong?" Jeremy says. "Here we go again, with Paul being wrong."

"Well, in this case I'm willing to give him the benefit of the doubt," Marj says to him. "He might not be doing it on purpose. But Schüssler Fiorenza claims that if there is any reference to party strife in the letter, the parties exist in Paul's own mind."

"And of course we can't know that," Jeremy says. "We can't read the thoughts of a dead man."

Yvonne is getting restless again. "Why are we doing this?" she asks. "We're back in Greek-land, and now *we're* breaking into factions."

You might well wonder why we've spent so much time turning over tiny sections of the text of 1 Corinthians, only to question and doubt their importance for our reading of the letter. Let me help: we've been examining some of the "received wisdom" about this letter. Commentators have waxed eloquent (and at length) about the possible causes of dissension at Corinth. Was it faction versus faction? Paul versus the Judaizers or Peter? Apollos versus Paul? Paul versus the majority of the Corinthians?

"No disrespect intended," Jeremy says. "But as Yvonne just asked, so what?"

Finally a question I can easily answer! We needed to evaluate these different theories on the chance that one of them would save us a lot of trouble and answer our original question about Paul's use of social terminology in the opening of 1 Corinthians. So, did any of these theories answer the question?

"No," Jeremy says. "Not really."

Well, I think I have an answer. Let's head back to the excavation house and catch the bus back to Old Corinth.

"But we haven't talked about wisdom and the gnostics yet," Thad says.

"And did I hear you right?" Jeremy asks. "Did you say you thought God was some kind of fool?"

The foolishness of God. Wisdom. Power. All these are part of the theory I want to test out on you. But first a shower, a little siesta, and then maybe we can talk a bit before dinner.

It's Yvonne's turn to pay the bill, and as we rise, our waiter smiles warmly at her.

"*Muchas gracias,*" he says.

For Reflection and Further Discussion

1. As you followed along the text of 1 Corinthians, did any questions occur to you that we didn't discuss?

2. This chapter is filled with detailed discussion. Note any points you are still unclear about and bring them to your group for clarification if you are reading this with others.

3. In this chapter we have seen our "naïve readers" tossing out the work of prominent scholars and pitching their ideas to one another. What do you make of this? Is this a legitimate way to do Bible study? Do you think this sort of approach is appropriate in a classroom? What are the strengths and weaknesses of such an approach?

The courtyard of the fountain of Peirene.   Photo by John Lanci

Chapter Sixteen

A Little History, a Little Wisdom, a Little Mystery

Well before dawn two men approach the Corinthian forum on the road from Cenchreae. They had arrived at the Corinthian port the previous day and now are walking to the city to find friends who keep a shop for leather-workers, where they can get work.

They cross through the South Stoa and enter the upper level of the broad, open plaza that constitutes the Roman city's forum. Normally the commercial and governmental hub of the city, at this hour the great square is quiet. But even now the men are not alone. Several people huddle around a fire in front of one of the shops on the other side of the broad expanse. Here and there a faint light indicates that other people in other shops are preparing for the coming day. Two women carrying water jars cross the square below on their way to the fountain of Peirene. A tent flaps in the breeze off the Gulf of Corinth to the north. A man stirs as he sleeps on the steps before an altar to the Divine Julius. One can hear the slow rico-chet of hooves on stone as a horse pulls a cart in the distance. When the sun rises, the bronze statues that dot the lower forum will cast long shad-ows across the open space. Now Athena and Heracles stand in the dark on their pedestals like shades.

The men walk past the speaker's platform, the *bēma,* at the edge of the upper forum and down the stairs to the plaza below. At the center of the open space they stop, for they are new to the city. Ahead of them, reflected in the light of the campfire, a line of columns defines the shops that form the northern edge of the city center. The firelight barely hints at the archaic Doric temple looming in the darkness above the stoa's colonnade. To their right they see a Roman basilica, where merchants much more influential than they will mingle in a few hours under the gaze of a large statue of Augustus. Behind them stretches the massive colonnade of the South Stoa, the longest uninterrupted line of columns in Greece. They stand in a dark forest of columns to their north, south, and east.

Turning to the west they proceed toward a series of four small buildings and a fountain house on a raised terrace. Three of the buildings are temples in the Roman style; the fourth is a tall, round display of columns forming a haven for a statue within. The men hail a woman passing by and ask for directions to the road to Lechaion, Corinth's northern port, where they hope to find their friends. The woman, also a foreigner and probably a freedperson with a shop of her own, seems surprised that they don't know the way; she points across the square to the large north gate, and the men turn to go.

But one of them stops abruptly. The darkness has grayed with the approach of dawn, and the faint stirring of morning light has caused the marble façade of one of the temples on the western terrace to begin to glow a pale pink. The small sanctuary is exquisitely proportioned and executed, and the man beckons to his companion to join him in taking a closer look.

They cross to the temple and ascend its steps. As they reach the top of the temple's platform a sudden flash of light from the sky distracts them. They look, and far above the city on the brow of Acrocorinth the sun has struck the bronze and gold decoration of the famous sanctuary of Corinthian Aphrodite.

A pinpoint of sharp light burns from the center of the temple. They do not know it, for they have not yet made the climb to the top, but the light is sun's dawn reflected off a warrior's shield in the temple, the one that the statue of Aphrodite, the city's protector, holds in her graceful hands.

Corinthian Musings

While the others shower and enjoy a brief siesta before we gather, I perch on a low wall of rock in the forum and imagine what it might have been like to arrive at the center of the Roman city for the first time.

I sit here among ruins of two cities, not one. The Roman architecture of the forum is overshadowed even today by the remains of an impressive Greek structure, the massive Doric columns of the archaic temple, which many believe was dedicated to Apollo. We will spend our time rummaging through the remains of the Roman city, but to understand the situation of the first Corinthian Christians we must familiarize ourselves with the Greek city as well.

The land of the Corinthians was suited for the urban center and surrounding towns that developed there. Watered by many springs, gifted with a

A portion of the Lechaion Road with Acrocorinth in the background.   Photo: TLP Archives

broad and fertile plain to the north and Acrocorinth's secure fortress to the south, the escarpment upon which I now sit has been inhabited since Neolithic times; the earliest evidence of human habitation dates to a thousand years before the arrival of the first followers of Jesus. Situated at the center of the eastern Mediterranean, Corinth in each stage of its prosperous career was as enriched by commerce as it was nurtured by agriculture. Craftsmen and -women, traders, speculators, runaways, tourists—the Greek city welcomed them all, though it did not invite any of them to an easy life. Rough and tumble at the best of times, at its worst Corinth was a crossroads of commercial and political ferment—and devastating wars. In the Peloponnesian Wars the Corinthians sided with Sparta, their neighbor to the south, against Athens, but their hatred of the Athenians got the better of them. When Sparta conquered Athens in 404 and refused Corinth's demand that it be destroyed, the Corinthians turned on their powerful ally and precipitated yet another conflict, this time fought on and off for decades mostly in Corinthian territory, which was ravaged.

That war wound down just in time for Philip II of Macedonia to invade Greece. Philip, the father of Alexander the Great, arrived from the north, and while it dodged this bullet, Corinth fell under the control of a Macedonian garrison on Acrocorinth. Its luck ran out with the appearance of the Romans. The Greek cities resisted the rise of Roman influence in the region. As a result, after a few difficult diplomatic skirmishes, the Roman consul Lucius Mummius arrived on the scene in 146 and proceeded to defeat and sack the city.

For a century much of the city was in ruins. Then in 44 B.C.E. Julius Caesar authorized the city's refoundation. Italy was having severe population problems as country folk, uprooted by a century of civil wars, were flooding the cities, particularly Rome. Caesar's plan was to entice this urban overflow to migrate to lands of new opportunity, colonies in the provinces. Some of these colonies, like Philippi, were populated with discharged soldiers, but Corinth became a magnet for civilians, in particular the urban poorer classes.

Julius met his dramatic end before this process could really get underway, but Caesar Augustus, his successor, saw to it that Roman Corinth grew to be the most prosperous city in Greece. It was a city of Italian immigrants and Greek locals, of rich speculators and working-class entrepreneurs, traders and potters, workers in bronze and leather and stones and gems, hardscrabble farmers and Roman priests, politicians and prostitutes, slaves with their masters and runaway slaves and those recently freed from slavery, men and women looking for new beginnings and new prosperity. The money was certainly new, and the life was probably fast.

This manifestation of the city flourished, and its people, many of them, found what they were looking for. Corinth was at the center of Greek commerce but it was not predominantly Greek; its architecture, its social and governmental structures, its coinage, inscriptions, and pottery were thoroughly Roman.

This Roman incarnation of Corinth is the city Paul slipped into one night, perhaps, alone or with one or two traveling companions.

Now it is Marjorie who slips into the forum and approaches me.

"The others are waiting for you," she says. "I figured I'd find you down here."

We survey the remains of the Roman forum in the filtered light of the late afternoon sun, devoid of tourists and their gassy buses at this time of day.

It's time to return to 1 Corinthians.

A Little Light Exegesis Before Dinner

Marj and I round the corner and enter the courtyard of our guesthouse. Yvonne and Thad are sitting in padded lounge chairs at a table under the low pine trees that serve as a canopy for the patio. Jeremy is off in the corner playing his flute, a simple wooden instrument his grandfather made for him.

We are greeted and seated, and it's time to begin.

We left off with some rather significant strands of theology twisting in the wind—

"Please," Marj says. "Leave off with the mixed metaphors."

—including notions of wisdom, power, and the foolishness of God.

"And the gnostics," Thad says. "Don't forget them."

I'm not convinced that they play much of a part in this journey. But because Thad is so eager and because gnostics of various types do find their way into most commentaries on 1 Corinthians I suppose we should take a look. Besides, that will lead us to a consideration of wisdom, and that, in turn, will lead us to the mystery of God's foolishness.

"All right!" Thad says. "Let's talk gnostic!"

What did you find out about the gnostics? Where did they originate?

"No one knows," he says.

When did gnosticism develop?

"No one knows," he says again.

Were they Christian? Jewish? Pre-Christian Gentile?

"Different people think differently about this," he says.

Perhaps you begin to perceive my problem with gnostics. Although fragments of a number of gnostic texts survive, and at least one gnostic gospel—the Gospel of Thomas—has been recovered in its entirety, the origins, dating, theological themes, and even the category "gnostic" are all—

"Up for grabs," Jeremy says.

You could put it that way. The big problem is with our sources. Most of the gnostic texts have disappeared, destroyed by their opponents, and the few that survive were, not surprisingly, written for gnostics by gnostics. That presents a problem.

"The same problem we had with the letters of Lillian and Alphonse?" Marj asks.

Exactly. They left out most of what we need to understand them.

"What about non-gnostic writers?" Thad asks. "Do they tell us anything?"

Other Christian groups tell us plenty. But you know the saying, "History is written by the victors." The Christians whose theological beliefs became the orthodox Christianity we know today bequeathed to us some scathing critiques of the gnostic views they opposed. They present their enemies' theology in the worst possible light. As a result it's difficult to say very much with confidence about any of the gnostic groups and what they believed and taught.

"But you can say *some* things about them," Thad insists.

Well, yes. Such as—

"I like the way some of them explained the reality of evil in the world," Thad says. "They believed that matter was evil and that God—the real God—didn't create it."

"Well, then, who did?" Jeremy asks.

"A demi-god, a sort of lesser or half-God, invented the world and everything in it," Thad says. "Including us."

"You like the idea that we were created evil?" Marj asks.

"No, no," Thad says. "Our bodies are evil, but each of us has a divine spark inside. The goal is to live a good life so that we can liberate the spark within our hearts so it can go back to its original source, the true, higher God."

"That sounds right to me," Yvonne says. "We die and our souls go back to God."

"It sounds pretty pagan to me," Jeremy growls. "Two gods? What about Jesus? Does he play any part in this weird riff on salvation?"

"He does!" Thad says. "The Christian gnostics saw him as the Divine Redeemer, the one who brings humanity the knowledge necessary to be saved."

For gnostics, knowledge was the key. The word for knowledge in Greek is *gnōsis;* hence the designation "gnostic," which, I believe, is not a name that most of these people would have answered to. What people refer to as the gnostic movement was actually an assortment of groups with a variety of different theologies. However, it seems that most of them sought salvation by means of knowledge or wisdom, some secret, special information that set them apart from other people.

This idea of gnostic "secret knowledge" or "secret wisdom" is what many close readers of Paul have discerned in 1 Corinthians, since he does make quite a lot of references to wisdom, including wisdom that is hidden. But is he referring to a gnostic kind of hidden wisdom? Or to something very different? Let's take a look.

I did a bit of quick concordance work a couple of days ago in preparation for our discussion. I looked up two Greek words: *sophos,* "wise," and *sophia,* "wisdom." I checked out where and how often they appear in Paul's letters. We find the adjective *sophos* fifteen times in the letters. Eleven of these are in 1 Corinthians and four are in Romans. Perhaps of relevance here is the fact that two of the uses in Romans are found in the last chapter, which, as we have seen, is probably a letter of recommendation Paul wrote for Phoebe, a highly placed woman in the Christian community at Cenchreae, Corinth's port. Paul uses the noun *sophia* nineteen times: once each in Romans and 2 Corinthians and seventeen times in 1 Corinthians. Of those seventeen *sophias,* fifteen appear in the first two chapters of the letter.

Something's going on here, and most of the major commentators have weighed in on the theme of wisdom in the letter. One prominent scholar, Hans Conzelmann, suggested that Paul founded a "school of wisdom" at Corinth; another, E. A. Judge, posited that Paul was in the habit of founding "scholastic communities" that debated theological matters in a style akin to ancient schools of rhetoric and philosophy. And then there are the theories about gnosticism at Corinth, found in books and articles too numerous for us to survey.

"Thank you, Jesus, for that!" says Yvonne.

"I'm still not clear on the most basic part of all of this," Marj says. "What exactly do you all mean by 'wisdom'?"

Paul appears to define what he means by wisdom in plain and simple terms: "But we proclaim Christ crucified, a stumbling block to the Jews and foolishness to Gentiles, but to those who are the called, both Jews and Greeks, Christ the power of God and *the wisdom of God*" (1 Cor 1:23-24).

Christ is the wisdom of God. Is this a title? Is Christ the personification of wisdom? The Divine Redeemer? The possibilities continue to accumulate as Paul "unpacks" his ideas about wisdom; he appears to be of two minds concerning its general availability to people. First he claims that "when I came to you, brothers and sisters, I did not come proclaiming the mystery *(mystērion)* of God in lofty words or wisdom" (1 Cor 2:1). So Paul's message is not some hidden mystery. But then he seems to claim that's exactly what it is, that there is indeed something secret or hidden about the wisdom he imparts: "We speak about wisdom among the mature, although a wisdom not of this age, nor of the rulers of this age, who will be brought to nothing. But we speak of *God's wisdom hidden in mystery,* which God decreed before the ages for our glory, which none of the rulers of this age understood" (1 Cor 2:6-8; my own translation).

This apparent contradiction has bedeviled scholars, and their resulting reflection has produced no consensus. The hiddenness of wisdom in the latter passage provides the launch pad for a great deal of speculation about gnosticism in Corinth, as does the word *mystērion,* which comes to us with a number of religious connotations. Is this a gnostic term, since we find it in other ancient gnostic texts? Is Paul making reference to the mystery rituals found in other religions of antiquity?

In point of fact, the term *mystērion* was perfectly at home in a number of religions in antiquity, including the non-gnostic, nonsecretive Judaism that Paul grew up with. In addition, *mystērion,* like "mystery" today, was used widely in its metaphorical sense. Schools of philosophy used it, as did just about everyone else, to indicate a very private secret. So how is Paul using the term? At this point let's see if we can follow what Paul says in the first part of the letter.

"You're sure we need to do this?" Yvonne says as she opens her Bible.

Absolutely! With or without gnostics at Corinth, wisdom seems to have been a big issue there.

"At least in Paul's mind it was," Marj corrects me.

Duly noted. Now, Paul first mentions wisdom in 1 Corinthians 1:17, where he implies that "eloquent wisdom" (*sophia logou,* literally "wisdom of speech") would render empty the cross of Christ, which is the power of God. In 1:19, citing Isaiah 29:14, he portrays God in opposition to (literally as "destroyer of") the "wisdom of the wise." He goes on to make a distinction between the wisdom of the world, which God renders foolish, and the wisdom of God.

In 1 Corinthians 1:17-25 Paul presents true wisdom—the wisdom of God—as connected to power (1:17, 18, 24) and connected, too, with the crucified Christ. This association of power with crucifixion, a method of destruction reserved for the least powerful people in ancient society, is what Paul calls folly and a stumbling block for those who oppose God's wisdom (1:18, 23).

How this could be? How could the slaughter of a Judean peasant on a cross be a manifestation of the power of God? That is what Paul is referring to when he speaks of a mystery. This mystery is not disclosed in words of excellence or wisdom, but it *is* disclosed. It is disclosed to those who have been called to it by God (1:24). The truth, the wisdom behind the mystery is nothing more (or less) than Christ (1:30) and Christ crucified (2:1-2).

Later we'll explore the content of Paul's "mystery" in some detail. But first, another question: When Paul claims that the wisdom of God is "secret and hidden" (2:7), from whom is that wisdom hidden?

Silence reigns as they stare at the text.

Recall the proem of the letter (1:5-7), where Paul praises the Corinthians. There he acknowledges that they lack no spiritual gift and have already been enriched with all speech *(logos)* and all knowledge *(gnōsis).* Look at the text. From whom is the mystery hidden?

"I'm looking at chapter two," Marj says, "and wondering if I'm missing something."

"How so?" Thad asks.

"Well, it seems pretty straightforward to me," Marj says. "The wisdom is hidden from 'the rulers of this age.'"

Exactly.

"Well, then, why all the scholarly jumping around?" she asks.

"I think I see the problem," Thad says to Marj. "Look at 1 Corinthians 2:6. He says he imparts wisdom 'among the mature.'"

"Yeah," says Jeremy. "And if you keep reading, it looks like Paul is talking about the Corinthians. Some of them are mature, and some of them aren't. Maybe the wisdom is hidden from some Corinthians and not others."

Very good, exegetes! Scholars wonder who are the mature and what is their connection to the "unspiritual" people Paul mentions in 2:14.

"And what about the 'babes' in 3:1?" Jeremy asks, consulting his King James Version of the text.

"Babes? There are babes in Corinth?" Thad says with a sly grin. "All right!"

"'Babes in Christ,' moron," Jeremy replies, though not (too) unkindly. "Mind out of the gutter."

So you see the problem? This section of the letter could be understood as Paul writing about several types of Christians at Corinth, some with more knowledge/*gnōsis* than others. We find such levels of spiritual knowledge among believers in other early Christian texts. Toss in a few gnostic terms, like *mystērion* and *sophia,* stir, and voila! Gnosticism at Corinth.

"So there were no gnostics at Corinth and all these scholars are, to use Jeremy's felicitous term, morons?" Marj asks.

Things are never that simple.

"So which is it? Gnostics or not?" Yvonne asks.

Let's go back to the text. But this time put on your "minimalist" glasses. I turn to Marjorie: What do you see? What is the wisdom here? What is the mystery that is hidden?

"Well," she answers, "the wisdom is Christ, according to 1:23-24. Christ crucified."

Excellent. What is the mystery?

"As you said, the mystery seems to be how a crucified man could also be the power of God."

Excellent. Next, from whom is the mystery hidden? For this we turn to Jeremy, our veteran Bible reader. We still have the people he flagged earlier, the "mature" and the less mature "infants" (the King James Version's "babes") among the Corinthians. Are these the people who are in the dark? Jeremy, you know this letter cold. Is there any evidence later in the text that would indicate that the people from whom Paul's mystery is hidden are part of the Christian community at Corinth?

Jeremy thinks for a minute.

"Well, there are the 'strong' and the 'weak,'" he says. "Paul tells the strong that they must not scandalize the weak."

Here Jeremy refers to 1 Corinthians 8:10, where Paul challenges community members who think they can continue to visit Gentile temples with their friends and even take part in the dining rituals that take place there. In the context of his argument Paul refers to some people possessing knowledge that others do not (see 1 Cor 8:1-13). But Jeremy, is the knowledge he writes about connected in any way to the hidden mystery he speaks of in 1 Corinthians 1 and 2?

"Not that I can see," he says. "In 1 Corinthians 8 the knowledge seems to be about the reality of the existence of other gods and their idol-worshiping pagan followers."

Yes, the knowledge that the "strong" have that can destroy their weaker companions is the knowledge that idols and even the food that is sacrificed to them mean nothing. That is a different issue than the one he's raising in the beginning of the letter.

Now, Thad, go for the gold. From whom is this mystery hidden?

A long Thaddean silence ensues.

"OK," he finally looks up. "If I just look at what I see here, the mystery is hidden from . . . not from the Corinthians, but as Marj said before, from the rulers of this age."

Bingo.

"But who are the rulers of this age?" Marj asks.

Well, if you go back to the secondary literature, most scholars think that elemental spirits or demons are the rulers Paul means here. They're the evil ones who engineered Christ's death. But—

"Wait," Yvonne says. "Put those minimalist glasses through their paces in a hurry so we can get this done and get over there to dinner. Look! They're bringing out the bread and retsina."

OK. Do it. What do you think?

Yvonne sighs, but hunger is a great motivator. She takes another look at the text I point to, 1 Corinthians 2:6-8. "It seems to me that the rulers of this age are the ones who crucified Christ, right? But it also seems as though Paul is saying that if they had understood the wisdom, they wouldn't have crucified him."

Good. Good.

"But would demons have changed their minds?" she asks.

Good question.

"I don't know about them," Thad says, "but the Romans might have changed their minds, and they were the ones who crucified him, right?"

Here is a situation in which our minimalist approach serves us well. There is little in the text to confirm the "received scholarly opinion" that the rulers of this age to whom Paul refers are supernatural, spiritual entities. And nothing in the text prevents us from identifying the rulers who crucified Christ with, well, the rulers who crucified Christ, that is, the Romans.

"So," Thad says. "The mystery that Paul refers to has to do with how hard it is to understand that the same person who was crucified is also the very power of God."

"And this is the mystery that's hidden," Jeremy says.

Precisely.

"I get it so far," Marj says. "But I don't really know what you mean when you talk about power. How can the crucifixion be 'power'? What is power anyway?"

"Oh, God," Yvonne sighs. "Can this wait?"

I think so. We've looked at Paul's use of wisdom and mystery terminology in 1 Corinthians, and I think we can set aside the "gnostics" as a primary influence at this point in the religious life of the Corinthian community. I suspect you could use a break from all of this close textual reading—

"And all this theology," Yvonne says.

And all this theology. As it happens, Marj's questions about power will lead us out of the text and back into the social and political world that Paul and the Corinthians inhabited.

"It's time for Rocks again, is it?" Thad says.

It is indeed. And that is where we will pick up this conversation tomorrow morning.

For Reflection and Further Discussion

Our brief discussion of gnosticism raises a number of questions we cannot pursue on this journey but that you might want to think about. Among them:

1. Recall how some of the gnostic groups explained the presence of evil in the world via the idea of a creator separate from the high God. How does your religious tradition (if you have one) make sense of evil? Do you accept this teaching? Does it make sense to you?

2. Many of the gnostics believed that we possess at our essence a divine spark that is trapped in our body. In this way of thinking, the body is evil and holds us back from becoming all that we could be. What do you think of this? Is the fleshly body evil?

3. Again, playing off of gnostic ruminations about the divine spark, do you agree with them that your body is a vessel your "real" self or your spirit inhabits? Or is your body an integral part of that real self? Put another way, is your body *you*? Or is it something you possess, is it *yours*?

Chapter Seventeen

The Rigmarole of Roman Power and Corinthian Rocks

The century before the birth of Jesus of Nazareth saw the birth of the Roman empire, and it was a difficult delivery. As we mentioned earlier, Julius Caesar brought to a conclusion a series of civil wars that almost destroyed the fabric of Roman society and necessitated the export of the urban poor to places like Corinth. His assassination in 44 B.C.E. set off another cycle of wars among the Roman elite, this time between Caesar's heir, Octavian, and one of his most important generals, Marc Antony.

In 31 B.C.E. one of the most significant battles in Western history was fought off the west coast of Greece at Actium. The Roman navy, loyal to Octavian and the Roman senate, confronted Antony and the great fleet of his powerful ally, Queen Cleopatra of Egypt. The Romans beat the pants off the forces of Cleopatra, and her hopes for a new world order, with Egypt at its center, were crushed. Octavian has cleared away the last obstacle between him and uncontested rule of Rome.

The obscure Roman writer Macrobius tells the story that when Octavian finally returned to Rome he was met by a crowd of people who had set out to greet and congratulate him. Out of the throng stepped a man holding a raven that, when prompted, proclaimed *"Ave Caesar victor imperator!"* ("Hail, Caesar, victorious emperor!"). Astonished by this unusual declaration of allegiance, Octavian (who was not yet, but would soon become, the emperor Augustus) promptly purchased the loyal bird for a phenomenal sum of money. Octavian was immediately accosted by another man, an associate of the first, who had been shut out of the deal. The disgruntled colleague in avian education disclosed the existence of a second bird that, when produced, declared on cue, *"Ave victor imperator Antoni!"* ("Hail, victorious emperor Antony!"). The wind presumably out of his sails, Octavian ordered the first man to share his bounty with his comrade.

This simple story depicts in miniature the position of the emperor in the early days of the Roman Empire. Octavian, fresh from his decisive victory over Antony, arrives on the scene. Two industrious men perceive him as someone from whom they may expect both generosity and fairness. The men are only two of a number of people who cultivated the favor of the new leader for personal gain.

Throughout the story Octavian's role is underplayed: not yet a tyrant who exerts absolute control over his people, he observes and reacts. He is described as surprised at the apparition of the talking bird; apparently he has not stage-managed this encounter. He offers riches and justice with his Solomonic sense of fair play, but he also receives something: he comes away from the scene with his reputation and honor enhanced.

As we contemplate urban life in the first century we would do well to remember that everyone, even the emperor, was attentive to relationships that maintained one's position and increased one's honor. We have no evidence that the first Corinthian Christians were immune to such concerns. Indeed, the maintenance of power relationships that enhanced one's social and financial position was a prominent aspect of the social, political, and religious life of Roman Corinth. Archaeological remains allow us to explore how these factors played themselves out in the lives of some individual Corinthians, and what we discover will shed light on the lives of the people Paul was addressing in his letter.

The Power of Relationships

At the east end of the Roman forum in Corinth lie the ruins of a large basilica. Although the name "basilica" is Greek (it means "the king's house"), the style of architecture is Roman. A basilica was a roofed rectangular hall, often surrounded by rows of columns. Basilicas served a variety of public functions such as courts of justice, shopping centers, banks, showplaces for art and, on occasion, the location of religious ritual. The basilica at the east end of the Corinthian forum, which probably dates to the mid-first century, is called the Julian basilica because within its ruins were discovered a number of statues depicting members of the Julio-Claudian family, the family of Augustus and his first successors.

Among the pieces of art discovered in the ruins of the Julian basilica is a statue of Augustus himself, which we now stand before in the museum at Corinth. It is carved from high-class white marble, and is larger than life size, almost seven feet tall.

The Roman Forum and center of power in the city of Rome.   Photo by John Lanci

Caesar Augustus in robes of priest.   Photo: Museo Nazionale delle Terme

The likeness to Augustus is clear; here he is a mature man with his toga pulled over his head, veiling it and indicating that he is offering sacrifice. The portrait may have been created toward the end of the emperor's life, although it is more likely posthumous.

A great number of portraits of Augustus have been found depicting him in a toga with his head modestly veiled in prayer. Statues such as this one were probably placed in public places to portray Augustus as a humble and pious Roman citizen giving thanks to the gods.

These statues are reminiscent of another portrait type common in the Roman period. We know that Roman citizens had little household shrines in their homes, niches in walls or small enclosures in the backyard in which they placed statues of household gods worshiped by the family. One of those spirits represented the soul or male spirit of the clan. This spirit resided in the patriarch of the clan, called the *paterfamilias*. The veiled Augustus looks a lot like the cult statue of a family's *paterfamilias*. This leads some scholars to suggest that the statue in the Julian basilica represents an attempt to present the emperor as the *paterfamilias* of the Roman empire. If that is the case it is only one example of the way Augustus ruled, not by force but by virtue of his power.

"Aren't force and power the same thing?" Thad asks.

Not at all!

In everyday conversation we often assume that power is something that people possess and can use, like a tool. Your boss "has the power" to compel you to do what he wants, or a Roman Catholic priest, it is often assumed, "has the power" to forgive a penitent's sins.

"What?" Yvonne objects. "Are you implying that priests can't forgive sins?"

Not at all. But in each of these examples the "power" that at first may appear to be a possession, almost an object, is in reality nothing of the sort. Both your boss and the priest exercise power because they're in relationship with others—the boss is part of a hierarchy of power relationships in your office, and the priest is understood to be in relation not only with other Church members but also with God (who in Catholic tradition is the one who forgives sins, not the priest).

"Right," Thad says. "My boss gets his power from someone else, and the priest gets his from the Church."

Yes, that's part of it. But no matter what they might "get" from someone else, neither boss nor priest has power unless she or he is in relationship with other people. Look at my own situation. I'm a college professor. Well enough credentialed, I might add. When I walk into a classroom, I'm accustomed to a pall of silence slipping into the room with me. Students know I am the teacher; they think I have a teacher's power of life and death—over grades if not human lives.

But as I often point out to a class, I am in reality a human being just as they are. Strip us all down to the essentials, and the only real difference between me and my students is that I am shorter and rounder, a bit of a wimp more than twice their age, which means that just about any of them, including the women, could overpower me with a well-placed kick if they wanted to. I don't normally pack heat in class, so I have no force with which to repel attacks. You cannot beat people off with the parchment of a doctoral diploma. My power doesn't consist of force; the only power that I "have" I receive from my students. Whether they know it or not, on that first day of class we agree to create a relationship in which I tell them to jump, and they ask how high . . . or I flunk them. If they don't want to honor this relationship I have no way to make them do so.

"You could report them to the dean, right?" Marj says.

True, I could use *my* relationships with other employees at the college to move my students or get them removed. But don't you see? Power, whether in a college or a church or a company, is less a possession than it is a network of relationships. No matter how much power a person "possesses" it means nothing unless it is exercised within the context of relationships with others.

"Unless it is power accompanied by force," Marj says.

"But can power ever be exercised by force without being the result of relationship?" Thad asks.

"Good question," Jeremy jumps in. "I was wondering the same thing. An army is a bunch of soldiers all related to one another and to their commanding officers."

"And an army is in relationship to its government," Thad says.

Yes, even this sort of power is the result of relationship, though sometimes it's maintained by brute strength. In general, however, power is the fruit of a network of relationships. Any social group, be it an army or a clique in high school, constitutes at some level a network of power relationships.

The Power of the Bible?

In the ancient context, when we speak of people having power we mean that they successfully integrated themselves into the networks of relationship that made up their society.

"Whoa," Yvonne says. "You're losing me in the vagueness of jargon."

"I think I get it," Marj says. "What he's saying is that who you knew was pretty important."

Your relationships were of ultimate social importance. If you wanted to get ahead you needed to cultivate connections with the people around you. The goal, actually attained by few people in antiquity, was to achieve and maintain some measure of control over one's own life and the life and reputation of one's family or clan. Even the Roman emperor and his associates had to cultivate a host of networks of interlinking power relationships.

"Why would that be?" Jeremy asks. "He had access to armies. Couldn't they enforce his decrees?"

The Roman empire was huge even by today's standards. During the first century it stretched all the way from Spain and northern Africa up to Britain and eastward to the fringes of the Arabian desert. No government, even resourceful Rome, could support an army big enough to police such a territory. In many provinces—among them Greece—a governor and a minimal staff were all the central government could afford.

"So what did they do to prevent civil wars and revolutions?" Thad asks.

Ah! A critically important question. In addition to the threat of force, which they used ruthlessly when they felt it was necessary, the Romans used propaganda to convince people that they should give thanks for the fact that they were subjects of the empire. They publicized all the good things Rome could provide: a superb network of roads, fewer thieves and pirates out and about, and especially an end to rather nasty regional wars, which ushered in a time of economic prosperity for many people.

"You're saying that the Roman empire was held together by a publicity campaign," Jeremy says.

You could say that, though the task was much more ambitious and sustained than the campaigns we experience. For instance, even today we find copies of the statue of Augustus in museums all over the Mediterranean world. Apparently they were set up like billboards strategically placed throughout the empire to promote Augustus as the central figure and most important symbol of Rome. The man and his successors took on an almost mystical significance for the inhabitants of the empire; indeed, he and a number of later emperors came to be worshiped as gods. The point wasn't to make the emperor feel good about himself but to provide a human image to which all people in the empire could relate. If that didn't work they could send in the troops, as they did when they squashed the Jewish revolt about forty years after the death of Jesus. But that was a last resort; their normal way of operating was to develop relationships with their provincial subjects, especially, though not exclusively, the important ones.

Thad is looking a bit agitated. "How did they get away with that?" he asks. "If they didn't overwhelm people by naked force, how did they persuade all those people to trade their freedom for the ancient equivalent of interstate highways?"

Keep in mind that ancient societies were very different from our own. For one thing, personal freedom, when it existed at all in antiquity, wasn't worth much in a world without uniformly enforceable laws. For another, ancient peoples didn't have the same kind of relationship to governmental structures that we do. In particular there were few social "safety nets" like welfare or medicare. In times of massive crisis, such as a regional famine, a government might step in and coordinate the feeding of those in need. But under normal circumstances, if the poor of a region were in trouble, they looked to the more affluent citizens of their locality, not to the government, for assistance. As a result, even before the Romans arrived, elaborate networks of power relationships were in place and questions of personal freedom took a back seat to communal survival.

Today we refer to these relationships as networks of patronage, and we need to know a little about how patronage worked in the first century.

"Because . . . ?" Yvonne asks.

Because Paul and his Corinthian friends were immersed in networks of patronage, and if we ignore this social reality as we interpret his letter we might misinterpret Paul's use of social terminology in 1 Corinthians 1:26, or worse, we will spiritualize this section of the letter into irrelevance for modern readers.

"Wow," Marj says. "Them's fightin' words."

"I feel a lecture coming on," says Thad.

Patrons and Clients: Personal, Reciprocal, Unequal

It's all about goods and services. Oh, and about honor.

"Isn't that the way it is today?" Marj asks.

It might look that way, but we should guard against interpreting a preindustrial society like that of Rome in terms that apply only to the modern society to which we are accustomed. Modern societies are political and economic systems in which numerous goods and services are provided by the state. At least in theory, highly centralized bureaucracies see to it that all citizens have equal access to those goods and services.

Ancient Mediterranean cultures, on the other hand, were not founded with such a concept of equality. People's access to the services they needed depended upon the status of their relationships with others.

"It was who you knew," Thad says.

Connections—personal relationships—were all-important. In this climate networks of patronage developed because some people needed services and others, through their own connections and affluence, could provide them.

The Roman social historian Richard P. Saller identifies three aspects of ancient patronage systems: they were personal, reciprocal, and unequal. These social interactions were pervasive in society, and so we need to look at them in a little more detail.

This model of relationship was first and foremost *personal,* although it existed at every level of public as well as private life. In fact all societal relations, both public and private, were conceived in terms of personal relations. Patronage systems bound together the rich and the poor, slaveholders and current or former slaves, politicians and their protégés, landowners and tenants, and the emperor and his subjects. In each of these situations individuals and families were connected through the exchange of honor and personal obligation.

"Personal obligation," Thad muses. "You mean, 'You scratch my back and I'll scratch yours.'"

Exactly. The patron-client model was at its essence *reciprocal.* When one gave a gift or provided a service, one expected something in return. Patrons might not have put explicit conditions on their benefactions, but a return was expected. You follow me so far?

"So far, yes," Yvonne says. "We still have benefactors today."

Lastly, patronage relationships were *unequal.* But not too unequal. Since people expected a return on their investment, the bulk of their generosity was directed toward those who could give more back. When some people got more than others the distinction was not based on need; those who got the most were people who could give more of what the benefactor wanted in return.

"But why give to people who already had more?" Yvonne asks. "What good is there in that?"

"The poor seem to get left out of this," Marj says. "What could they give back?"

Actually, the poor were part of the patronage network because they did have something to offer the rich. Think it through. In the reciprocal patronage relationship the client—the person receiving the gift—received financial assistance, sometimes in the form of cash, but more often as services rendered. For example, Regilla and her husband, the Greek philosopher Herodes Atticus, took it upon themselves to renovate a fountain in the center of Corinth, thus providing an improved water source for everyone in the city as well as a pleasing place for people to gather and rest. What do you think they got in return?

"Many thanks?" Jeremy offers.

Exactly. Public gratitude. In fact, the city used some of the money to erect a statue in Regilla's honor. When people came to get their day's water they might enjoy a moment of shaded rest and thank the gods for this prominent woman's generosity.

Such public honor was important to all social strata of people in antiquity. We moderns can easily underestimate the significance of this social dynamic. In ancient Mediterranean cultures honor was of supreme importance, often outweighing even wealth or access to political power in the determination of one's social status. Honor, according to Aristotle, was the supreme external good; assigned to the gods, desired by the distinguished, it was the highest award for the victorious.

"Honor used to be important in our culture, too," Yvonne says. "At least it once was. Nowadays . . ."

"What you say is true," Jeremy cuts in. "Nowadays who pays any attention to behaving honorably? Even presidents . . ."

"We'll not be going there," Marj says.

People from all walks of life sought to increase their prestige and honor in any circumstances they could find. No voluntary association of tradespersons, for instance, was too humble to attract the attention of an influential patron, and even within the humblest of such associations the prime motivation for participation was to increase one's personal honor and status.

"This is getting a bit too abstract," Yvonne cautions.

"Can you define more clearly what you mean by honor?" Thad asks.

Two New Testament scholars, Bruce Malina and Jerome Neyrey, put it this way: honor is "the positive value of a person in his or her own eyes plus the positive appreciation of that person in the eyes of his or her social group." This is, of course, an abstract idea, Yvonne, but we have almost brought this lecture home.

Honor gets enfleshed in different societies through different customs and practices. Through these practices, honor functions as what Malina and Neyrey call a "register of social rating." This rating enables people of unequal standing to interact with one another in ways that the culture deems appropriate. One person might be born into an honorable situation, but another might pursue and acquire it. Such pursuit of honor, in particular through the giving of gifts and benefactions, was a matter of great import in ancient Mediterranean societies. If one of you has been able to follow this, you can tell us why.

I look to Thad, our abstract thinker.

"I think I see what you're getting at," he says. "If everyone seeks honor, then they all need each other. Rich or poor, everyone gets interconnected and the culture . . ."

"The culture thrives," Marj says. "The desire for honor leads to patronage, which helps the poor survive. I see what you mean," she says. "Patronage ties people of all different social statuses together."

Exactly. Modern interpreters debate about who derived the greatest benefit from this ethic of reciprocity, this "ideology of patronage," as Saller puts it. But there is no debate concerning the effect of patronage upon the society as a whole: people sought social relationships in order to get what they needed or what they wanted, be it goods and services or honor and prestige. The ideology of patronage involved just about everyone in Greco-Roman society, even slaves and women, two groups often ignored by both the ancient literature and modern commentaries upon it, and just about everyone was socialized to value this ideology's goals and seek them.

"At the risk of looking like a fool," Yvonne breaks in, "I still don't see the connection here with 1 Corinthians."

Fix in your memory this phrase: *primary socialization.* I'm going to suggest that in the face of this dominant cultural network of patronage Paul proposed a new and different way to relate to society. That may be why he uses social terminology in his letter, and it may be a heretofore unexplored source of the conflict between him and some of the Corinthians.

But enough of this! Let's take a walk over to the forum in Old Corinth. I want to show you some interesting rocks.

Two Honored Corinthians

We stand in the forum and face west toward the remains of a raised terrace that once boasted a series of small, ornate structures, many of them temples. At the north end of the terrace we stand before a cement block about seven or eight feet high and eighteen feet wide. This foundation belonged to a small monument, a round building with eight columns and a conical roof topped by a big marble pine cone, which rests on the ground nearby. Other parts of the white marble structure indicate that the builders worked with materials of excellent quality. As we circle the cement block we walk over to an inscription that was chiseled on a large curved marble architrave.

"Architrave?" Yvonne asks.

The part of the structure that sat on the columns and supported the roof.

"Was this a temple?" Jeremy asks.

We're not sure. One way or the other, though, this pile of elegant marble was an ideal showcase for some expensive artwork and this inscription; your eye would catch sight of the columns and follow them up to this architrave.

"Sort of like an ancient billboard, perhaps," says Thad.

Interesting that you suggest that. Let's take a closer look at the inscription.

"I can't make it out," Yvonne says. "It's Latin, right?"

"Yeah," says Thad. "But what with all the chips and nicks, and . . . are these abbreviations? I can't make it out either."

The carving of the letters is among the finest found in Corinth. The inscription, as it was published, without the nicks, and with the abbreviations spelled out, reads:

(C)N • BABBIVS • PHILINVS • AED(ilis) • PONTIF[EX]
[D(e)] • S(ua) • P(ecunia) • F(aciendum) • C(uravit) • IDEMQVE • IIVIR •
   P(robavit) •

"Which means?" Yvonne waits.

"Gnaeus Babbius Philinus, aedile and pontifex, had this monument erected at his own expense, and he approved it in his official capacity as duovir."

The Commodus inscription found in the rubble of Temple H.   Photo by John Lanci

"Look," Yvonne says, and she points to a series of letters. "This guy was a pope!"

"What?" Jeremy says. "Where do you see that?"

"It says he was a *pontifex*," Yvonne says. "That's a title for the pope: *pontifex maximus*. It's just about all the Latin I remember."

Actually, Yvonne is half-right. Gnaeus Babbius Philinus was not a pope; he wasn't even a Christian. But he and the pope do share the Roman title *pontifex;* in fact, a common term for the pope—pontiff—comes from this official designation for a high priest in ancient Roman religious practice. When the Roman empire waned and the bishop of Rome gained importance he got the title, as did his papal successors to this day.

Gnaeus Babbius Philinus (we will call him Babbius for short) prospered in Corinth during the first half of the first century C.E.; this monument may date to the time of Augustus or Tiberius.

"And Paul," adds Thad.

Inscriptions mentioning Babbius in Corinth are numerous, for he provided the city with a variety of benefactions. In addition to this monument he underwrote a fountain dedicated to the great sea-god Poseidon, he was involved in the construction of the Southeast Building at the other end of the forum, and he sponsored a statue of Poseidon, the base of which was discovered near the Propylaia, the main gate to the forum.

"This guy was into Poseidon," Jeremy says.

His devotion to Poseidon may indicate that he was in the shipping business and was in the deity's debt.

"The inscription says that Babbius was a *duovir.* What's a *duovir*?" Marj asks.

The *duovirs*—literally "the two men"—were the chief magistrates, almost like the mayors of the city. They were the executive officers of the city council and the chief justices of the court system, elected every year.

"They probably couldn't get much done in a year," Yvonne says. "How many times could they be reelected?"

Actually they weren't reelected, at least not year after year. The job brought with it some political responsibilities, but its main attraction was prestige. To be elected *duovir* was a great honor that the city bestowed on its most illustrious citizens. Babbius was apparently a very wealthy and honored man in Corinth.

"Why are we looking at all this?" Yvonne asks.

You'll see. We now head north out of the forum to the remains of the theater. As archaeological rubble goes, Corinth's theater is not very impressive. It was long ago looted of most of its seating and now isn't much more than a hollowed out half-bowl with some limestone pavements at the bottom. Our destination is one of these pavements; on it we find the most famous inscription from Corinth. It reads:

ERASTVS • PRO • AEDILIT[at]E / S(ua) • P(ecunia) • STRAVIT

and it translates: "Erastus in return for his aedileship laid (the pavement) at his own expense."

"Why is this so famous?" Yvonne asks. "I've never heard of it."

What about the rest of you? Does the name Erastus ring a bell? As expected, Jeremy nods suddenly.

"Erastus!" he says. "Paul mentions him at the end of Romans."

Yes. As we've seen, chapter sixteen of the letter to the Romans contains a number of references to people Paul probably knew at Corinth. Among them is Erastus, the *oikonomos*—Greek for city treasurer.

"Wow," says Jeremy. "Now we're getting somewhere! We're standing on physical proof of Paul's association with Corinth," he says to his colleagues. "I like this."

I hesitate to deflate this unusual outburst of Jeremian exuberance. However, there is a problem. A possible problem.

"I think I see it," Thad says. "You just said that Erastus was the city treasurer. What was the word?"

Oikonomos.

"Here he's an *aedile,*" Thad points to the limestone slab at our feet. "Is that the same thing?"

Alas, no. An *aedile* was one of the two business managers of the city; they were in charge of public buildings, streets, markets, and city revenues.

Jeremy is frowning. "It seems like nothing is ever simple on this journey of yours," he says. "Nothing is what it seems to be."

The Erastus inscription in the theater at Corinth.   Photo by John Lanci

"Couldn't Erastus have been both an *oiko . . . eiko . . .*" Yvonne fumbles. "Couldn't he have held both of those jobs, maybe at different times?"

"I'll bet the job descriptions were similar," Thad says. "It sounds like they both handled money and business-type stuff."

"Or maybe Paul got the title wrong," Marj suggests.

It's certainly possible that Erastus the *aedile* is identical with the Erastus the *oikonomos* mentioned by Paul in Romans 16:23. The excavators thought so, though of course they weren't biblical scholars. We really cannot know.

"That's the problem," Jeremy says. "We spend all this time studying and reading and talking, and we never seem able to prove anything."

Jeremy's right. Biblical study can be frustrating. We really would like some straight answers to our questions.

"I'd just like to have a passage—any passage!—say what it seems to be saying," he sighs. "Without all the academic rigmarole."

"Rigmarole!" Yvonne exclaims. "I haven't heard that word in years."

With a reluctant smile, Jeremy shakes his head and the tension breaks. Frustration or even anger is a reasonable response by believing Christians to the "rigmarole" of our journey. But remember, this excursion's not over until the fat exegete sings. By the time we're done, many of your more important questions should be answered, much of your frustration calmed. I think you'll find that the rigmarole will be worth the effort.

"I have a question," Marj says. "Didn't I read somewhere that the elite of a first-century city like Corinth weren't attracted to the message of Christianity?"

I nod.

"If that's the case, would this Erastus be a Christian?" she asks.

"That's a good question," Thad says. "Even if these Erastuses are two different guys, they're both prominent in Corinth and Paul does mention one of them in Romans 16."

Excellent observation. Let's go back up to the west temple terrace to check out a stone that will help answer some of these questions.

A Second Jeremian Ventilation

Back at the forum we stand before another block of white marble covered with letters.

"They look like names," Thad says.

They are. Robert Scranton's translation goes like this:

> "Emperor Caesar, son of deified Marcus Antonius Pius Germanicus [Marcus Aurelius], grandson of deified Pius [Antoninus Pius], great-grandson of deified Hadrianus, great-great grandson of deified Traianus Parthicus, great-great-great grandson of Nerva: Marcus Aurelius Commodus Antoninus Augustus Pius Sarmaticus Germanicus Maximus, by tribunal power, Emperor . . . Consul . . .

Father of his country. From the testament of Cornelia Baebia a certain person made and administered [this]."

Archaeologists believe that this inscription graced the front of a temple, though we don't know to which god. It was erected as the result of the last will and testament of a wealthy woman, Baebia, and it consists almost entirely of the name of the person to whom it was dedicated, the emperor Commodus.

"Commodus!" Thad exclaims. "He was the bad guy in that Russell Crowe movie *Gladiator*, right?"

"The one played by Joaquin Phoenix," Marj says.

"Commodus certainly wasn't a Christian, was he?" Yvonne asks.

No, that's not why his inscription is important to us. Look at the way the emperor is named.

"It's almost like a litany," Yvonne says.

"Or a family tree," Thad adds. "Right up to his great-great-great grandfather."

In the ancient world the names of your parents, grandparents, and their ancestors were an important signal to others of your social status. In fact, it was as important as your wealth, probably more so. Thus when you put up a public inscription—a billboard to yourself—you always included the names of the individuals and the family from which you came. The more ancestors you could rustle up, the more prestige and honor you could claim and, of course, few could claim as much honor as an emperor. Hence this inscription.

"Well, why don't Babbius and Erastus name all their ancestors in their inscriptions?" Yvonne asks.

The woman is reading my mind. Care to make a guess?

"It certainly wasn't modesty," she says. "That doesn't seem to be much of a value in this culture."

"I'll take a chance here," Marj says. "Could it be that they didn't want people to know the names of their ancestors? Were they ashamed of them?"

"Maybe they were crooks," Jeremy suggests. "Their ancestors, I mean."

"Or maybe," Thad says, "their ancestors were of lower social status."

There it is. Neither of these two honored men, Babbius or Erastus, sees fit to mention his ancestral heritage. As I said before, we have recovered a number of inscriptions mentioning Babbius, but none of them refers to his ancestors, though some of them seem to go out of their way to name his descendants. The reason? We can't be sure, but it's quite likely that Babbius and Erastus were freed slaves.

"Elite ex-slaves?" Marj asks.

When Corinth was refounded in the century before Paul arrived, the city was populated with people of the Italian lower social orders, especially poor folk and ex-slaves. The result was a land of opportunity for those who wanted to augment their pocketbooks and their social status. The city was filled with tradespeople who were ex-slaves or freedpersons (in Latin *liberti* [males] and *libertae* [females]). The freedpersons of Corinth could aspire to great prominence. While the achievements of Babbius and Erastus were the exception and not the rule, and not many freedpersons achieved great political power, virtually all of them were socialized (there's that word again) to better themselves, to put as much distance as they could between themselves and the dishonor of slavery.

We have seen in this chapter that the social world of Paul and the Corinthians was dominated by Roman power. All the people of Corinth, from slave to privileged, were socialized to value relationships of patronage. The major goal of this network was to enhance one's social and economic status as well as to promote the honor of one's family.

"To get ahead," Marj says.

"That seems so superficial," Yvonne says. "All this energy over a person's place in society."

"Yeah," Jeremy says. "I'll bet that's why Paul is so angry or at least so impatient with them."

Possibly, but don't sell the Corinthians short. Higher social status in the first century was not always a superficial goal for superficial or frivolous people. As we will see in the next chapter, status seeking was much more important to most people than that.

In some situations, it could be a matter of life or death.

For Reflection and Further Discussion

1. How would you describe the nature of power as it is exercised in modern Western society? Do you agree that power is not a possession but a network of influence? What are some examples of your exercise of power?

2. The Romans were very concerned with honor. How would you describe our modern attitude toward it? Is honor something you're concerned about? In what ways? What are some of the strengths and weaknesses of a culture as fixated as the Romans were on issues of social status?

3. Imagine that you're an ex-slave in first-century Corinth. You go to a Christian worship service and hear 1 Corinthians read to the congregation. Skim through the letter and write down your reactions as a freedperson. Do any particular passages give you hope? Do any take it away?

Chapter Eighteen

The No-Relax Tour Continues into Darker Realms

Yvonne and I are enjoying the light and warmth in the small courtyard of the museum at Old Corinth. We sit on a wooden bench surrounded by the collected odds and ends of Corinthian rubble—uneven stone blocks bearing faded inscriptions, random pieces of statuary, and small architectural chunks of long tumbled and looted buildings. It's afternoon and the tour buses have returned to Athens, so we have the museum practically to ourselves.

"Where are the guards?" Yvonne asks. "We could steal anything here we wanted." She observes a limestone block to her left. "If we could pick it up."

Our fellow travelers arrive, huffing with irritation.

"Those guards!" Thad says.

"We were just talking about them," Yvonne says. "They seem to have disappeared."

"They were outside yelling at us," Marj says with a sheepish grin. "Don't worry," she says. "We weren't stealing anything. Weren't even rearranging anything."

So, your crime?

"Jeremy and I were sitting on a column drum in front of the museum," Thad says. "To get out of the sun."

"Yeah," Jeremy says. "Minding our own business, and this guy comes up and starts shouting at us."

"'No relax!'" Marj barks, imitating the guard. "'No relax!'"

"No relax," Yvonne says. "I like it. That could be the theme for this journey of ours."

"Do you think it's OK to sit here?" Thad asks as he points to a spot near our feet. "These pavements may be priceless."

We begin our conversation as Yvonne uncharacteristically leads off.

"I will probably regret this," she says as she pulls a folder from her bag. "I tried to get through these inscriptions you gave us to preview, but I am just lost."

She holds up a photocopy of one of the Corinthian texts we are about to examine. "I understand the translations, of course," she says. "But I'm still having trouble seeing how this relates to the Bible."

"Jeremy has a confession to make," Thad says before I can answer. "Go on," he prods his friend.

"Aw, it's no big deal," Jeremy says. "It's just, well, I told Thad that I think I'm beginning to see where you're going with all of this archaeology stuff."

"And . . . come on, admit it," Thad says, but Jeremy remains silent.

Marj laughs. "Jeremy thinks he likes the track you're on."

Well, this is news.

"Say more." It is Yvonne's turn to prod him. "Seriously! Enlighten me."

Jeremy gestures toward me. "He's telling us that the rocks, as he calls them, are going to help us interpret the Bible as a text, right?" he pauses. "The only connection I can see is this: the Bible is written for poor folk, not for the rich and the powerful, but for people just like the ones mentioned in these inscriptions he had us read for today. And I like that. I like it because I think it's true."

"We all may be on the same page after all," Thad says with that sly smile of his.

Let's take advantage of all of this amiability—and of Jeremy's insight—and explore a bit more of this alien socially constructed world. Let's talk about the poor in antiquity. In particular, let's uncover the situation of the most unfortunate of the poor: slaves.

Ancient Slavery

In the ancient Mediterranean world slavery was a fact of everyday life, not a moral issue. People assumed the validity of enslaving other human beings, and their economic systems depended on it. What's more, slavery was not limited to a certain continent, culture, or race. Virtually no one was free from the possibility that he or she might become a slave. If our town or country were conquered, those who were not killed would be given as booty to the victorious soldiers or sold to others on the open market. As a result, slaves could come from every race and social class—rich, poor, old, young, highly educated, children, women, or big, burly men.

"So slavery was part of their primary socialization," Thad says.

Exactly. Except for the writings of one or two philosophers very few people in the ancient world questioned the idea of enslaving other people.

Even in the New Testament, Jesus and Paul seem to assume its legitimacy, the way you or I might take for granted the validity of keeping pets. Slaves were the possessions of their owners, who could do with them as they chose. You could beat them, use their bodies any way you liked, or work them into an early grave. In some places and times owners had the power of life and death over their slaves. They could brand them or have an iron collar welded around their necks to be sure that even if they escaped they would not get far. The timely return of an escaped slave might bring a nice reward. Slavery, in all of its particulars and cruelty, was a legally sanctioned institution in first-century Roman Corinth. As a result, another primary socialization involved the desire among the enslaved to become free.

"They could do that?" Yvonne asks.

In a number of ways. They might spend years saving what little money they made in tips and eventually buy their own freedom. Some groups of freed slaves pooled their money to buy freedom for friends and family members still enslaved. An understanding owner who was grateful for faithful service might free his or her slave or, as sometimes happened, a poorly treated slave might manage to run away, though this was not easy to do if they had been branded or otherwise marked.

"Branded!" Yvonne says. "Like cattle?"

"You said 'his or her' just now," Marj says. "Women owned slaves?"

Absolutely. Even former slaves owned slaves. As I said, we are not dealing with a moral issue here, but with a difficult fact of life. Although accurate figures are impossible to come by, some historians estimate that as much as a quarter or even a third of the population of the Roman empire was enslaved during some periods.

"That's a lot of slaves," Thad says.

It is, indeed. And those numbers, even though they are just estimates, serve as a powerful reminder to us that the world of the first Christians was very different from our own.

Quiet reigns in the courtyard. It is time to take a closer look at some more Corinthian inscriptions.

Corinthian Freedpersons Make Good

Ancient sources tell us that the Roman colony of Corinth was populated with freed Italian slaves. Over the following decades the city continued to be a magnet for slave and freed. These people created at Corinth Greece's largest city and commercial center. Individuals as well as groups of freedpersons left monuments and inscriptions attesting to their quest for achievement and social recognition.

Most of the freedpersons of Corinth were probably of low social status; as a result, very little evidence of their experience survives. Take a look, though, at the following inscription. It is from a small, white marble plaque, badly damaged, which was found in 1937. The inscription reads:

[m • v]IBVLEIVS	[Marcus V]ibuleius Heracliu[s]
[viv] • M • L • HERACLIV[s]	freedman of Marcus,
	[during his lifetime],
[sib]I • ET • HELPINI • L • V[ibulei]	for himself and his (wife) Helpinis,
[uxori] • SVAE • ET • SVEIS • P[osteris]	freedwoman of V[ibuleius],
	and their descendants,
	(acquired this burial place).

This modestly carved grave monument, which may date from the first century C.E., is a rare piece of evidence for the presence of less affluent freed-persons at Corinth. The couple probably both came from the same household. We know little about them except that they were able to provide a burial site and an inscription; they could apparently take some pride in that.

"Wait," Yvonne says. "How does the translator get all this English from those few letters?"

"I was wondering about that, too," says Thad. "Why are some letters capitalized and others not? And what's with the brackets?"

Letters that are capitalized are inscribed that way on the block of stone as we have it. Inscriptions, then as now, were not cheap; as a result, people developed a series of abbreviations. A freestanding M, for instance, stands for Marcus, a common name. Positioned as it is here, L stands for *libertus* or *liberta,* freedperson, and it is incorporated into a person's name. If they were freeborn the couple would have an F, which indicated that they were the *filius* or *filia* of someone, which means . . . ?

"That one's easy," Thad says. "'Son' or 'daughter.' As in 'filial devotion.'"

"And the brackets?" Jeremy asks.

Notice where they fall in the inscription.

"On either side," he says.

The brackets indicate that a section of the inscription has been lost and had to be reconstructed. Usually we see them at the ends of lines, since the original blocks got chipped away at the edges to reshape them so they could be used in new structures or pavements.

"How do they know what to fill in?" Thad asks.

They guess, but not randomly. In this case, for example, the first line as we have it reads IBVLEIVS. Ibuleius (Latin had no U; hence the V does double duty) is not a name found in antiquity, as far as I know, while Vibuleius is widely documented. Since the stone looks as though there was something in front of IBVLEIVS, a V seems likely, especially since we find a V in the third line, which may indicate that Helpinis was also a freed slave of Vibuleius Heraclius.

"That seems like a bit of a stretch," Marj says.

Not really. What better place for a slave to find a spouse than in the large household in which she is a member?

"Well," she says, "what about the rest of the reconstruction? 'During his lifetime' and 'acquired this burial place'?"

Kent probably posits the abbreviation VIV ("while living" or "during his lifetime") because there is space for three letters and because certain typical phrases like this are found on a large percentage of the gravestones of humble folk.

"So it's part of the genre," Marj says.

Yes, you could say that. The last parenthetical phrase is added to give the modern reader a better sense of the context, which ancient passersby would have known, since they understood their cultural genres of grave inscriptions.

"Sort of like the dates on our tombstones," Thad says. "We know that they indicate the dates of birth and death, but someone from another time and place might not."

Exactly. Now take a look at the next inscription.

[p(?) • aefi]CIO • P • F •	To [Publius?] Aeficius Firmus Sta[tia]nus,
[ae]M • FIRMO • STA	Son of Publius, of the tribe [Ae]milia,
[tia]NO • AED • ORNAM(entis)	who was honored by the decree of the city
[o]RNATO • D • D •	council with the perquisites of aedile;
[p • aef]ICIVS • ATIMETVS	[Publius Aef]icius Atimetus
[lic]INIANVS • PATER •	[Lic]inianus, his father (and)
[p? • aef]ICIVS • ATIMETVS • ET •	[Publius (?) Aef]icius Atimetus and
[. . .]NIA • GAIENE • AVI	[. . .]nia Gaiene his grandparents (erected this statue).

This inscription was found in the forum at Corinth. It probably dates to the second quarter of the second century C.E., about a hundred years after Paul's visit. It commemorates Aeficius Firmus Statianus, a man to whom the city council granted an honorary aedileship (remember Erastus the aedile?). This honor probably allowed him to become a member of the city council and brought other opportunities for enhanced status and influence. Do you see the three generations mentioned?

"Yeah," Jeremy says. "I was thinking that this looks like that emperor's inscription, but on a small scale."

Precisely. Look in particular at the names of the men. The youngest man is Publius, the son of Publius. When the elder Publius is mentioned, his father Publius, too, is identified. But the grandfather—and the grandmother—have no ancestors listed. The lack of further ancestors suggests that what we see here is a *libertus* (Atimetus) and perhaps a *liberta* (Gaiene), who in their old age take pleasure in the fact that their grandchild, freed of the stigma of servile origins, has made good.

"Whoa! Stretch Alert!" Marj says. "Maybe they just ran out of space on the stone."

"Or they ran out of money," Yvonne adds.

Certainly these are possibilities. However, there's another clue here that suggests that I'm right: the grandfather's name. Atimetus ("dishonored" or "despised") was a common name for slaves and freedpersons. They probably acquired it from some owner as a nickname. Look closely: the grandfather Atimetus passes the name to his son, but by the third generation it's laundered away. The grandson earns a nice bouquet of honors for the family, and a statue in the civic center as well. The family is literally "dishonored" no more. This depicts precisely the aspirations of freedpersons and their descendants all over the empire.

"If slaves were everywhere," Marj says, "why do we see them so rarely in the New Testament?"

Those who have provided our modern biblical translations gloss over most of the references to slaves in the New Testament; for instance, they often render as "servant" the Greek word *doulos,* which means "slave." The slaves are there, in the original text, anyway.

"Then why haven't any of us heard about this?" Marj asks. "The brutality of this 'world.'"

Good question, without an easy answer. My guess is that it's because until very recently many historians characterized ancient slavery as a rather benign form of bondage, a transitional experience that people endured for a while but then got free of. For instance, the prominent social historian of ancient Christianity Gerd Theissen writes that a slave "could expect to be freed after about thirty years, and often sooner," and that most people were liberated by the time they were thirty-five years old. He seems to have found this not in the ancient sources, which provide no evidence that most slaves were eventually freed, but in the writings of early twentieth-century historians of ancient Rome.

"I wonder how many galley slaves lasted thirty years," Thad says.

"Or people sent to the mines," Jeremy adds.

"Thirty *years* of slavery?" Marj says. "I don't think I could last that long even with a cushy job in some rich woman's villa."

We turn to the last inscription on the sheets I distributed. Found in 1950 in the Corinthian forum and dating perhaps to the early second century, it reads:

- - - - - - - -	[This monument was erected by]
[decernente] • COLLEGIO • LARVM	the decision of the association of the
• DOMV[s]	Lares of the Imperial Household.
• DIVINAE •	
CVRAM • AGENTIBVS • COLLEGIANI[s]	Those who had charge of the erection were the two most outstanding members of the association,
PRIMI[s] • T • FLAVIO • AVG • LIB • ANTIO[cho]	Titus Flavius Antio[chus], freedman
ET • TI • CLAVDIO • PRIMIGENIO •	and Tiberius Claudius Primigenius.

Here we have evidence at Corinth for a *collegium,* or religious association, devoted to the family hearth gods (the *lares*) of Augustus and his successors. Notice that one of the people mentioned was a former slave of the emperor.

"The emperor lived in Rome, right?" Thad asks, and I nod. "So what is one of his freed slaves doing in Corinth?"

Good question. Any member of the emperor's household, even a slave, probably lived rather well compared with the situation of even freeborn peasants or people with a trade. When an imperial slave was freed he or she probably left the emperor's service with a nice bank account. Of course, we can't know the precise circumstances of Titus Flavius Antiochus here, but Corinth would be an excellent place for an affluent freedman to establish a new life and enjoy his wealth.

Let's see. Titus Flavius Antiochus. Erastus. Babbius. Atimetus and Gaiene. Vibuleius and Helpinis. Although the standard books on the social world of early Christianity give the impression that there was a single homogenous category—*libertus*—the archaeological remains of Corinth indicate that the city was a place where a variety of freedpersons, both influential and poor, male and female, made a living and aspired to increased social standing. New Testament commentaries fail to convey the complexity of the social situation of *liberti* and continue to render invisible the existence of *libertae,* the women. Contrary to what modern biblical scholars assume, there were many different types of freed men and women; not all were freed in the same way, and most did not enjoy anything close to what would pass for freedom today.

The Complex World of Freedpersons

"Didn't freedpersons achieve some sense of security in the networks of patronage you talked about?" Thad asks.

Some did. For instance, the freed slaves of Roman citizens might become citizens themselves, thus inheriting a somewhat privileged social status within the city and the empire. They could vote, they got breaks on some taxes and, importantly for citizens in the provinces, they received some protection from the powers of local magistrates, like officials today who are likely to be corrupt or capricious in their enforcement of the rules. But the situation of most freedpersons was anything but secure. For instance, as we have noted, many freedpersons were women. If a Roman citizen freed a female slave she didn't become a full citizen. She couldn't vote and in most places in the empire most political positions were not open to her.

"But at least she was free," Yvonne says.

Yes, but freed slaves could lose their freedom at any point, for instance if they committed certain crimes. In Rome the emperor Claudius ordered some freedpersons back into slavery for showing disrespect to their patrons, and the historian Tacitus recounts a senatorial debate concerning the same question under the notorious Nero.

"This sort of situation seems hopeless," Yvonne says.

And yet, as we have seen, freedpersons were not without all hope. There were ways for some to increase their honor and status. They might petition the authorities for a positive change in their status or get an influential friend to do so. A woman might increase her status through childbearing. Augustus in particular was concerned about declining birthrates. If a woman produced as few as two children she and her husband might earn the right to a social upgrade.

"I suppose they could marry rich, right?" Yvonne asks.

Indeed, some did. But most freedpersons improved their status by providing services to the state. They might serve in the local police or fire brigade or they might, if they had the bucks, offer benefactions to their city or state in times of emergency, such as a famine.

The upshot of all of this was that *liberti/ae* came in both genders and enjoyed a whole array of different civic statuses, and many of them had a vested interest in increasing their social and legal position if the opportunity arose.

"Did any of these people just strike out on their own?" Jeremy asks.

Despite the dangers of being disconnected from a web of patronage relationships, a great number of such *liberti/ae* traveled throughout the Mediterranean world. Importantly for our purposes, in many areas of the empire, and in particular in port cities such as Corinth, these independent freedpersons dominated trade and industry and often swelled the ranks of voluntary religious associations, like Christianity, as well.

Puffed Up in Corinth

Most interpreters acknowledge that Paul's Corinthian correspondents probably enjoyed a variety of social status positions; after all, he spends much of his time and rhetorical capital encouraging those who are strong to be careful with those who aren't. What has not been noticed is that every single person associated with Corinth in Paul's letters *could* have been a freedperson, even Erastus, as we have seen. Check out the trio of supposed leaders whom Paul commends in 1 Corinthians 16:15-17. They may be leaders among the Christians, but they all appear to bear nicknames: Stephanas, a.k.a. "wreath man" or "crown," Fortunatus, "the fortunate one," and Achaicus, the "Greek guy." Where'd they get such no-account names? From their owners? Or their freed parents?

"So you're arguing that the Corinthian Christians were all freedpersons," Marj says.

No, there's no way to prove that. But if it consisted of a significant number of freedpersons, the Corinthian Christian community incorporated folks very much concerned with questions of social position and access to power.

"I have a question," Jeremy says. "Does all this concern with social status explain why Paul's so worried about the Corinthians being puffed up?"

"Puffed up?" Yvonne looks bewildered.

"They boast a lot," Jeremy says. "According to Paul anyway."

I suspect that all this social status stuff has everything to do with Paul's concern about boasting at Corinth. Look again at the context of our passage. "Consider your own call," Paul begins in 1:26. What is the "call" or the "calling" of the Corinthians?

"He says that God chose them to shame the wise and the strong," Thad says.

And?

"And," Marj jumps in, "to make sure that no one boasts before God."

Bingo! In 1:29 this is the Corinthians' vocation: to assure that no flesh will boast in the presence of God. And then he ends this section with a quote from the prophet Jeremiah: "Let any who boast, boast in (or 'of') the Lord."

Now, what's interesting about this . . . I am shuffling through some of my papers and lose my thought. Yes, here it is. What's interesting is that the word-group that in English we render "boasting" *(kauchaomai, kauchēma, kauchēsis)* appears fifty-nine times in the New Testament. Fifty-five of these fifty-nine uses of the word are found in Paul's letters, thirty-nine in 1 and 2 Corinthians. In addition, a word related to boasting, *physioō* (Jeremy's "to be puffed up") occurs in the New Testament only in 1 Corinthians.

"So Paul's especially worried about boasting here in Corinth," Thad says.

"Boasting of your achievements doesn't seem like it's always a bad thing," Marj says.

True. The Greek word-group associated with *kauchaomai* has a double set of meanings, positive and negative. On the positive side it refers to the idea of boasting or glorying in the Lord.

"That's not exactly what I meant," Marj says. "Sometimes when we succeed at something it's kind of nice to boast a bit about it."

"Hey," Jeremy interrupts. "Paul boasts sometimes, right?"

He does indeed, but in this letter it's clear that Paul frequently intends the pejorative sense of the word, and in every instance but one when he does he uses it with the Corinthians in mind. Obviously something about them and their particular situation brings this out of him.

"And you think it's their hunger for honor and status," Jeremy says.

Makes sense to me. Paul is writing to people whose whole lives have been centered on increasing their status, on earning their own manumission and then freeing enslaved spouses and children.

"So," Thad says, "in this context freedom is not merely a 'theological' issue."

Exactly. Some members of the assembly might be very concerned with physical freedom and resistant to being mistaken for the unfree. Others might be struggling to gain enough capital and influence to redeem family members still enslaved. New Testament interpreter and social historian Richard Horsley characterizes the people of Roman Corinth as "a conglomeration of atomized individuals cut off from the supportive communities and particular cultural traditions that had formerly constituted their corporate identities and solidarities as Syrians, Judeans, Italians, or Greeks."

We are looking, then, at a whole collection of different types of freedpersons. Some would have been physically weakened by servitude and did not feel the stability of freedom but the vulnerability that comes with illness or quick changes in status. Some of the Christian *liberti/ae* may have had a lot more wealth and influence than some of the freeborn in the community and may have been quite used to independence and to taking responsibility for themselves and their families. This could account for some of the dissension at Corinth. Is this independence behind the Corinthians' resistance to Paul's authority? Is Paul trying to put himself into the role of patron when he claims to be their "father" (4:15)? How would participation in the patron/client relationship influence a believer's understanding of Christ as Lord or Master?

The freedpersons of Corinth spanned a whole range of social positions, from rich to poor, prestigious to humble and perhaps despised. The Corinthians to whom Paul wrote may have spanned much the same gamut. The Corinthian Christian community to which Paul wrote was not one composed of settled people with status, with a minority of upper-class members and a majority of the lower social strata. Rather, the community was comprised of people of various means and hopes for the social betterment of themselves and their families. All of them would have been socially disadvantaged; many were probably destitute.

It's gotten chilly in the museum courtyard, and Yvonne is packing up her papers.

"Will I need to save these inscriptions?" she asks. Before I can answer, she spots a disapproving look from Marj.

"Don't give me that stare of yours, young lady," Yvonne says with mock seriousness. "Are *you* going to carry my suitcase all over Greece? You have to clean out the nonessentials when you're on the road," she says as she snaps her bag shut. "You gotta travel light!"

For Reflection and Further Discussion

1. Take some quiet time, and in your imagination put yourself in the place of a slave in the first century. How do you feel? What do you miss most? Can you think of anything good about being a slave in that period? If not, go deeper; there must have been advantages to being a slave, or else wouldn't there have been more frequent slave rebellions?

2. Despite everything we have read in this chapter one could still argue that ancient freedpersons were inappropriate "social climbers." If some Corinthian Christian freedpersons came to you for help in constructing an argument against people like Paul (who told them not to be so concerned with status), what points would you suggest they make?

Chapter Nineteen

The Great Reversal

"Yuch."

Yvonne is disgusted.

"Can we go back to the Weather Channel?" Marj says.

After dinner I invited everyone to my room to watch some film clips that a couple of my students compiled for a class exploring different images of Jesus. At this point an actor, Willem Dafoe, is moving toward the camera in slow motion. He is spattered with blood, his head a haze of thorns and hair covering a skull of torn flesh. His shoulders are weighted down by the timber of a crossbeam.

Of course, he is Jesus and this is the way of the cross as depicted by film director Martin Scorsese in *The Last Temptation of Christ*. My students slowed down the action and changed the music score; the effect was to heighten the horror, to rub one's nose in the blood.

"This is very gross," Thad says.

Yvonne stands up and walks toward the door of the living room. "That isn't how I think of the crucifixion of Christ," she says. "I can't watch this."

The scene is very graphic. Graphic, and probably very accurate in its depiction of death by crucifixion.

"No wonder so many churches protested this movie," Marj says, as actors playing Roman soldiers put "Jesus" down on the cross and drive a nail into his hand. Dafoe/Jesus screams and writhes in agony.

I think the protests against the film had more to do with Scorsese's handling of Jesus' sexuality than with the gore of his death. Some people thought it irreverent to speculate about what it would have been like if Jesus had dodged the cross, married Mary Magdalene, and settled down to raise a family.

"You're saying that this"—Yvonne points to three naked men contorted on crosses—"this isn't Hollywood exaggeration? This is accurate?"

I nod, and she walks back to the doorway as the crucified actor is ridiculed by passersby. "Tell me why we are watching this," she demands.

Well, what are you seeing here?

"A pretty gross experience of torture," Thad says.

How is this different from the crucifixes you saw when growing up?

"Our church doesn't have crucifixes like Catholics do," Jeremy says. "But the ones I've seen show Jesus almost at peace, like he knows that this will pass and it'll be OK in the end."

"And he wears a loincloth," Marj says. "Not naked like this."

"Here," Yvonne says, as she looks through her handbag and comes up with a rosary. "Here is the crucifix as I know it."

She hands me the glass beads with their small silver cross, and I hold it up to the others. See? This cross is a symbol, a clean, stylized theological statement of Christian belief. The Son of God who died for us, so that we might live.

That cross—I point to the television screen—is a device used by legitimate governing authorities to accomplish a public execution. It was the electric chair, the lethal injection that eliminated people found guilty of serious crimes. That cross is also a symbol, but what it symbolized in the first century was vastly different from the faith statement conjured by the cleaned-up Christian icon.

Why are we watching this gruesome scene? Because most of us have theologized the crucifixion of Jesus. We've sanitized it, and in the process we've tamed it. One could say that we have robbed it of its power.

We need to discuss crosses.

Ancient Crucifixion

Yvonne looks worried as she returns her rosary to her bag, but she needn't be. This won't take long. A few examples from the past will, in broad strokes, make the point:

- In 71 B.C.E., at the conclusion of a slave rebellion led by Spartacus, the Romans crucified six thousand slaves and their coconspirators.
- When Pedanius Secundus, a wealthy Roman, was murdered by one of his slaves, the magistrates followed Roman law and executed both the perpetrator and all the other slaves in the household. In this case four hundred men, women, and children were crucified.
- According to the historian Josephus, in 4 B.C.E. the Roman general Varus quelled an uprising in Judea and crucified two thousand rebels.

- The Roman procurator Florus ran into resistance when he looted the treasury of the Jerusalem Temple. Roman soldiers put down the rebellion by scourging and crucifying thirty-six hundred men, women, and children.

"Ugh," Yvonne says, "Enough!"

One more. The Roman general (and later emperor) Titus besieged Jerusalem during the Jewish War of 66–72 C.E. and gathered up and crucified up to five hundred refugees from the city *every day;* in his history of the war Josephus records that very soon there wasn't enough room for all the crosses, and the Romans were in danger of running out of wood. Some people were spared crucifixion; instead, they were tortured in other ways— eyes burned out, whipped flesh shredded from bones. Sometimes the victims' hands were cut off and they were driven back into the city to strike terror in the hearts of the Jewish citizens within.

"I get the point," Yvonne says. "The Romans crucified a lot of people."

The Romans did not invent crucifixion. Our first citation is in the Code of Hammurabi, when—

"No more!" Yvonne whispers.

OK. No more statistics and no more gore. But we need to examine this topic just a bit more. For instance, who do you think got crucified?

"My guess would be the poor," Thad says, correctly. "People of low social status."

High-status enemies of Rome, such as foreign kings, were sometimes executed in this manner, and Roman citizens might be crucified if they committed particularly heinous treason against the state, but Thad is correct: the people who were crucified were most often of low social status, so low and poor that they had no right to appeal and their families could not afford to bribe a local magistrate into executing their loved one in a more humane way, perhaps by means of a quick beheading.

"So what you're saying is that freedpersons in Corinth might have faced actual crucifixion," Jeremy says.

Well, the Roman judicial system was essentially prejudiced against *liberti/ae*. Freedpersons didn't share in one of the most important rights of a Roman citizen: exemption from torture. They could be put to the rack, just like slaves, if they were suspected of a crime or if their patron had been assassinated. When Paul talks about the cross in 1 Corinthians 1 we today hear him expounding an edifying theological concept. But he's not speaking primarily of a theological symbol, not in the early first century. He's talking about a Roman political and juridical practice, and a practice to which *it is conceivable* some of his audience might succumb. It's quite possible that these people had seen a crucifixion.

"Most of the examples you mention come from Judea or maybe Rome," Thad says.

"I noticed that, too," Marj says. "Were there crucifixions at Corinth?"

Well, in 146 B.C.E. the Romans destroyed the great cities of Corinth in Greece and Carthage in Africa. In each case thousands of citizens were slaughtered or enslaved, though we have no explicit reference to Corinthian crucifixions.

"Would the Corinthians have known about crucifixions?" Thad asks.

The number of references we find to crucifixion in our ancient sources would suggest that they did. Many cultures and societies, not just the Romans, seem to have used this method of execution as a form of social control to keep the lower classes in line. The sources we have indicate that it was mainly used as a deterrent; that would not work if crucifixions were private affairs. Thus they were public events, and most probably everyone knew about them.

Most importantly for our study, no member of the lower social strata was exempt from the possibility of being crucified. As we just noted, when Paul spoke of Christ crucified his audience not only knew what he was talking about, but they also probably knew that it was conceivable that crucifixion might be their own personal fate as well.

"You mean if they followed Jesus," Yvonne says.

No, I mean that if they were not citizens and not well-connected in the social order just about everyone had the prospect of crucifixion hanging over their heads if they or their family or city got on the wrong side of the local Roman authorities.

"I think I see what you mean," Thad says. "Bad as things might get for us, we don't have to consider that aspect of the cross of Christ."

And as a result we read or hear Paul's letter very differently than his first audience did.

"I never thought I would say this," Yvonne grumbles, "but can we get back to 1 Corinthians? Bury me in Greek," she says as she stares at the continuing scene of agony on the television, "but just turn this off."

Lift High the Cross

Your wish is my command.

As we have seen, 1 Corinthians is a letter that is also a rhetorical text. The thesis of Paul's sustained rhetorical argument is found in 1 Corinthians 1:10 (his appeal that there be no dissension), and his first proof begins with 1:18 and continues through the end of chapter four. Most scholars believe that this first proof is more theoretical than those that will follow. Paul lays out the underlying problem as he sees it, and then throughout the rest of the long letter he applies what he has said in the first four chapters. While we could follow Paul's argument through the proofs he makes, in the interest of time and space I suggest that we pass up an extended discussion of the structure of the letter and concentrate instead on the content and force of Paul's words in the first few chapters.

"Sounds great to me," Yvonne says.

Take a look at how the first proof begins. Paul has just disclosed that he does not preach with clever or eloquent speech, "lest the cross of Christ be emptied of its power" (1:17). A while back we wondered how eloquence of speech could negate the power of the cross.

"Quite a while back, actually," Marj says.

Yes, well, now we can look for an answer to the question. Paul launches the first proof with a series of statements putting the wisdom of God into opposition to the wisdom of the wise or the wisdom of the world. In light of our previous discussion, what *is* the wisdom of God and the wisdom of the world?

"I still don't see it in the text," Yvonne says. "All these words seem pretty vague to me."

Exactly. The concepts that Paul discusses here—wisdom, signs, mysteries, power, even the cross—seem like abstract theological concepts to us. But it's most unlikely that a first-century audience, unschooled in centuries of Christian thought, would find what Paul says to be so abstract.

Let's start again, leaving aside for a time the wisdom of the world. What does Paul say about the wisdom of God?

"That's a bit easier," Thad says. "In 1:24 Christ is the wisdom of God."

"Same thing in 1:30," Jeremy says.

Look again. Is it Christ?

"Well, yeah," Thad says. "It says it right here in 1:24, 'Christ the power of God and the wisdom of God.'"

"Are we missing something?" Marj asks, and I nod yes.

"Is it a translation problem?" Thad wonders.

No, it's a reading problem. Look again at the passage.

No response, just the shaking of heads.

The wisdom of God is not Christ, but Christ *crucified:* "But we proclaim Christ crucified . . . the power of God and the wisdom of God" (1:23-24). The key image here is the cross, and it is an image that Paul uses with great skill and eloquence, despite his disclaimer in 1:17 concerning his rhetorical delivery.

Even humbly skilled ancient orators understood the value of "hooking" listeners with riveting imagery as they attempted to engage and convince their audiences. Aristotle compared public oratory to scene-painting, and other ancient writers recognized the importance of placing visual reminders before the eyes of the audience. Metaphors in particular served this purpose, placing things vividly before the eye of the mind.

Paul was rather good at using visual metaphors to cut through clouds of theory and make his point sharply. Hans Dieter Betz has pointed out that

Paul uses the rhetorical device of conjuring up visual imagery when referring to the cross of Christ: in Galatians 3:1 he reminds his addressees that Christ has been exhibited as crucified *before their eyes.* He doesn't mean that the people of Galatia in central Turkey were eyewitnesses of the actual crucifixion; rather, Betz suggests that the cult formula "Christ crucified" is a "word-picture" that Paul paints before the eyes of the hearer and that achieves its impact not so much by persuasion as by the almost visual impact of the image.

Paul, then, offers the Corinthians the image of Christ on the cross, an image for his audience to ponder. Can you see it? Not the theological symbol stuck to the end of a rosary, but the image of a man in excruciating pain, hung in public humiliation like a bleeding slab of meat because he and his family were too poor to avoid this form of death. Do you see? Paul says that the cross has power; indeed, it *is* the power of God (1:18). It is Christ's crucifixion, not his teachings or his miracles or his being anointed by the Spirit, that Paul claims to be "the power of God and the wisdom of God" (1:23-24).

"I think I see how eloquence could empty the cross of its power," Thad says.

"Me, too," Jeremy says. "Paul doesn't want us to see the cross as a cleaned-up symbol."

That's it!

Paul first mentions wisdom in 1 Corinthians 1:17, where he implies that "eloquent speech" *(sophia logou)* would render empty the cross of Christ, which is, he says in 1:18, the power of God. In 1:19, citing Isaiah, he portrays God in opposition to (literally as "destroyer" of) the "wisdom of the wise." He goes on to make clear the distinction between the wisdom of the world, which God renders foolish, and the wisdom of God. Each of Paul's references to a wisdom opposed to that of the worldly wise makes coherent sense if the content of the wisdom Paul proposes is Christ crucified, and in 1:23-24, his summary of this section of his letter, he states in clear terms that this is what he means by wisdom:

> But we proclaim Christ *crucified,* a stumbling block to Jews and foolishness to Gentiles, but to those who are the called, both Jews and Greeks, Christ the power of God and the wisdom of God (1 Cor 1:23-24).

While the teachings of Jesus could be a stumbling block for some, most of what he said was consistent with the instruction of other first-century Jewish preachers. And I'm not sure how much of a problem belief in his miracles would have been; the ancient world was littered with wonder-workers of genuine power. Most people in this pre-scientific-revolution culture would have assumed the reality and validity of miracles (or signs, as Paul refers to them).

Stay with me. Paul identifies the wisdom of God with Christ *crucified*. In 1:17-25 he presents true wisdom—the wisdom of God—as associated with power (1:17, 18, 24) as well as with the crucified Christ. The linkage of power and being crucified—a method of destruction reserved for the scum of the earth—now this is something new to the ancient world, and this is what Paul calls folly and a stumbling block for those who oppose God's wisdom.

Whew. Let's take a break and reconvene upstairs. It looks to be a lovely evening.

Rooftop Ruminations on the Wisdom of the World

We are up on the flat roof of our guesthouse, sitting under the summer night's canopy of stars. A slight breeze rises from the gulf to refresh the orchards all around us. We watch a full moon rise over the flat horizon of plains north and east of Old Corinth. The pale moonlight smoothes the craggy limestone cliffs of Acrocorinth. The eyes play tricks and the mountain seems to stir.

Yvonne shivers in the cool of the night and draws her sweater close.

"We're not free of you and your exegesis yet, are we?" she asks.

Not quite. We aren't done with wisdom.

"It's been another long day and I'm exhausted," she says. "I think the wisest thing we could do would be to head for bed."

The wisdom of the world to which Paul refers. What is it?

Yvonne sighs, and Marj asks, "What do the commentaries say?"

We've already touched upon much of what the "experts" suggest. The wisdom of the world? Perhaps it's a Hellenistic or Jewish school of wisdom like that of Philo, brought in from Alexandria by Apollos. Others think it's a brand of gnosticism with secret, special knowledge, or even a kind of mystery religion with secret rituals. Still others throw up their hands and identify the wisdom of the world as a whole collection of diverse views with which Paul disagrees. What about you, though? What do you think Paul means?

"I have an idea," Marjorie says. "If we know what Paul thinks true wisdom is, the wisdom of God, perhaps the wisdom of the world is simply the opposite of that."

"That would make sense," Jeremy says, "since Paul seems to imply that the two wisdoms are polar opposites."

So, what is the wisdom of God?

"It's the power of the cross," Marj says.

And what would be the opposite of that?

"Wait!" Thad, who has been scanning the stars, comes alive. "I think I have it. The power of God is the power of weakness, right?"

"The power of God is foolishness in the eyes of the world," Jeremy adds, "for the worldly reject the cross."

"Right," Thad says. "What's the opposite of the power of the weak?"

"Obviously, it's the power of the strong," Marj says.

"Could the wisdom of the world have something to do with understanding—or for Paul, misunderstanding—power in the world?" Thad asks.

Now we're getting somewhere. As we have seen, Paul's problem in 1 Corinthians is not with different kinds of theology; at least we can't find much evidence for such a problem. And in the first two chapters we see that God's wisdom is hidden from the Romans, not the Corinthian Christians, the Romans and anyone else who shares their—

"Their values!" Thad says. "The clash of wisdoms here is a clash of social values, not warring theologies."

Precisely. The wisdom of the world is not a matter of religious speculation but of cultural values and norms that were fixated on amassing more and more power and social status.

"The primary socialization," Jeremy says, "toward honor and status."

God's wisdom, on the other hand, is found in the very people that the dominant Roman culture thought were foolish and of little consequence, "the low and despised," as Paul puts it in 1:28.

"The low and despised," Jeremy says. "And Christ."

Yes, Christ crucified. Christ crucified is the power of God and the wisdom of God, remember?

"With you repeating 'Christ crucified' so often, how can we forget?" Yvonne says. "What I don't remember is why we're doing all of this. For a minimalist approach, this surely is a lot of stuff to digest."

As we watch the moon rise, let's consider what we have done. We have looked closely at a text. We have teased out of it a number of questions and consulted the experts. They've been of some help, but they have not provided us with THE correct interpretation. Rather, they've prodded us to do our own thinking about the passage.

We've discerned that Paul is worried about dissension that results from a clash between values. For him, the contrast between the wisdom of God and the wisdom of the world plays itself out in terms of power and perhaps social location. Conventional wisdom would place Christ at the bottom of the social scale, for he's a crucified person, an outsider, and a threat to the Roman social order. But in God's wisdom the one who should be at the bottom is raised to the pinnacle of the divine order of things.

In fact, we are not alone in noting this "great reversal" of social values. Let's head downstairs out of the evening chill and press ahead for a few minutes to explore some of the implications of what we've seen on the journey thus far.

Puffed Up in Corinth. Again.

We settle into one of the common rooms in the guesthouse. Yvonne, who had pleaded for an early end to this session, has been placated with a cup of tea.

Recall the number of times Paul uses the terminology associated with boasting and being "puffed up" and the fact that most of his denunciations of such behavior are directed at the Corinthians.

"That reminds me of a question I had before," Marj says. "What were the Corinthians boasting about?"

"I was wondering the same thing," Jeremy says, and as he speaks he pulls out his Bible.

"Are you sure their boasting has anything to do with social status?" Thad asks.

Look again at the context of our passage. "Consider your own call," Paul begins in 1:26. What is the "call" or the "calling" of the Corinthians?

"He says that God chose them to shame the wise and the strong," Thad says.

And?

"And," Marj jumps in, "to make sure that no one boasts before God."

Precisely. In 1:29 this is the Corinthians' calling: to assure that no flesh will boast in the presence of God. And then Paul ends this section with a quotation from the prophet Jeremiah: "Let any who boast, boast in the Lord." Clearly something about the Corinthians and their particular situation brings this out of him.

Look at the next mention of boasting: the end of 1 Corinthians 3. This passage—3:18-23—wraps up this section of Paul's argument; in it we find the key. What does he say? Put it in your own words, Yvonne.

"He says that if you want to be wise, be a fool," she says. "'For the wisdom of this world is folly with God.'"

What else do you see?

"He says everything is theirs already," Thad says. "Ah, maybe this is a reference to their seeking possessions."

Yes! All things are theirs—life, death, leaders, the whole world! But the Corinthians belong to Christ, while Christ is God's. The passage ends with the spotlight on God.

"So," Thad says, "the Corinthians' boasting gets in the way of a focus on God."

And therein lies our last crucial exegetical insight.

God's Great Reversal

Now take a look at 1 Corinthians.

"Oh, no," Yvonne moans. "Not again."

Yes, again, my friend. This is how a community reads a text. We read it together and share our insights. Then we read it again. And again.

"Haven't we gotten just about everything out of it yet?" she asks.

We have only scratched the surface. Indeed, we'll be able to do little more than scratch the surface in the course of this journey. But we can—we must!—go a bit more deeply into the text if we are to tie together our study of the texts and rocks of Corinth in a way that will have any relevance whatsoever to your lives once we close the book on this journey. Trust me, it won't be long now. One or two more high dives into Paul's prose and we will dry off, trot quickly around a bend, and enter the home stretch of "Talk."

We have been focusing on the first two chapters of the letter, and in particular we have seen that Paul spends a lot of his epistolary energy contrasting the wisdom of the world with the wisdom of God, which he identifies as the cross of Christ. Let's take a closer look at 1 Corinthians 3.

As this chapter begins, Paul is concluding a bit of a tirade concerning the revelation of God's Spirit to those who can receive it. He begins in 3:1-4 by identifying his audience as still "of the flesh" just like everybody else because of their adherence to individual teachers. Look closely at how he argues against such devotion to mere men.

Beginning in 3:5 he uses a rhetoric of contrast once again, this time between God and the named leaders of the Corinthian community: Apollos, Cephas, and Paul himself. Paul and his fellow teachers are "servants" (3:5; 3:9; and "servants of Christ and stewards of *God's* mysteries" in 4:1). They plant and water, but *God* gives the growth (3:6-7). The community is *God's* field, *God's* building (3:9). Paul laid the foundation of this building through the grace of *God* (3:10). The building is *God's* holy temple, a sanctuary of *God's* Spirit and protected by *God* (3:16-17).

Do you see? Paul counters what he perceives as dissension by an exhortation to see reality as it is: all is God's.

"Actually," Thad says, "isn't that exactly how he ends this section of the letter?"

Indeed:

> So let no one boast about human leaders. For all things are yours, whether Paul or Apollos or Cephas or the world or life or death or the present or the future—all belong to you, and you belong to Christ, and Christ belongs to *God* (3:21-23).

All is God's. All is not Paul's or Apollos's or Cephas's.

"So it's all about God," Marj says.

Yes, God and the relationship of God to God's people, in this case the Corinthians. Paul opposes the boasting we saw as part of the Corinthians' primary socialization, because when they get puffed up with boasting about their own achievements or their honorable positions within the community they miss the whole foundation of the gospel that Paul and the others have been proclaiming.

"Which is?" Yvonne asks.

"I've got it," Thad says. "God deliberately chose the weak, not the strong. To boast is to try to change your status, to get out of the situation of being weak."

"And to do that is to go against God's will," Jeremy says.

In Paul's words, to do that is to empty the essence of God's message of its power.

"And that essence—your word, I think, not Paul's," Jeremy says, "the essence of God's message is . . ."

"The cross," Marj says. "We have come full circle back to the cross of Christ."

Indeed we have. Now do you see the wider implications?

"I think I do," Marj says. "Paul means that we can see the nature of God, God's wisdom and power, in Jesus Christ crucified, just as we noted earlier."

As Pauline scholar Victor Furnish puts it, "God's self-disclosure in the cross places all human pretensions to power and wisdom under judgment." Paul is presenting a complete reversal of the understanding of what it is to live right and live well. If the cross of Christ, which the world sees as a sign of weakness and shame, is actually "the defining event of God's power and wisdom," Furnish concludes, "then every merely human notion about these is turned completely upside down." In other words, Paul presents a radically new set of values and context for life in the world.

"A second socialization?" Thad asks.

Precisely. As Jerome Neyrey puts it, Paul presents God's reversal of "the map of honorable persons" that people in first-century Roman society, both Greek and Jew, adhered to.

"Ah," Yvonne says. "Now I see why you force-fed us those inscriptions in the museum."

"Yes," says Marj. "The Corinthians in the inscriptions were seeking to enhance their social standing in society. That way they could be seen as honored and secure. But Paul is proclaiming the complete opposite—the value of weakness and lack of security."

Yvonne looks relieved, but Jeremy's brow is clouded and his eyebrow arched.

Putting God to the Test

"Wait!" Jeremy says. "I see a problem."

He is staring at his Bible, so we turn to ours.

"Your mention of Jews and Greeks reminded me of something. Look again at 1 Corinthians 1:18-25," he says. "Paul says that the wisdom of

God, the crucified Christ, is a stumbling block to Jews and folly to Greeks. But these Jews and Greeks aren't seeking honor, are they?"

What are they seeking?

"The Jews want signs and the Greeks want wisdom," Jeremy says. "But why? To increase their social status? That doesn't seem likely."

"I see what you mean," Thad says. "Paul acknowledges that the Jews and the Greeks are seeking God—"

"But Paul thinks they are doing it the wrong way," Marj completes his thought.

"Well," Yvonne looks at me and says dryly, "there goes your thesis about honor and social status."

Not quite. Look again at the passage. What is wrong with the strategies of the Jews and Greeks?

No answer. I try again.

Think about it. If people got the signs or the wisdom that they wanted with respect to God, what would they have? Why do people seek out miracles or attempt to follow a philosophical argument? What are they looking for?

"Proof?" Marj ventures.

Yes! And why would Paul be opposed to a search for proof when it comes to God?

"Because there is no way to prove anything about God," Jeremy says. "You have to have faith."

"Yes!" Thad says. "And if you could prove something about God, you wouldn't need faith."

What would you have instead?

"Knowledge?" Yvonne says. "But what would be wrong with that?"

"Oh, wait," Marj says. "I think I have it. For us, of course knowledge is a good thing. But think back to the Bible. Knowledge of God, *knowledge* that God has withheld. Where is that considered a bad thing to seek?"

"In Genesis," Jeremy says. "Adam and Eve seek knowledge and get kicked out of the Garden of Eden."

"And what's wrong with knowledge in that context?" Marj asks.

"Whoa," Thad says. "I see where you're headed. They want power. Control over their own lives. They want to be able to do what they want when they want. If they want to eat of forbidden fruit, well, they can just go ahead and do it."

"Isn't that what the sign-seeking Jews and wisdom-seeking Greeks—and the status-seeking Corinthians—are all doing, at least according to Paul?" Marj asks. "They're all trying to control their destinies, to somehow control God and God's actions."

They all look to me. I haven't interrupted because I'm enjoying their dialectical analysis and because, as I now tell them, they are headed right where I thought we'd go. They have played right into my waiting hand.

"How so?" asks Jeremy.

You folks have landed right where the scholars do, at least the ones I read, even though you don't boast your Ph.D.'s. Yet.

"What do the docs say?" Thad asks.

Pretty much just what you have said. Thad's secondary socialization is presented by Raymond Pickett in his book *The Cross in Corinth.* Pickett, building upon the earlier work of social theorists Peter Berger and Thomas Luckmann, argues convincingly that what we have in 1 Corinthians is Paul responding to a clash of two different universes of meaning.

"I'm lost," Yvonne says.

Recall what we said earlier about the Corinthians having a primary socialization: that is, they have been taught how to relate to those around them in certain ways, just as we have been socialized, albeit somewhat differently, by our own Western culture today.

"Can you give me an example?" she asks. "This is sort of fuzzy."

An example. OK. My father and his brothers and sisters were born and raised in a little village in rural Italy. My oldest aunts remember riding burros into the fields in the morning to work on the crops. Peasant country living was my father's primary socialization. When my father was thirteen his family emigrated to America. This new world offered him a series of secondary socializations, new ways to behave, new avenues through which to find meaning in his life. Now, decades later, they have acclimated themselves to a new universe of meaning: my father and my aunts, born in a village without electricity, struggle to make sense of Web-TV so that they can send e-mail to their grandchildren.

You see? They were raised with one set of beliefs and values and then forced to integrate themselves into vastly different social and cultural circumstances. So too the Corinthians. Raised poor and perhaps enslaved, they were primarily socialized to get free and to amass as much capital and security as they could. Now Paul comes along preaching a new socialization: the cross of Christ as the wisdom of God and all that that entails. According to Paul's letter, the Corinthians respond by using their new spiritual gifts and knowledge, and perhaps their affiliation with different teachers, to enhance their status within the Christian community.

"And that causes the dissension," Marj says.

Yes, and in the process of this clash of universes, this contest of cultural values, Paul sees the Corinthians losing sight of one of his most fundamental principles: the primacy of God. Peter Lampe, another New Testament interpreter, suggests that for Paul the danger of seeking signs or wisdom is that by doing so one submits God to proofs. God is no longer allowed to be God. As Hans Conzelmann puts it, Paul thinks that those who seek signs or worldly wisdom expect God to submit to their criteria. And Leander Keck—

"I think even I get the point," Yvonne interrupts me.

Yes, Paul denounces all attempts by anyone to turn God into some sort of manageable creature.

"All is God's," Jeremy says. "Yes!"

I was going to take us right here and now into the last stage of this Corinthian sojourn—"Talk"—but I suspect it is time for another break. All in favor—

I look around, but they have already dispersed.

TALK: COUNTERIMAGINING THE WORLD

Pilgrims in the Basilica of the Holy Sepulchre during a Holy Week service.
Photo by Nova Development

Chapter Twenty

Three Umbrellas and a Sea Change

We are about to round a bend in the metaphorical road of our journey and enter the third movement, the final stretch: "Talk." But wait! It seems as though we will begin this section with a major skirmish. I hear raised voices.

As it turns out, Thad and Jeremy have been discussing with some passion the question of biblical interpretation. Again. Thad had claimed that there is no such thing as an uninterpreted text. As soon as someone hears or reads it, that person has to take it in and make sense of it, and that is the first act of interpretation. Jeremy objected, "How, then, could anyone read the Bible and find Truth with a capital T? Real truth is Truth, no interpretation necessary."

Marj looks dismayed, and Yvonne bewildered.

"I have been listening to each of these guys," Marj says, "and they both make sense."

Yvonne nods. "I agree with both of them. That makes me very uncomfortable."

This is one of the most difficult of the thickets we have to chop our way through: the question of objective truth. I knew it was going to come back to haunt us.

Try to Be Objective!

My friends Mary and Ben once arrived at the dorm only to discover Mary's roommate in tears. Carla's boyfriend had just dumped her for another. Ben attempted to console the lovelorn girl. "Try to be objective," he soothed. "You're better off without Spike." Mary hugged her roommate and looked her straight in the eye. "You *know* you don't really need a drug addict in your life," she observed, "even if he did remember to bring flowers on your birthday."

Try to be objective. How often we hear ourselves say this. But come on, really now. Who can be objective when we are in the midst of anything important to us? Objectivity requires that we step away from all feeling and attain complete detachment. We are filled with ideas, emotions, whims, plans, and personal agendas, all of which are a part of the *subjectivity* in which we live and move and have our being.

We are subjects, not objects, and it is in our very nature, when the stakes are high, to approach the situation subjectively. So it is that when we come to a biblical text we are not and cannot be strictly objective. As philosophers and literary critics have shown, there is no conceivable way that anyone, even an expert, can come to a text completely free of his or her own biases. With due respect to all who have gone before and all who currently comprise Church leadership and the magisterium—and to Jeremy—there just is no way to prove that any one person's reading of a given biblical text is objectively the correct one.

"But we're talking about objectivity here," Marj says. "You can't deny the reality of objectivity."

What if I told you that what we call "objectivity" is a relatively recent social construction? It is, you know.

"Are we heading toward postmodern deconstruction?" Thad asks. He is a philosophy major and discussion of things such as the nature of reality definitely perks him up. "The deconstructionists claim that objectivity is nothing more than 'an agreement of everyone in the room.'"

Where we are heading is toward a very cursory survey of the history of ideas, in particular the Enlightenment.

"Ah, yes," he smiles.

"Oh, no," Yvonne frowns. "I hear a history lesson coming. Please try to keep it brief."

The Rise of the Rational

We've already discussed the idea that societies develop or construct their own values and views of reality, right? Well, for hundreds of years after the decline of the ancient world the people of western Europe lived in a social world they constructed to be first and foremost a stable one. For most folks change was considered bad; any notion of progress, which might induce change, was suspect. As a result both the political world and the Church developed rigid hierarchies of authority and clear social distinctions. Like it or not, everyone knew who they were and where they fit in.

But plagues and wars and human ambition took their toll, and in their upheavals things changed anyway. More rural peasants moved to towns and cities, and there they discovered new ways to make a living; some accumulated a nest egg and even more money, others traveled as hired hands or merchants. A middle class arose and people who had not inherited wealth and status began to claim them anyway.

Standing in the way of these new social developments were the rich hereditary aristocrats and the Catholic hierarchs (as yet there were only scattered protesters to the dominant Catholicism). By the eighteenth century western Europe had endured what have come to be known as the Reformation, the Counter-Reformation, and the Renaissance. Philosophers were thinking new thoughts, and these ideas gradually had an impact on the wider society. Eventually the social construction of Europe shifted, and the "enlightened" ideas of people such as Descartes, Hobbes, Rousseau, and Locke flowered. Nation-states replaced many of the ancient hereditary kingdoms, and scientists became eager to reconfigure how they understood the universe. All this became the basis for the way we modern folks grew up thinking about our society and our reality.

"I'm following you so far," Yvonne says, "but can you be more specific?"

"Let me," Thad says.

Go for it.

"With the Enlightenment, reason became more important than faith," he says. "In fact, reason became the most important faculty we have."

"Not for me," Yvonne says. "Faith is more important to me than reason."

Good point! One of the results of the Enlightenment and the revolution in scientific inquiry that accompanied it was an increasing gap between the highly cultured elite and everyone else. In fact, one could argue that the Enlightenment movement has had very little effect on most people.

"No way!" says Thad. "Even people who don't read the philosophers have been affected by their worldview."

"An example, please," Marj says.

Thad looks as if he is about to stumble, but he recovers.

"We wouldn't have science if it weren't for the philosophers of the Enlightenment," he says. "They're the ones who first claimed that the universe can be understood through rational inquiry. They're the ones who gave us the sense that progress is good and that human experience is important, that we can derive answers from our rational evaluation of that experience."

Thad is correct on all counts. Moreover, these were the people who asserted that the individual and the individual's experience must be considered as of critical importance. Thad's philosophers had other effects, though, which some of us lament today. For one thing, such an emphasis on pure reason, which had always been associated with the male principle, led to a further decline in the valuing of women and the faculties traditionally associated with femaleness: emotion and intuition.

More to the point of our journey, the Enlightenment thinkers also quite effectively proclaimed that religion and religious doctrines cannot tell us anything significant about the physical world and little about what it is to be fully human either. It was during this period that God was forcibly relocated to the distant and unapproachable high heavens. Religion and the Bible were not dismissed out of hand, but when they were studied, the roles were reversed. As one scholar has put it, "Traditionally, the Bible was the means by which the world was perceived. Following the Enlightenment, the world became the means by which the Bible was understood."

"Will this be on the test?" Yvonne asks, but with a smile for Thad and me. "You both get so worked up about all this."

The point here is that while objectivity seems to most of us to be of the highest value, the standard by which all is measured, things haven't always been this way. There are other ways to make meaning of our experience that, even though they're not objective, may be just as valid as "objective" truths.

Take a minute. Go to your own experience. We spend our lives not in the isolation of clear, abstract thought, but in conversation, knowing very little for certain, interpreting everything we hear as we go along. Yet we manage to survive. So it is with biblical texts: if they are, as we have suggested, the product of the conversations of those who have gone before, and if scriptural texts are conversation partners for us today, then there is no way we can gain objective access to them. They are the product of subjectivity; they must be listened to and what they say to us must be interpreted.

"Settle down, dear," Yvonne soothes.

"Let him go!" Thad says. "He's on a roll."

Even so tradition-laden a source as the recently promulgated "universal" Roman Catholic catechism recognizes the dynamic nature of Sacred Scripture. It reminds the reader that the Word of God (both Jesus Christ and the Bible) is not a "written and mute word, but incarnate and living." To view it otherwise is to run the risk of turning the Word into a "dead letter."

A dead letter.

Reality Check: It's OK to Be Subjective

Jeremy shakes his head. "But if there is no such thing as objectivity," he says, "what can we know about the Bible?"

"Yeah," Marj adds, "way back at the beginning of this journey you talked about what you called 'parameters of interpretation,' remember?"

Yes. We discussed that in Chapter Three.

"Well," she says, "do we throw them out now?"

"And if we do," Jeremy says, "can we all read it the way we want to?"

It does look as though we are back at square one, this journey taken in vain. If there is no objectivity, then all that exists is subjectivity, and we are trapped within it. Double-check for me, but when we talked about guidelines or parameters I recall that we touched upon the reality that troubles us now: even with clearly articulated parameters for interpretation we'll never isolate THE objective meaning of a biblical text.

I suggest that the way out is to accept reality: not a single one of us can be objective about anything that is important to us.

"Not even the scholars? The bishops? The pope?" Marj asks.

Interpretation—making sense of the data we take in—is a necessary condition of knowing anything. Thus, as long as churches are made up of people, and as long as scholars are human, even our religious leaders and our finest and most disciplined minds are limited in what they perceive. Any given expression of truth is relative to the perspective of the person or community expressing it.

"In other words," Marj says, "all truth is relative."

"And you deny the existence of objective Truth," Jeremy adds.

No, I believe that objective Truth with a capital T exists and is not relative. But our *perception* of Truth is subjective—this side of the grave at least. To be a human being who thinks about these things is to join a quest for understanding of the content and the nature of Truth. That is the classic definition of theology: faith seeking understanding. We *believe* in the Truth at the same time that we seek it. And we seek it because we want to *live* it, to experience it, not just believe in it.

"If there's no objectivity and we have no access to the Truth," Thad says, "why bother with any of this Bible study in the first place? Why not just give up?"

None of this means that we should just give up. Besides, we couldn't give up this quest for knowledge even if we wanted to. Thad of all people knows that! Instead, confronted by this inevitable inability to be objective, let us follow the example of a number of other wise pilgrims on this biblical journey. They recognize the fact of human subjectivity, and they attempt to be as aware as possible of the attitudes, values, and beliefs they bring to their interpretation of biblical texts. They "own" their biases and put them right up front. Then they continue their work of analysis and interpretation.

"That's nice and liberal of you," Jeremy says, somehow without sounding sarcastic. "But it doesn't really solve anything. Paul Hill could own his biases and still go out and buy a shotgun."

"This is a rarity! I think I agree with you," Marj says to him.

"Well," Thad says, "if it's OK to be subjective and there's no way to read a biblical text for its objective meaning—and, I presume, we should not look to scholars or to Church authorities for a definitive interpretation—it sounds like a free-for-all, and who's to say that *any* interpretation is beyond the pale?"

Marj, Thad, and Jeremy have a good point. Nothing prevents us from reading and understanding a biblical text any way we like, and as Paul Hill demonstrates, people do just that. Hey, it's a free country.

So . . . Anything Goes?

"So," Thad says, "there's no way to determine the correct interpretation of a biblical text."

Not objectively, no. How could one do that with a text written in tensive language? There is no one correct way to decipher a symbol, is there? And yet it's not the case that anything goes. The biblical text itself imposes some constraints on the range of possible interpretation. As commentator John Burgess puts it, Scripture sets out or defines a "field of meaning." Within this range some interpretations will be more powerful or compelling than others. Burgess uses the analogy of a music score. Anyone who plays the music is guided, but also constrained, by the notes on the page; nevertheless, there is ample room for interpretation and even improvisation. The musician brings the text of the score to life.

"I see what you mean," Thad says, "but with a piece of music it's pretty clear who decides which version of the score is within the acceptable limits and which isn't: the critics and the audience. But with a biblical text?"

As we shall see, discernment of "valid" interpretations of Scripture comes about in much the same way: it is the Christian community that determines the acceptable field of meaning.

"But what criteria do they use to make such a determination?" Thad asks. "It all sounds so, well, blurry."

The easy answer is that, yes, the interpretation of any tensive text is going to be ambiguous. That's why scholars and communities of Christians have developed so many different techniques with which to uncover what the texts are communicating.

"And the difficult answer?" Marj asks.

That involves getting beyond the Three Umbrellas.

Beyond the Three Umbrellas

I think that our problem lies here: we're trying to determine the "correct" meaning of Scripture. In other words, we are still laboring in the shadow of the Three Umbrellas of Fernando Segovia.

"Sounds like an art film," Thad says.

"Or a Latin American novel," Marj says.

Most of this journey has been spent "unpacking" the scholarly approaches that Segovia characterizes as three traditional overarching umbrellas: historical, literary, and cultural criticism. These critical movements are important for people who are attempting to interpret the Bible; they help us to narrow the field of meaning by putting the texts into historical, literary, and social contexts. That's why we've spent so much time exploring them. But as Segovia points out, these three traditional "competing modes of discourse" don't take us far enough; something is lacking.

Yvonne sits back in her chair and crosses her arms.

"We've been at this journey thing of yours since Christ was a cowboy," she says. "And now you say 'something is lacking'?"

"Christ was a cowboy?" Thad wonders. "I missed that gospel."

Something is lacking, Yvonne! You.

"Me?" Yvonne looks startled. "Why, honey, I'm right here!"

Segovia criticizes traditional scholarly approaches to biblical studies because in addition to fostering a false sense of objectivity, they focus almost exclusively on the text. Or the author of the text. Or the world that produced the text. Or the world described by the text.

"Exactly," Thad says. "So what's the problem?"

Traditional biblical criticism doesn't encourage us to consider as valid and valuable interpretive concerns of the world of the reader. The present situation of the reader. The reaction of the reader. The community of the reader. Instead, the reader is passively "informed" by the people holding the umbrellas, informed about what the text meant or perhaps means today.

Something is lacking. We need a paradigm shift.

"A what?" Yvonne asks.

A sea change in our approach to the Bible. The critical methods we have examined can give us the material we need to analyze the texts with some sophistication, and they alert us to take care not to read our own modern prejudices and social constructions into ancient texts. In that sense they promote the "edginess" that can encourage us to read the Bible afresh in every situation. But we have yet to call out the power of Scripture to affect our lives in any forceful way. To do this we need to shift the paradigm, that is, the conventional framework or set of standards we have been using.

"You don't mean, I hope," Marj says, "we now throw out everything we've done so far, do you?"

No. But we cannot settle for a passive, armchair, intellectual approach to Scripture. We have to look at the Bible in a radically new way.

"Oh, dear God," Yvonne says.

As it would happen, some biblical scholars are doing just that, developing new ways of examining the texts. In the process they are going beyond conventional readings and are taking into account the role these texts play as Sacred Scripture in the lives of Christian communities. Biblical theologian Sandra Schneiders summarizes this shift well. She suggests that the sacred text has three aspects or "worlds" for us to explore: the world behind the text (the social world of the author); the world in the text (the content of the documents we have); and the world before, or in front of, the text (the world of the audience). Traditional criticism—the three umbrellas—investigates the worlds behind and within the texts. What has been missing on our journey is Schneiders's third world: the world in front of the sacred texts; in other words, how the reader of the texts interacts with it.

"She's echoing Segovia here," Marj says.

Her work predates his, I think, but they land in roughly the same place.

"But what does that have to do with the Bible itself?" Jeremy asks. "The inspired word on the page doesn't change when the audience experiences it."

No, but the point is to read an inspired text for inspiration, right? And what is inspiration? Just the words on the page? No, it's God's living word speaking to us in our current situation. The significance of Scripture is not that it's a text, but that it's a means by which to launch a conversation with the divine. To understand and appreciate a literary text, a novel like *Catcher in the Rye* for instance, we need only examine the text. The audience, even the author, can be considered irrelevant (a good thing, since J. D. Salinger has allowed so little access to his person).

But reading a sacred text is different. You can sit in your room and read a Gospel or a book of the Pentateuch for your class in literary traditions as though it were an accomplished work of art. But to read the same book as Sacred Scripture is to approach it not just as a text but as an encounter, an encounter with God. Thus if we want to explore how the Bible works as Scripture we have to do the work we have done and learn about the details of its historical background or the complexities of its literary composition. But we must also do more: we have to ponder how it is that Scripture offers us an experience of God. If our reading is going to be more than an informative intellectual exercise, we have to *enter* the text.

"Enter the text?" Marj asks. "How do we do that?"

The same way you enter the mind or the heart of another person: by kindling your powers of imagination.

Imagination and Fire

Picture a big, roaring bonfire late at night. We have been strolling around it, admiring its beauty, maybe even warming our bodies in its light. We've fueled it and probed it and poked at its embers and ashes. Now it's time to steel your nerves and jump in.

"I've been able to follow you so far," Yvonne says. "But now you're losing me. You want us to jump into a fire?"

You may have thought that the goal of our journey was to learn the facts about biblical texts and to gain exposure to the skills needed to interpret them. But that was only part of our objective. Ours is a journey that transcends the pursuit of information. Up until now we have kept the Bible at arm's length; it has been the object of our inquiries. Now we will plunge into its fire. If this final stretch of road works for us we will transcend matters of information and sample our potential to be transformed by the journey. At the end we will not be done, we will not be newly complete and transformed. But I suspect that many of us will have a nose for the next road, an ear for the next excursion on our way to divine transformation.

"Catch your breath," Marj says. "You're floating into the heavenly spheres."

"We're up pretty high," Yvonne adds. "I need a little oxygen."

"Yeah," Jeremy says. "Can you let us know what we're getting into?"

Let me come down to earth and approach this from another angle. Do you recall your original conversations with me?

They nod and I ask them to remind us.

"I came to you because I didn't know what to tell my kids when they asked me why they should go to church," Yvonne says.

"I was rip-roaring mad at people like Paul Hill," Marj says.

"I couldn't understand how anyone can consider the Catholics and other liberals—" Jeremy begins, but Marj's whoop of laughter interrupts him.

"Sorry," she says. "Only you would lump Catholics and liberals into the same camp."

He shrugs. "I didn't see how any of them are really Christian," he continues. "Not with the way they play fast and free with the Bible."

"My question was pretty basic," Thad says. "Who cares about any of this? Why is the Bible important to people?"

OK. Now, have your questions been answered?

They pause, look at each other, and together shake their heads.

"No," Thad says. "I don't think you've answered any of our questions."

"Actually," Yvonne says, "I have more questions now than I did before."

I am not surprised.

"You're not offended?" Yvonne asks.

Of course not. The journey isn't over.

"But I still don't have a clue," she says.

Oh yes you do. And now is the point where you'll come to understand how clued-in you really are. Now we'll begin to apply what we've learned to your original questions as well as to some that have arisen along the way.

How do we get around the problem of our innate subjectivity?

Are there other ways to appreciate our experience if we decline a lock-step adherence to the point of view of the "enlightened" philosophers?

How do we converse with God through Scripture?

Who is God anyway?

What are the implications for our lives today, here and now, of the idea that the word of God is living and active and not a dead letter?

"And what does this all this mean," Yvonne adds, "all this talk of imagination and fire?"

For Reflection and Further Conversation

1. What do you think about all this talk about objectivity? Does it make sense to your experience? Why or why not?

2. Do you have any preliminary ideas about how one "enters" a text? Perhaps you have encountered this idea in another field of study.

3. All of this talk about jumping into fire! Have you ever fire-walked? Do you know anyone who has? Is it a miracle? Do you know how scientists explain it?

Chapter Twenty-One

Counterimagining the World

We have just danced swiftly through a brief account of the Enlightenment and the rise of science. But I'm thinking of the beginning of our journey. Remember? We talked about something called "the Great Fallacy."

"I remember," Thad says. "You told us about that liberation theologian . . . what's his name?"

Robert McAfee Brown.

"Right," Thad says. "He argues that there is no difference between the real world and the good world."

And what was at the center of his insight?

"That God is not far off somewhere up in the sky," Thad says, "detached from what's going on down here on earth."

"God is here, in our midst," Jeremy says.

I suspect you can see now what Brown is reacting to.

"Yeah," Jeremy says. "He's reacting to the Enlightenment. The idea that God is up in heaven, not present or active in our world."

"I've been thinking about that," Yvonne says. "It's been nagging my mind since we first started."

Go on.

"I'd hardly call myself an enlightened person," she says. "But I think that I've fallen into that trap too. When I think of God, I think of him up in heaven, not here in the room with us."

And in that you are not alone. As Thad said earlier, the assumptions we make concerning the nature of reality have been bequeathed to us by the great writers, thinkers, and scientists of the Enlightenment period and their modern successors. Their conclusions have reached the point of general acceptance, "common knowledge" in the West, and even the most traditionally religious in our midst assume that this is the only way to describe life in "the real world." And yet, Scripture as we are coming to understand it does not fit easily into this world of ours. Nor does God.

"*I* don't fit easily into this world," Jeremy says.

"Actually," Yvonne says, "I don't either. Though I never really thought about it before."

I suspect these two are not the only ones to feel this way; most of us could not do without the fruits of enlightened positivism.

"Positivism?" Marj asks.

"Positivism," Thad repeats. "How to describe it . . . ? It's the assumption that observable phenomena, verifiable facts, are what make up reality. Positivism is the basis for science and the study of logic, among other things. What's really real can be objectively known as real."

"And that, of course, leaves out God and religion," Jeremy says.

Not always. Religious people can be positivists, either by choice or accident.

"I could be an accidental positivist?" Jeremy asks.

You might well be.

"But I reject any belief system that rejects God," he says.

Yes, but when one promotes religious beliefs as though they are undeniable, objective facts, how is this different from the program of scientific positivists? The subject matter (God) is different, but the method is the same.

Jeremy's dander is up. "You're saying I'm no different from an atheistic scientist-type?" he asks.

Marjorie, defuser of pointless conflict, jumps in here. "It sounds like we're all so steeped in the modern world that it's hard to imagine anything different," she says.

Bingo.

"You know," Marj says to me, "you really date yourself whenever you say that. No one plays bingo anymore."

"My grandma does," Jeremy says.

"So come on, Gramps," Thad says to me with the sly smile. "Where are we heading next? Into the fire?"

Radical Imagination

Not just yet. As Marj says, it's hard to envision a different way of looking at the world, but as luck would have it, Walter Brueggemann, an insightful interpreter of the Old Testament, comes to our aid. In his little book *Texts Under Negotiation* he counsels that we might as well accept the fact that we inhabit a world in which most people still equate truth with the knowledge of verifiable facts. But, he says, they're wrong.

"He says that?" Thad asks.

Well, not in so many words. He says that knowledge really "consists not in settled certitudes but in the actual work of imagination."

Imagination is the key. He goes on:

> By imagination, I mean very simply the human capacity to picture, portray, receive, and practice the world in ways other than it appears to be at first glance when seen through a dominant, habitual, unexamined lens. More succinctly, imagination as the quintessential human act is a valid way of knowing.

In other words, reality—life in the world—is "an on-going, creative, constructive task in which imagination of a quite specific kind has a crucial role to play."

"And that kind of imagination would be . . . ?" Thad says.

The kind of imagination that can construe or understand our world in a radically new way.

"But how are we to do that?" Marj asks. "This sounds awfully theoretical."

For once, the answer is simple and direct: turn to the sacred text.

John Burgess puts it this way: "Scripture," he says, "like poetry, engages our imagination. Scripture is an invitation to construe the world in a different way."

"It sounds like these scholars are telling us that it's OK to free ourselves from some sort of mental straightjacket," Marj says.

An interesting way to put it.

"So this is what you meant before," Thad says, "when you said we have to enter the text."

Marj nods in agreement. "I remember what you said: we have to kindle our powers of imagination and enter the text."

"And plunge into the fire," Yvonne adds. "That was where you lost me."

Now do you see what I meant? We moderns have lost touch with the reality that scientific positivism is a relatively new development. It hasn't always determined how people understood what is "real" in the world. We have lost sight of the role that imagination continues to play in shaping our reality. We make sense of our perceptions of the world by imaging that world in certain ways.

"Back to the Bible," Jeremy asks. "What has any of this to do with how we read it?"

The Dangerous Denigration of the Truth of Myth

For a couple thousand years the stories in the Bible functioned for most people both as history and as myth, and both as history and as myth the Bible was understood to be true. When Enlightenment thinkers began to define scientific fact as the only arbiter of what is real, they drove a wedge between myth and history, and myth became synonymous with falsehood (as in "It's only a myth").

"So the Bible wasn't true anymore," Marj says.

Before history and myth were split up and mythic thinking was dismissed, people understood the power of mythic truth. Most medieval folk didn't spend a lot of time worrying about the historicity of biblical texts because the texts were more than historical records for them. They understood the power of these texts in a way we don't: the power that religious myths have to *create* reality. In a world based on the Bible and religious ritual, God was a present reality in life. Christ was not a fondly remembered teacher or an intellectual article of faith. Christ was alive, present in their midst. Could they prove, say, the Resurrection as a historical fact? Of course not. But they knew that Christ was resurrected because they experienced him in current time, living among them.

"Did they see him?" Yvonne asked.

No. But they sensed him, they knew him to be present, and they experienced his power.

"So," Thad says, "are you saying we should dump our modern knowledge of science and the truth of history and go back to an ancient way of constructing the world?"

You know we couldn't do that. But we need to enhance and enrich our understanding of history and how the Bible works. To study the Bible well, as Wilfred Cantwell Smith has suggested, we have to attempt "to understand human history as the drama of our living our life in history while being conscious of living it in a context transcending history."

"English, please," Yvonne says.

To appreciate and understand the Bible we have to see it as a channel, a conduit, between humankind and the transcendent, in other words, between us and God.

"So the Bible is a conversation partner," Yvonne says. "As you've been telling us all along."

And if the Bible is a conversation partner, or rather a tool that we can use to enter into a conversation with the divine, we enter the discussion by exercising our powers of imagination.

"Even though," Marj adds, "we've been taught that 'imagined reality' isn't reality at all."

Precisely. If we can approach Scripture with our imaginative abilities in high gear, the premodern, traditional way of understanding Scripture allows us lots of room for movement, lots of space in which to listen for God and to interpret what we hear.

Now, rather than tossing out the three umbrellas of traditional biblical criticism, I suggest that we cherish and engage them, for they can guide the conversation between God and God's people. They will offer us tools that we can use to determine some parameters for the discussion and help us form a base line so that we can test the interpretations.

"And avoid the position of Paul Hill," Marj says.

Yes! Brueggemann puts it this way: we Christians are invited to form a community that is a place "where people come to receive new material, or old materials freshly voiced, that will . . . nourish, legitimate, and authorize a counterimagination of the world."

"We are to counterimagine the world," Marj says.

Thad has been darkly quiet for some time so I ask what's troubling him.

"I'm a philosophy major," he says. "I'm not comfortable with this post-Enlightenment imagination stuff."

"What's wrong with it?" Yvonne asks him.

"It goes against just about everything I was taught," he says. "If I were to walk into class and talk like this, they'd think I was crazy."

After a brief silence, Marj stirs. "Let me make a connection here," she says. "It might help."

"Please do," Thad says.

"What you just said about being considered crazy reminded me of something," Marj says. "The foolishness of God. The call to counterimagine the world is of a piece with the 'foolish' way of God."

"Yes," Jeremy says. "The wisdom of the world—in this case, the Enlightenment way of seeing reality—sees God's way as foolish."

"And," Marj says, "I'll bet the so-called Great Reversal can only be accomplished through imagining a new way of being."

"But not everybody who believes in the Enlightenment's view of reality thinks belief in God is foolish," Thad says.

"No, but . . . oh, wait!" Marj says. "I just thought of something else. Enlightenment thinking is the equivalent of the Corinthians' primary socialization!"

The neurons are firing, and we are once again on the right road. The reversal we alluded to definitely involves reimagining our culture's values and aspects of our primary socialization. As I said before, I'm not inclined to dismiss all the Enlightenment's thinkers or their achievements as anti-God, but it does seem to me, Thad, that if you accept the challenge to counterimagine the world you will most likely be negatively judged by some of the worldly wise.

"I'm not sure this is particularly comforting," Thad says. "Maybe we should move on. What's next?"

How did that man in the gospels put it? Come follow me.

For Reflection and Further Discussion

1. What's your attitude toward imagination? Think of some instances when imagination was a valued asset to you. Can you think of any situations when imagination was not helpful? On balance, why is imagination a good thing? Or why not?

2. Thad just whispered to me that this material seems to validate all those times when he tuned out his teachers and got caught up in his daydreams. How is daydreaming similar to, or different from, the sort of imagination we discussed in this chapter?

Chapter Twenty-Two

We Confront the Passion of God

I was going to title this section "Practical Imagination." After our last, brief encounter with theoretical concerns, now we move to the hands-on aspect of what we have been studying. In the process we will discover an answer to each of our four friends' questions. At least a partial answer. The beginning of an answer.

We sit in a circle of blue-padded chairs in the quiet chapel on the college campus that is my current work site. We are escaping the late summer's heat and have the place to ourselves. The south side of the church is radiant with the bright colors of two tall, narrow windows of stained glass. The left window presents stylized images from the first book of the Bible. Cool blues and greens of a dome of water give way to the browns and yellows of a fresh creation, culminating at the bottom with two figures resting under a tree. The right window begins with a slumbering figure, a man on an island, and as one's eyes move up this window, past seals and lamps and a woman clothed like the sun, we arrive at a vision of the new Jerusalem descending to the earth from the book of Revelation.

Presupposition number one for our journey has been that God abides in our midst. From its depiction of divine evening strolls in the garden of Genesis right through to the final harrowing visions granted in the book of Revelation, the Bible makes this claim: God is not somewhere up there far away! God is here, God is with us. God offers us first not a memorizable program of laws for moral behavior but a living experience, an invitation to a conversation.

Christians discover the Bible to be their primary access to this conversation. Sacred Scripture is different from other texts. Yes, Scripture is a source of information for instruction and guidance, and it can function, too, as the object of conversation. But Scripture is more than that. In the words of

Hebrews, "the word of God is living and active." Wilfred Cantwell Smith went so far as to insist that "scriptures are not texts"!

"Then what are they?" Yvonne asks.

According to Smith, "Scripture is a human activity." It is a "bilateral term" that "inherently implies, in fact, names a relationship" that people sense they can have with the transcendent.

"My simultaneous translator is not working," Yvonne says as she fidgets with an imaginary headset.

Thad jumps in. "It sounds to me as though your scholar friend Smith is saying the same thing that Hebrews says: Scripture is organic, alive, not inscribed on a stone."

That's it exactly. The Catholic bishops who gathered at the Second Vatican Council, hardly a bunch of flaming humanistic liberals, put it this way:

> Through tradition the holy scriptures themselves are more thoroughly understood and constantly actualized in the Church. Thus God, who spoke in the past, continues to converse with the spouse of his beloved Son.

"'The spouse of his beloved Son,'" Yvonne says. "That's the Church, right?"

"The people of God are the bride of Christ," Marj confirms.

Elsewhere the council documents claim that Christ is present to us today, "since it is he himself who speaks when the holy scriptures are read in the church." And again: "In the sacred books, the Father who is in heaven comes lovingly to meet his children and talks with them."

The recently revised, official *Catechism of the Catholic Church,* building on the documents of Vatican II, makes this dynamic clear as the light pouring through those windows. It claims that the followers of Jesus form a "religion of the Word of God, not a written and mute word, but incarnate and living." I've made reference to this before. The text is a living word, an ongoing communication. The alternative, as the Catholic catechism puts it, would be to see Scripture as—

"A dead letter," Marj says, completing my thought.

"That's OK for Catholics, I suppose," Jeremy says. "But what about the rest of us?"

The idea that sacred texts hold the potential for imaginative encounters with divine realities is not limited to Catholic Christians.

"So it's a Christian thing," Jeremy says.

In fact, it's more than that. When we look at the scriptures of other major religious traditions we discover that they serve as an invitation to an encounter very similar to the Christian experience of the "living word." We find that cross-culturally sacred texts are seen as authoritative because communities look to them in search of values, rules, and proper rituals. Paul Achtemeier takes this a bit further and claims, as we have hinted earlier, that these special texts have the sort of vitality that can "author" reality. Scripture's authority lies in "its power to create and shape reality" for its readers. It has this power because people believe that it has its source in the divine.

"I see what you mean," says Marj. "Scripture functions differently than other texts do. But this all seems a bit abstract to me," she says. "Can you show us how this idea of Scripture might work?"

Once again, your pleasure is my command. Let's return to the Song of Songs.

Ruminations on the Bridegroom and the Bride

Recall the chapters of our earlier journey concerning the Song. We looked at the text from a number of viewpoints, attempting to discover its genre and *Sitz im Leben*. One traditional way of understanding this alluring book, one we did not pursue, suggests that it can be understood as an allegory. In allegory a story or narrative is interpreted in such a way that the people and events symbolize something else. Texts written in tensive language, the playground of symbol, are particularly conducive to allegorical interpretation. So, for instance, Adam and Eve in Genesis can be cherished as rich, nuanced symbols of all humanity, while the innocence of the garden may symbolize the pristine state of human consciousness before we mature and give ourselves over to the darker side of human nature, the part that wants control and power.

"Yes, I see," Marj says. "Through allegory we enter the text. We share the experience of Eve and her husband."

A text like the Song of Songs is ripe for this sort of analysis, and it should come as no surprise that the text's interpreters over the centuries have discerned in its lush imagery a number of profoundly allegorical meanings. Jewish sages saw in its poetry a vivid description of the love shared by God and the people of Israel, while Christian writers as early as Hippolytus of Rome wrote volumes of commentary in which the Song's bride and bridegroom symbolized the love of God for the Church.

But over time a different strand of allegorical tradition developed. Between 240 and 245 C.E. Origen, the wise Christian scholar in Alexandria, composed a ten-volume commentary on the Song of Songs. Only fragments survive, but they suggest a solidly exegetical treatment of the Song in which Origen revisited earlier Christian interpretation of the lovers as God and Church. However, he added a new dimension, a new twist, if you will. For him the bridegroom is Christ, and the bride is not just the Church but the individual Christian soul. Do you see the significance of the difference?

"I think so," says Yvonne.

"Yeah," Thad says. "It sounds as though he personalized the text."

He did. He proposed that the author of the poem was attempting to "instill into the soul the love of things divine and heavenly," and in the process the text provided the reader with what Roland Murphy calls "an advanced course in spirituality." In doing this Origen set the stage for a flowering of subsequent interpretations that encouraged Christians to see in its poetry an allegory representing a pervasive spiritual reality: both the Church and the individual Christian are united to God through Christ.

The fullest development of this allegorical tradition can be found in the writings of the Spanish mystics of the sixteenth century. Teresa of Avila, founder of an order of Carmelite sisters, saw in the Song a great hymn about the "spiritual marriage" of the soul and its beloved Christ. She began a commentary on the text, a rare thing in her time for a layperson (and a woman at that!) to attempt. Her book sings with rapture of the love that God has for each of her nuns. "What endearing words!" she proclaims. "What sweetness! One of these words would have been enough for us to be dissolved in you!"

Her fellow Carmelite, saintly John of the Cross, was perhaps even more profoundly moved by the text. He wrote a poem about union with Christ, a "Spiritual Canticle" laden with imagery reminiscent of or directly taken from the Song of Songs. "Love, cover those bright eyes!" his Christ/bridegroom insists.

> I'm lifted! off on air!
> Come settle, dove.
> The deer—look yonder—lies
> hurt on the hill above,
> drawn by your wings he loves the coolness of.

His poem was so well received that John was prevailed upon to write a detailed commentary on it, one that comes to over five hundred pages in its English translation.

Marj is appreciative of all of this information, but impatient. "I'm not sure how this relates to the idea of Scripture as the living word," she says.

"My problem exactly," Yvonne says. "What does all of this mean for us?"

The Implications for Yvonne

Back to the text! Turn to chapter six of the Song of Songs. Here we plunge into the middle of a discussion between the bride and her companions, who wonder where the bridegroom has gone. Suddenly he reappears and begins a litany of praise of the bride and her beauty. In the translation of Roland Murphy he sings:

> Beautiful are you, my friend, as Tirzah,
> lovely as Jerusalem,

awe-inspiring as visions.
Turn your eyes away from me,
   for they disturb me (6:4-5).

"Whoa," says Thad. "My translation is different."

Actually, all the English translations differ here, particularly with regard to Murphy's third line. That's because the translation of the Hebrew words here is in dispute; what Murphy renders "visions" may also refer to the banners or trophies of an army. Your translations may also render the last line differently.

"Mine has the groom 'dazzled' rather than troubled," Marj says.

"The King James Version has 'Turn away thine eyes from me, for they have overcome me,'" Jeremy says.

And the NRSV—the New Revised Standard Version?

"'Turn away your eyes from me, for they overwhelm me!'" Thad reads.

Even the ancient sages who translated the original Hebrew into Greek for the Septuagint apparently had some trouble with this verse. The root meaning of the Hebrew verb has something to do with "assault" or "oppress," but the Greek spins this a bit and incorporates the notion of flying away, perhaps like a flock of birds disturbed by a sharp sound.

In any case, these variations change little when we are attempting to discern the significance of the text for Yvonne. Look again at the context.

"Wait," Thad says. "I remember how weird some of the allusions are in the Song of Songs. But to compare the bride to a city like Jerusalem? I don't get it. And what or who is Tirzah?"

Jerusalem was an important symbol of beauty in Israel's collective imagination, beauty and delight, for it was home to the Temple, the place where God dwelled. For the author of the book of Lamentations, Jerusalem was "the perfection of beauty, the joy of all the earth" (2:15). Tirzah—the name may come from one of the Hebrew roots for "delight"—was one of the garden cities of ancient Israel, remembered long after its destruction for its beauty.

Good question. Now, back to the significance of this text for Yvonne. In light of the history of Christian allegorical interpretation, what do you see?

We all look at Yvonne.

"Well . . . ," she begins, "the groom is saying this to the bride, right? He is telling her that she's pretty good-looking."

And . . . ?

"He seems to like her eyes," she says.

And . . . ?

"And what?" she asks.

What effect do her eyes have on him?

"I guess it depends on the translation," she says. "They dazzle him, or overcome him, or in my translation, torment him."

The Wailing Wall and Plaza in the old city of Jerusalem. Photo by Corel

Good. Now, who is "he" again?

"The groom?" she asks.

Yes, but in the context of the allegorical tradition? She looks at me blankly.

"I think I get where you're going," Marj says. "Can I jump in here?"

"Absolutely," says a relieved Yvonne.

"The bridegroom is Christ, right?" Marj asks Yvonne, who nods in agreement.

"That means that what we have here is Christ speaking to his bride," Marj continues. "If you or I am the bride—"

"Ah," says Thad. "I see it."

"Yes," Marj says. "This passage is saying, in effect, that you, Yvonne, your eyes, your soul, are so beautiful that you disturb Christ, you dazzle him. You torment him."

In the words of an early version of the Jerusalem Bible, Christ the bridegroom says to the bride, "Turn your eyes away from me, for they hold me captive." The Song proclaims a love so strong that the bridegroom, Christ, is rendered almost powerless before it. This is how God in Christ feels about Yvonne, and by extension, about the rest of us.

Yvonne has been silent, but now she pulls back in her chair.

"You make it sound as though God is a drunken college student," she says. "Sorry, guys."

A God drunk with love for you! That's a fine way to put it.

"But that's not what I was taught," Yvonne says.

No, you were taught a more conventional, primary-socialization version of God: God is up there in God's heaven, all-powerful and looking down on us, waiting for us to die so he (God is conventionally a he, right?) can judge us.

"God does judge us," Jeremy says. "You aren't going to deny that, are you?"

When we die we are held accountable, but this reading of the Song implies that we are held accountable for the way we responded to God's unconditional, almost drunken love for us.

"That doesn't sound very biblical to me," Jeremy says.

Ah, but it is. Turn to Psalm 63. Here we see a situation that I am sure is familiar. The psalmist prays:

> O God, you are my God, I seek you,
>   my soul thirsts for you;
> my flesh faints for you,
>   as in a dry and weary land where there is no water.
> So I have looked upon you in the sanctuary,
>   beholding your power and glory.
> Because your steadfast love is better than life,
>   my lips will praise you.
> So I will bless you as long as I live;
>   I will lift up my hands and call on your name (63:1-4).

This is the common view of the relationship between the believer and God: we pine for God, hope in God, yearn for God. This hunger for God is at the essence of the life of the person of faith.

"Well, of course we hunger for God," Jeremy says. "But you sound like you're saying that God hungers for us."

Ah, but there is another figure in the Bible who yearns and hungers for intimacy. Look at Psalm 147. In the midst of this great hymn of praise for all that the divine does for us, we read this about God:

> His delight is not in the strength of the horse,
>   nor his pleasure in the speed of a runner;
> but the LORD takes pleasure
>   in those who fear him,
>   in those who hope in his steadfast love (147:10-11).

Do you see? The psalmist offers the fullness of praise to the all-powerful God, but recognizes a degree of mutuality. God delights, God feels pleasure as a result of the divine interaction with God's creatures. We see this again in Psalm 149:4, "For the LORD takes pleasure in his people." The Lord, in some translations, "delights" in us.

"But wait," Jeremy says. "When the psalmist refers to God's people he means Israel, right?"

Yes, that is the primary reference. But more is present here than the primary meaning, because that's the way the tensive language of Scripture works.

"If this were written in steno language," Marj says, "none of this would apply to us, since we aren't part of the original audience, the people of Israel."

In the Psalms, in the Song of Songs, and elsewhere in the Hebrew Bible (see, for instance, Isaiah 61:10–62:5), words are put into the mouth of God that indicate that the relationship between God and God's people is passionately mutual. True, God does not, strictly speaking, *need* Yvonne or Thad, or any of us or even all of us; God is complete in and of God's self. But for whatever reason (probably to be found only in the mind of God!), the divine force that we call God takes delight in us, and in the Song of Songs the divine has inspired a text to tell us that.

"Well, I suppose I see what you mean," Jeremy concedes. "If God didn't passionately love us, why would he have sent his only Son to die for us?"

"Still, I've never thought of God that way," Yvonne says. "Passion? God a God of passion?"

And that, I humbly suggest, may be the reason you had a problem and came to see me in the first place.

"I don't see the connection," she says.

Before this journey, what were you offering your kids when they asked you why they had to go to Mass?

"That was the problem," she says. "I wasn't sure what I *could* offer them."

"You offered them a rule," Thad says. "You have to go to Mass or else you go to hell."

And for better or worse, in this day and age that is not a very compelling argument.

"The hell it isn't," Jeremy says.

"No, he's right," Marj says to Jeremy. "I think a lot of us are looking for something more than a God to be afraid of. When it comes down to it, I think I'd rather go to hell than believe in a God who'd send me there just because I missed Mass one or two Sundays."

"I am getting very uncomfortable," Yvonne says to me. "I like what you are saying, but to miss Mass is a sin."

"I suppose it can be," Thad says. "If Mass is the way you stay close to God, skipping church on Sunday would cut you off from God. And that's the classic definition of being in the state of sin."

Thad's right, but I am getting a bit uncomfortable too. Our purpose here is not to sort out all the problems that Christian theology (and Christian practice) present. All we can do now is lay down a foundation for further discussion of these matters. That foundation is this insight: God is here, God is intimate with us, God and God's power to bless and to heal and to delight—all of this is available here and now, every day. If Yvonne grows in her understanding of this, no, that's not it . . . if she enables herself to *experience* this rather than just believe in it, then she will not only have something to say to others. She will become a model of the insight she wants to share. Do you see?

"Sounds like you're saying we have to teach by example," Marj says. "We can lead people to God by living the experience of God."

"OK. I see what you mean," Yvonne says as she sits back in her chair. "But how do I learn to experience God in this way?"

"Grace," Jeremy says. "Pray for God's grace."

Yes, the gift that we call "grace" is what we need in order to share in this experience, and that gift comes to us through prayer. Fortunately, the Christian community in its wisdom has developed a number of ways to put ourselves in grace's way.

"Grace. Prayer," Marj says. "Again, these are abstractions to me. Teach us how to pray."

Whoa! The way of prayer is very simple and very complex at the same time, and in any case that would be a different journey.

"So you're going to leave us hanging in the abstract?" she says.

"Let me put it another way," Marj says. "Teach us how to enter the text."

Now you're talking. Let's walk out on the quad and I'll introduce you to a very hands-on, practical form of prayer that might help put some flesh on the spiritually abstract.

The Three Rs: Read, Reflect, Respond

A cooling breeze rustles the leaves over our heads as we sit under a maple tree on a hot, lazy afternoon. The dry grass spikes exposed skin as if it were a haystack beneath us.

"Lexus what?" Yvonne asks.

Lectio divina. It's Latin for "sacred reading."

"You're saying we have to read the Bible in Latin?"

No. Let me begin at the beginning.

Early in my own spiritual journey a wise man taught me a very simple way to incorporate Scripture into my private prayer. This type of meditation is formally known as the *lectio divina,* though we need not trouble with the term. This "active" reading of a sacred text involves three stages: we read the text, we reflect upon it, and then we respond to it.

"Say more," Thad says.

Not surprisingly, active reading is the opposite of passive reading. To read actively, one puts oneself into the text. You play with it; indeed, poet Kathleen Norris calls the *lectio divina* "serious play."

"Serious play," Jeremy says. "I don't get it."

"That's because you're so serious," Marj says. "It sounds to me like reading poetry. You don't read a poem the way you read a textbook. You get into the poem, savor the images. You let the poem speak to you in your own life, right?"

Exactly right. The meditative techniques of the *lectio* invite us to an exercise of imagination and an experience of Scripture that is transformative rather than informative. Are you reading a biblical text for Scripture class? Then your goal is information, not transformation. But if you want to plug into the ongoing conversation between God and God's people, the *lectio divina* is an excellent way to begin.

"So, how do we begin?" Jeremy asks.

How do you begin any other sort of serious prayer?

"Well, I find a quiet place," he says, "and chill . . . er, calm down."

And that's exactly what we do with the *lectio.* Take your Bible to a place where you won't be distracted, and get into a comfortable position. Some people kneel or sit in church; others walk in the woods or wander over to the beach. The important thing is to try to shield oneself from anything that might distract from internal listening.

"Internal listening?" Yvonne repeats.

Most of my prayer involves me talking to God. The *lectio* provides God with an opportunity to talk to me. But this cannot happen if my mind is already distracted by the clutter of my own words or disturbed by people passing by or interrupting me with phone calls.

"I find it enormously difficult to quiet down inside," Thad says.

We all do. But with practice you can find the technique that allows you to be still. I invite my mind to imagine a stone in the center of a dusty road. I focus on that image, and when I get distracted, I come back to it again and again. After a few minutes the storm of excess thought settles a bit and I can begin to listen.

"Listen for what?" Yvonne asks.

Listen for God. We begin by reading a passage from Scripture. You can pick one at random or read through a particular book, as I prefer to do. Either way, the important thing is to banish from your intentions any need to make a particular amount of progress in your reading. In other words, in this form of prayer you let go of all control; in half an hour you might read and reflect on two verses of a story rather than finish it. You may hear the Spirit of God whispering to you, or you might hear nothing. The point is to put yourself in a position where you can hear God speaking if God wants to. This will only work if you can let go of all preconceptions of what prayer is supposed to be like or what God might say.

"This is still sounding vague to me," Yvonne says. "How do you hear God talk?"

I'm afraid it's different for different people. Many connect through this method of imaginative reading, reflecting, and then responding. Let's take an example: the story of the Good Samaritan. Where is it, Bible-Man?

Jeremy shakes his head, smiling. "Luke, chapter ten," he says.

Yes, let's open our Bibles to Luke 10:29-37. Now if I were teaching this text in a New Testament class, I would begin with the background material: Who were the Samaritans? What was their relationship to the Jews of Jesus' time? What is the point of the text within the context of Luke's gospel? I might even note that the priest and the Levite avoid a man lying on the side of the road, not because they're irresponsible and selfish, but because they're following Jewish Law: they are Temple officials, and the Law says that they must remain ritually pure to perform the sacred rites, which they couldn't do if they touched a bleeding or dead man. Then, within the restrictions laid out by this background information, I would ask the class what they think is the point of the passage.

The *lectio divina* provides me with a completely different experience of the Good Samaritan. In a quiet place I still the inner turmoil for a few minutes. Then I say a little prayer; usually I ask God for a clearing of my own stuff—the scholarly and the personal—so I can hear what God might want me to hear. Then I open the book and read just the first verse, 10:29. Actually, I stop after the first half of the first verse: "But wanting to justify himself . . . ." I don't worry about who the "himself" is, nor do I research any background information about the passage, about justification or Samaritans or ritual purity. I just sit with the words—"But wanting to justify himself"—and having read them, I try to empty my mind of everything but those words, not knowing at all what might happen next.

Sometimes, not always, unbidden thoughts begin to stir out of the silence:

Do I justify myself to others inappropriately? Have I been defensive lately in a relationship? Actually, I have. (I will spare you the details!) Why am I being so defensive with that person? Am I afraid?

And then I sense deep within myself something like a voice, though it's not a voice. It's an insight, and it comes from inside me but it is not of me. "Why be afraid? Why not trust?" it says. "Trust me to heal that relationship." And then, "Don't you think I can?" Oh, I respond, you can do anything. "Then trust me."

I sit in silence for a minute or two savoring what I have just "heard," and then, having read and reflected on that half verse, having perceived what might be the voice of God, I respond: Lord, I believe; help my unbelief. Help me to trust you.

Then I return to the text and read the next part of the verse and repeat the process. Or if the meditation on my misguided, defensive need for self-justification has gone on a while and now I have to get to work, I may end the prayer session right there, having read only five words.

That is how Christians have read Sacred Scripture for centuries. That is how they have engaged God in conversation. Trust me on this: if you take seriously the *lectio divina* (or centering prayer or any of a number of other styles of prayer), if you make an honest commitment to the discipline required to quiet down and enter onto this silent and solitary path, if you cultivate the necessary humility to allow God to lead the way, then God will come to meet you and will guide you into a new perception of the world. You'll begin to see life in new ways, and you will counterimagine one small part of the world.

A sudden gust of wind clamors through the trees around us like a meteorological exclamation point to my little speech.

"Message received," Yvonne says as the leaves quake above our heads.

"Not so fast," Marj says. "How do you know if the voice you hear is the voice of God?"

You don't know. Not unless you test it.

"How do you do that?" Jeremy asks.

Thad suggests, "As Jesus said, 'By their fruits you will know them.'"

Indeed. If the meditation bears fruit—in this case, if it turns out to be the first step in a healing process for me—then I believe God was speaking to me. The voice of God will only lead us to healing, integration, and wholeness.

"But there's a lot of room here for self-deception," Thad says, correctly. "What seems like healing now might later turn out to be just the opposite."

"Right," Marj says. "What if you're a conservative bishop and you decide to heal your community by excommunicating all the liberals?"

That's why even a bishop should have a spiritual guide, a mentor or director with whom to share his or her insights. A good spiritual director learns how to listen with you, staying out of the conversation but still asking the right questions to confirm the holiness of its course.

"I'm still not comfortable with this," Marj says. "We all know of people who have been misled by pastors or priests they trusted but who turned out to be anything but trustworthy."

Very true. Our mentors and guides must be tested as well. We do that as a community, as a Church. While it is true that even a large group can sometimes misread the voice of God, most Christians trust that when an earnest community comes together in honest prayer God will not allow them all to be deceived. Paul knows and shares this insight with the Corinthians. In 1 Corinthians 12–14 he exhorts them to test the many gifts they have received; you can probably guess the standard he suggests.

"I'll bet it has something to do with avoiding dissension," Marj says.

"It does," Jeremy says. "He tells them to use their gifts to build up the community. If what they say or do causes dissension, then that is not of the Spirit."

"I have another problem, though," Jeremy continues. "You said that when you pray you put aside all the information you know about the Bible, right?"

Usually, yes, when I'm praying alone.

"Then why do we have to know any of this stuff? Why learn about techniques of exegesis or archaeology or how a scholar reads a text if we can encounter God without it?"

"That is one excellent question," Yvonne says hopefully.

If our prayer life consists only of our own private prayer we don't need form criticism or rhetorical criticism or any of the other umbrellas of criticism—or the rocks—in order to enter a conversation with God. But is the life of Christian prayer limited to one's personal encounters with God? No, it is not!

The *lectio divina,* practiced alone, provides us with access to what we call "private revelation." Through private revelation God speaks to the individual about the concerns of that particular individual. The person need not be familiar with biblical scholarship in order to engage in this conversation. But as soon as that person believes that God has spoken a word for the community, that message has to be tested. And to discern what God is saying to a Church, that Church needs people familiar with some of the techniques and traditions of Christian biblical scholarship. If you don't know anything about how the Bible works in community you can't play your part in the discernment.

"But why does someone like me have to know these things?" Yvonne asks. "Why can't the Church trust the scholars to enlighten us?"

In the old days, perhaps, we could leave these weighty matters in the hands of scholars and pastors. The vast majority of such people were trustworthy and, if not always wise, at least well-intentioned. I believe that is still the case. However, Catholics in particular have a problem: where are all the priests, nuns, and brothers? By divine design or not, laypeople are being challenged to step up to the discernment plate and play their part in ways they have not done in a very long time.

"But I'm no theologian," Yvonne says. "Even after this journey I won't be qualified to test people's conversations with God."

"You sound like Jeremiah," the prophet's namesake says. "And Moses. And Gideon."

Jeremy is correct. Presented with God's call to minister to God's people, each of them demurs because he thinks he is unable or unworthy. How does Jeremiah put it when God attempts to commission him as a prophet?

"'Ah, Lord God, behold, I cannot speak,'" Jeremy quotes from memory. "'For I am a child.'"

Before God we *are* children, all of us, scholars and pastors too. But we are called as surely as Jeremiah was, called into this conversation, called not just for our own benefit but for the upbuilding of the Christian community, called to transformation, called to counterimagine the world. Called not alone but into community.

"Calm down, dear," Yvonne says as she reaches over to pat my hand. "You're getting all excited."

I admit I do get excited about these things.

"Well, why not?" Thad asks. "Isn't passion the point of this leg of our journey?"

For Reflection and Further Discussion

A lot of questions about the Song of Songs must remain unanswered on this journey. Care to consider a few?

1. Does this chapter shed any light on why Rabbi Akiba thought so highly of the Song of Songs?

2. With its graphic depiction of human sexuality, what do you think the Song might tell us today about love? About the significance of sexual expression?

3. Read the last chapter of the Song, in particular 8:6, which counsels that "love is strong as death." As Diane Bergant points out, "We all know that there is no force on earth that can withstand the power of death. . . . Death has the final word. If love is strong as death, then it must possess comparable strength and fierceness." What do you make of this observation? What do you think the text is saying about love, human or divine?

Chapter Twenty-Three

In Praise of Christian Flesh

Come in! Come in!

As my four guests enter, the feline terror twins David and Jonathan bounce down the stairs to sniff the intruders for extra-domestic evidence of life in the outer territories. Their inspection completed, they tear off in a raucous whirl of howling across the room up onto the wood stove (cold, as it is late summer), sending a votive candleholder with a crash to the floor. They streak past Jeremy, who, as usual, recoils ("I still think they are evil") as they thump back up the stairs to compare results in the privacy of the bedroom.

We approach the end of our time together, and I have invited my friends to dinner. A fractured wisp of song echoes from the kitchen. It sounds like: "I dreamed I saw [mumble . . . mumble] Hill last night . . . ." A pot falls out of a cabinet and bangs onto the floor. ". . . alive as you and me."

"Who is that?" Yvonne asks.

My friend Chemise in town from San Francisco.

"What is it she's singing?" Yvonne asks. "It sounds familiar."

It's an old labor song. Joan Baez sang it.

"Who's Joan Baez?" Thad asks.

Yvonne and I ignore the question although (because?) we are old enough to answer it.

Thad persists. "Did she just say 'Paul Hill'?"

"I think it's about Joe Hill, not Paul Hill," Marj says.

"You have a friend named Chemise?" Yvonne wonders.

Chemise is her *nom de cuisine.* Her real name is Jane. Anyway, she has volunteered to cook for us on the condition that we leave her alone in the kitchen and do not attempt to interest her in our conversation. I am not making this up; she's a minister, and she's on vacation from religion.

Removing the Bible from a Christian's Hands

We get settled in the living room and begin with a citation from a book by Stanley Hauerwas entitled *Unleashing the Scripture:*

> Most North American Christians assume that they have a right, if not an obligation, to read the Bible. I challenge that assumption. No task is more important than for the Church to take the Bible out of the hands of individual Christians in North America.

"Who is this guy?" Thad asks.

"Some pagan, probably," Jeremy says. "A worshiper of Wicca or something."

Hauerwas is a highly regarded specialist in Christian ethics at the Duke University Divinity School, who was raised in the liberal Protestant tradition.

"I've never met a Protestant who wanted to keep the Bible out of the hands of the faithful," Jeremy says. "Weird."

Does this next quotation help?

> The Bible is not and should not be accessible to merely anyone, but rather it should only be made available to those who have undergone the hard discipline of existing as part of God's people.

"I get it," Thad says. "He doesn't think a person should read the Bible alone."

In his book Hauerwas does indeed challenge the independent reading of Scripture.

"But doesn't that deny everything we just talked about?" Yvonne asks. "The *lectio divina* and all?"

So it would appear, at least at first. But look again at what Hauerwas says. What do you think he means by "the hard discipline of existing as a part of God's people"?

"Oh, I can answer that," Marj says. "He's talking about how difficult it is these days to be a part of a Church. Especially if you're a woman or gay or—"

"I think he's talking about more than that," Thad says. "He's referring to the idea we talked about before: we test the validity of an individual's biblical interpretation by sharing it with the wider Christian community."

Hauerwas asserts, as we have, that there is no such thing as objective interpretation of Scripture. If anyone can interpret a biblical text in any way he or she wants to, with no one else checking or testing it, the power of Scripture can be subverted and used as a weapon against others. And this can lead to . . .

"To Paul Hill and his shotgun-toting Jesus," Marjorie says.

Hauerwas takes issue both with biblical critics on the left and literalist fundamentalists on the right. He claims that theirs is a "debate between friends who share many of the same assumptions."

"Now what could a fundamentalist share with one of your liberal scholar friends?" Jeremy asks.

Both groups assume that the individual interpreter is, in Hauerwas's words, "capable of discerning the meaning of the text apart from the consideration of the good ends of a community." As a result, both biblical critics and fundamentalists render the Church "incidental."

Jeremy makes a move to respond, but Yvonne cuts him off.

"I repeat," she says. "What does that say about the private revelation you talked about before?"

I doubt that Hauerwas would object to your reading the Bible alone to tap into a private conversation with God. Individual spirituality serves as the bedrock of any religious group's collective experience. Problems arise, though, when people assume that the sole point of the divine conversation is the well-being and instruction of the individual. Religion is then reduced to a concern, as someone once put it, "with the individual's need of peace, rest and joy in the midst of the storms and billows of life."

"But isn't that what religion is all about?" Yvonne asks.

Actually, no, it's not. And you know it's not.

"I do?" she asks.

It's Not About You

Yes, you do. You're Catholic, and to be Catholic or Orthodox or Lutheran or Presbyterian or Episcopalian or a member of any of the major Christian churches means that to a greater or lesser extent your religion is based not just in your individual piety but in the faith experience of a community of believers as well. This Christian thing—it's not just about you and God, right?

She nods.

Theologians like Stanley Hauerwas warn us of another danger: some people believe that what they hear in private must automatically be valid for everyone else too. In other words, they confuse private revelation (meant for them) with public revelation (meant for everyone in the community). God may speak to Thad in the quiet of his heart, whispering to him that it would be OK with the divine if he decided to study for the priesthood.

"Perish the thought!" Thad mumbles.

But if the conversation continues and Thad believes that God is telling him that Roman Catholic priests should be able to marry, he does not have the right to stand up at Mass the next Sunday and announce this change as God's will for all Catholics.

"But then you're not allowing God to speak to the whole community through one member," Marj says. "I thought you told us that we need to know all this stuff so that we can help to change the Church."

Let me clarify. God might well speak to Thad about the need for change in the Church's policy of clerical celibacy. But if God intends this message for the whole Church, Thad must submit his message to the mediation of the Church.

"So leaders decide," Thad says, "not me."

Not so fast. I suggested that you would submit your discernment to the mediation of the Church, not the leaders.

"There's a difference?" Thad asks.

"What is a Church? Any Church? If it's not just the building, what is it?"

"I don't understand the question."

"I do," Marj says. "A Church is a group of people."

"But there are leaders in a Church, right?" Thad asks.

In Christianity the leaders are members of the community who receive from that community the authority to preside over that community and over the community's discernment of what God is saying to the community as a whole.

"You sure do use the word 'community' a lot in that sentence," Thad says.

You caught that, eh? The community as a whole is what makes up a Church, and the community must participate in some way in validating major decisions.

"But . . . ," Jeremy begins and this time I cut him off.

I know, many people, especially Roman Catholics, don't perceive this discernment process happening in their churches. That may be the case, but we need to steer clear of this discussion because . . .

"Because it's not part of our journey," Marj says. "You always say that when the conversation starts to get controversial."

"Or really interesting," Yvonne adds.

It sounds as though you two are getting primed for your next journey, in which you move from the study of the Bible to an exploration of the nature of the Christian community. That *is* the logical next step for many people who read the Bible as a conversation partner; as you'll see, we will lay the foundations for that theological tour of duty before we rest. But for now . . .

"End of discussion," Thad says.

"You got that right!" Chemise has appeared at the door with a casserole dish. "Dinner is served," she announces.

Twilight in the Sanctuary of God

We are back in the college chapel at the time of the day when dusk shadows into night. The summer staff has gone home, and the peacefulness of the rural campus outside is undisturbed. We rest in the stillness of the large, darkening room.

"I love sitting in a church like this," Yvonne says. "You can almost feel the silence, feel God watching you."

"It's so peaceful," Marj says. "I come here sometimes to calm the cares of the day."

The quiet mystery of a sanctuary, a sacred space. Religious communities build temples, mosques, and shrines—all kinds of gathering places that enhance our sense of divine presence and bring us inner peace. But . . .

"Here we go," says Thad.

But we aren't at the peaceful end of our journey yet. We still have a few loose ends to tie together.

Jeremy stirs hopefully. "For one thing," he says, "we haven't talked much about Paul and 1 Corinthians. I'm still trying to figure out what freedmen have to do with anything else we've talked about."

"And although it may be part of the next journey, I do want to know more about what you mean by Church," Yvonne says. "I'm still wondering why I should make my kids go to Mass on Sunday."

We Crack Open a Metaphor

By a truly marvelous coincidence, those are exactly the things I want us to discuss. One would think I put the words in your mouths! Jeremy, get us started. How does Paul describe the Christian community in 1 Corinthians?

"He calls it the temple of God," Jeremy says. "In 1 Corinthians 3 . . . um, I forget the verses."

1 Corinthians 3:16-17. Good. What else does Paul say about the community? In particular, how does Paul describe the connection between the community and Christ?

"Well, later in the epistle he says that the community is like the body of Christ," Thad says.

By now all of us have reached for our Bibles and Yvonne has switched on a tiny shaft of light. Where does Paul say that?

"In 1 Corinthians 6:15," Thad says, and reads, "'Do you not know that your bodies are members of Christ?'"

Good. In this section of the letter Paul is denouncing fornication with prostitutes. He argues that such activity is unwise because our physical bodies are parts (that's what he means here by "members") of Christ's body, and it is wrong to unite Christ's body to the body of a prostitute. Now where else in the letter does he connect the community with Christ in this way?

"In the twelfth chapter," Jeremy says. "He has a whole section on the community and how it's like the body of Christ."

There! You said it again.

"What? What did I say?"

Twice you've said that Paul describes the community as being like the body of Christ. Is that what Paul writes? Look at the text.

They turn to 1 Corinthians 12, and the sound of flipping pages flutters through the dark silence of the chapel. How well a Bible teacher knows that willowy whisper of paper!

The rustling subsides and Yvonne speaks for all. "I'm clueless," she says.

Does Paul write that the community is like the body of Christ? *Like* the body of Christ?

"Oh, I get you," Thad says and looks up from his Bible, but the others still look puzzled. "1 Corinthians 12:27. Paul doesn't write that the community is *like* the body of Christ. The community *is* the body of Christ."

He reads the verse, "'Now you are the body of Christ and individually members of it.'"

"But does he mean that literally?" Thad asks.

I'm not sure I would go that far. In the third chapter, which Jeremy just cited, Paul uses the same language to characterize the community as a field, a building, and a temple. The community is not *like* each of these things; it *is* each of them.

"But it's still a metaphor," Thad says.

I wonder if the word "metaphor" captures it. Gustavo Gutierrez, the father of Latin American liberation theology, asserts that readers

> often regard this theology of the church as simply a beautiful metaphor. However, we must, shocking though this idea may be, see through to the realism that characterized the Pauline approach. He is speaking of the real body of Christ, which he looks upon as an extension of the incarnation.

Is Paul creating merely a beautiful metaphor in 1 Corinthians? He wasn't the first ancient writer to depict a group of people organically as a body. The image was already an established tool with which to describe the unity of political and social groups in Greco-Roman thought. But the way Paul uses it to describe a human community as a spiritual reality, that does appear to be unique. Hence the problem we moderns have in interpreting it.

"I have an idea," Yvonne says, sounding rather pleased with herself. "Maybe he's talking about a sacrament here."

Say more.

"Well, I'm thinking of the Eucharist," she says. "The wafer is bread, but it's also the real presence of Christ. Maybe Paul is saying that the community, made up of people, is the real presence of Christ."

He does seem to be making a connection like that. Some Christian thinkers have suggested that he is articulating a spiritual truth here about the mystical or eucharistic nature of the Church, but I find no evidence that Paul thought that way. Christians don't begin to describe the Church as a mystical reality until one or two centuries after his death; our understanding of Christ in the Eucharist is later still. Besides, to call this image mystical or sacramental doesn't do justice to the text.

"I see the problem," Marj says. "Look at 1 Corinthians 6. When he is talking about believers not joining their bodies to the bodies of prostitutes I don't think he's talking metaphorically."

John A. T. Robinson, author of an important book on the use of body imagery in the Pauline letters, agrees. He finds it "almost impossible to exaggerate the materialism and crudity of Paul's doctrine of the Church as literally now the resurrection *body* of Christ." But Robert Gundry, another influential writer on our subject, correctly points out that in 1 Corinthians 12 the physical doesn't define the nature of membership in the body of Christ. Look again at the passage. Paul's emphasis is upon people's gifts and talents, not their—or Christ's—actual physical attributes.

"It seems as though the image is more than a metaphor but less than literal," Thad says.

"What it really seems like is that it's getting late," Yvonne says. "My husband is not going to believe that I spent half the night in church. Now how do we get out of this mess? I know you have an idea."

Warts and All

Try this out for size: First of all, while the Greek word that Paul uses for body—*sōma*—does mean physical body, the ancients could also employ it to refer to the whole person, one's body *and* personality. Check?

"Check," Thad says.

What if Paul is using the word *sōma* to refer not only to the physical body but to the *presence* of Christ? What if through baptism the Christian becomes a new person, a new reality?

"Paul does make that claim in Galatians," Jeremy says.

Indeed he does. In Galatians 2:20 he proclaims: "I have been crucified with Christ; and it is no longer I who live, but Christ who lives in me. And the life I now live in the flesh I live by faith in the Son of God."

Paul doesn't become a physical replica of Jesus Christ; nevertheless, Christ is alive in him.

"And he extends this to all believers in Galatians 3:27-28," Jeremy says. "He writes, 'For as many of you as were baptized into Christ have put on Christ. There is neither Jew nor Greek, there is neither slave nor free, there is neither male nor female.'"

"I like that last part," Yvonne says.

"And he concludes with 'for you are all one in Christ Jesus.'"

It appears that in 1 Corinthians 12 Paul is fleshing out that insight.

"Ouch," Marj winces. "'Fleshing out' the body image."

Now pull back and recall what we know of the purpose of the letter. Paul is trying to articulate a new reality for the Christian community. By virtue of their baptism, they are different. They don't merely symbolize that new reality; they embody it. They quite literally put flesh on a new social reality, though as Gundry points out, what Paul has in mind is not just a mystical, physical union with Christ.

"Then what is it?" Thad asks.

Gundry suggests that the Corinthian body of Christ is an ethical reality, not just a physical one.

"But what does that mean?" Yvonne asks.

I take it to mean that the Corinthians, when they come together as Christians, are not just the physical presence of Christ in the world; they are Christ *for:* Christ for others, Christ for the world. As the body of Christ, the Corinthians live as Christ lived; they do what he did. In this context Pauline theologian Jerome Murphy-O'Connor focuses on the experience of loving one's neighbor. He says that in the act of loving, Paul and the Corinthians are Christ, since they "make present in the world the essence of Christ's being."

"So, by extension," Thad says, "when Christians come together today, we are the very presence of Christ in the world."

Yes.

"Warts and all?"

Warts and all. As far as we know, this is the first instance in which a Christian formulates the idea of the Church as the body of Christ. Paul recapitulates it briefly in Romans 12:4-5, and centuries of later Christians have developed and embellished it so that it has become, I suggest, the core of the Christian experience.

"So what about Corinth and the freedmen?" Jeremy asks.

"Freed*persons,*" Marj says.

"Yes, and those inscriptions?" Yvonne says.

What was the purpose of Paul's letter? What was the central problem he was addressing?

"He perceives dissension at Corinth," Marj says, "and he thinks that's a bad thing."

And what did we come up with as the probable cause for the dissension?

"The social climbing of freedpersons," Marj says.

Any further thoughts on why he's so upset?

"Dissension is a threat to unity," Jeremy says. "But the Corinthians can only be the body of Christ if they are united."

"Paul's so worried about dissension," Thad ventures, "because the very presence of Christ in the world is threatened by disunity."

Paul exhorts the Corinthians to discern who they are in a radically new way. He asks them to lay aside their primary socialization and participate in the Great Reversal made manifest in Jesus Christ.

"But why does he use body imagery?" Jeremy asks. "All this emphasis on the flesh! Why didn't he keep it more spiritual?"

Excellent question. For some reason, Paul spends an inordinate amount of his ink on matters that concern physical bodies. Think about it. He deals with incest (1 Cor 5:1-8), fornication (1 Cor 6:12-20), marriage and divorce (1 Corinthians 7), food and eating meat sacrificed to idols (1 Corinthians 8 and 10), and what happens to the body when we die (1 Corinthians 15). It may be the sheer volume of body problems that leads him to use such a crudely physical image. Or he might be avoiding spiritual imagery on purpose if, as some suspect, the Corinthians were proposing a Christian practice that Paul judged too heavily weighted in the direction of disembodied spirituality.

It's even possible that the freedpersons of Corinth were reacting negatively to the terminology of an earlier Pauline discourse on the community as the body/*sōma* of Christ. *Sōma* was one of the Greek words used to describe a slave, and it probably had very negative connotations for those who had been freed from bondage.

"Meet Fortunatus, my *sōma*," Marj says. "My lump of flesh. Yuch."

Given the rhetorical nature of letters, we'll never know for sure what Paul was thinking. What we do know is that the Corinthians played a critical role in the development of early Christian ecclesiology. Remember what that is?

"The study of the Church," Thad says.

Whatever was going on among them, the Corinthians pushed Paul's theological buttons and pushed them hard. They forced him to enunciate clearly and powerfully how he understood the connection between the risen Christ and those who followed him. Paul would have been no fan of modern rugged individuality; for him, it would destroy the unity of the community.

"Now I see why you quoted that curmudgeon Hauerwas," Thad says. "About taking the Bible out of the hands of individuals."

Hauerwas isn't the only theologian to get cranky about this stuff, but he's surely one of the more plain-spoken. Christian tradition is clear on this point: the Bible needs a community in order for the text to be interpreted validly as Sacred Scripture. Although he's not a Catholic, Hauerwas quotes with approval the documents of Vatican II, which, in his words, make it clear that "Scripture can be rightly interpreted only within the practice of a body of people constituted by the unity found in the Eucharist."

So, Yvonne, perhaps you begin to see why it is indeed important for your daughter, if she is a Christian, to go to Mass on Sunday. The community's worship is more than an opportunity to come together and sing and reflect quietly on what God has done for me personally or to ask God in the privacy of my heart for yet more favors. It's certainly more than a convenient way to avoid mortal sin and the resulting eternal damnation. When the community gathers, it is Christ in the world who gathers. Christ for the world. We are encountering here more than fond memories of a great teacher from long ago, more than a beautiful metaphor.

"I have to think about that," Yvonne says. "But now I have to go. Tomorrow is indeed Sunday, and one way or the other I have to get to Mass."

"Let's all go to Mass together tomorrow," Marj says, and we stare at her with surprise. "I know; I did tell you that it's been a while since I went. Quite a while. But I want to see what it's like now."

"Would that be OK?" Yvonne asks Jeremy, who shrugs and says it would be fine.

"Can we meet here for Mass tomorrow?" Thad asks.

We could, but I have a better idea. Summers are pretty slow at a college chapel, since most of the congregation have been run off the property until September. Meet me in the parking lot tomorrow morning at nine. I have a different church I want you to experience.

For Reflection and Further Discussion

1. Reflect further on the notion that the Bible must be read in community. What are the strengths and weaknesses of the arguments presented?

2. Do you think a person can be a Christian (note I didn't say "be Christian") alone?

3. Does your primary socialization understand the individual to be more important than a group in most situations? Is that a good thing or a bad thing? How so?

Chapter Twenty-Four

The Journey, Not the Arrival, Matters

"I will never understand how a person can eat a mushroom as if it were a hamburger," Jeremy says to Thad.

"Here," Marj says, "taste mine. Portobellos actually do have flavor."

"All I taste is mustard," he says. "And a bit of relish."

Yvonne shoves him good-naturedly.

"I always wondered what's in mushrooms that should make me want to eat them," Thad says. "Are they high in fiber or charged with extra vitamins?"

I think you are avoiding my question.

"What was the question again?" Thad asks.

I asked you what you thought about the church service we just attended.

"It wasn't like any Catholic Mass I ever went to before," Jeremy says. "It reminded me more of our Sunday services back home. They were really raising 'em up."

"Raising them up?" Thad looks perplexed.

"You know. Singing and shouting praise," Jeremy says. "We raise our hands and our hearts and our prayers to God."

"It wasn't much like Mass in our parish," Yvonne says.

How so?

"It seemed, well, a bit out of control, over the top," she says. "Are you sure it counts?"

We had worshiped at Our Lady of Good Counsel, a Roman Catholic parish community made up predominantly of African-American and His-panic families. We had been invited to join the congregation for donuts and coffee in the parish hall afterward, and now we were lunching at a deli-catessen downtown.

"I liked it," Marj says. "I liked the way everyone looked and sounded—and boy, did they sound!—like they wanted to be there."

"Yeah," Thad says. "I liked that, too. It was neat the way the families sat together and the parents let their kids squirm around and make noise."

"I liked the diversity," Yvonne says. "And did you see the couple in wheel-chairs?"

"Did you see those two guys holding hands during the prayers?" Marj asks Jeremy.

"Yeah, I saw it."

"So, what'd you think?"

"About what?"

"About them being in church?"

"I think," Jeremy says, "we're getting off the subject again."

"No fair!" Marj says, pointing to me. "That's his line."

"You gonna eat those onion rings?" Thad asks her with an ingratiating smile, and I seize the moment to put us back on track.

The Power of the Meal

Meals. Speak to me of meals and of sharing food. They look quizzically at me.

Well, I wonder if Thad would have asked Marj for her onion rings when we first began this journey?

"No, of course not," Thad says.

Why, then, do you ask her now? What's changed?

"We know each other now," he says.

So you've developed an attitude toward the food on Marjorie's plate be-cause of your increased knowledge of her as a person?

"Don't be silly," Marj says. "His comfort with my onion rings isn't the re-sult of rational knowledge of 'my person.' It's because we've been through so much together. Isn't it, Thaddeus?" She passes him her plate, and he forks a pile of fried rings onto his own.

"Why do I get the feeling that this isn't about sharing onion rings?" Yvonne says.

The point does have something to do with the sharing of a meal. When we first met at my house each of you ate from your own plate, and while you were polite with one another, you maintained a rather formal distance from one another. Now you freely challenge each other's thoughts, swat each other on the back of the head, steal food—

"Hey! I asked," Thad says. "This time."

—practically off of each other's fork. We've gotten to know one another through time passed together, traveling, talking, eating, drinking.

"Remember Yvonne and the Albanian waiter?" Thad says, and she shoots him the dark glance of death.

We have memories of time together; diverse though we are in our religious backgrounds, we now form a community of shared experience. As a result, when we gather, even in the dark corner of a linoleumed delicatessen, our meals constitute more than the consumption of food. They feed us more than calories, don't they?

"I see what you mean," Yvonne says. "My husband Paul and I insist on having the girls over every Sunday afternoon for dinner. At least once a week we need to be together around the table. After all, we're Italian!"

It's no coincidence, then, that meals are critically important to religion. To eat together is to bond. Imagine, if you can, finding our friend Paul Hill starving at your door on a day when you are in a particularly foul mood. You resist the impulse to throttle him in his weakness, but you draw the line at inviting him in. Instead, your better self hands him a sandwich and sends him off. Can he still be your enemy, as hated an enemy as he once was, after you feed him?

"I don't see how," Jeremy says. "The mere fact that you fed him means that you don't hate him."

Oh, I suspect that the human heart is complex enough to hold generosity and hatred together for a while. But even if you go no further, you have taken the first step on the road to reconciliation. If we pay attention to them, meals accomplish more than the feeding of our bellies; they change us. And so it is that worship around a table of food at church—for that is what an altar is, a table of food—transforms us.

"I can't say I felt any different about the people in church as a result of going to Mass with them," Thad says.

"Neither did I," Marj says. "But I wonder if I'd still say that if we went to church there for a couple of months."

"I actually did feel something shifting," Yvonne says. "But it was after church in the hall. The way everyone was so friendly, pouring us juice and coffee and all. I started to really feel welcome, almost at home."

That's precisely my point. When the Christian community comes together, here today in urban America or a couple of thousand years ago in Roman Corinth, the community's worship around the table is an invitation to be transformed, to enter a new reality.

"Going to church on a hot summer morning, even one as good as that one was, doesn't seem very transforming to me," Thad says.

It doesn't? Let me ask you this: What happens at a Catholic Mass when the priest and the congregation pray the Eucharistic Prayer, the prayer over the bread and wine?

"It becomes the body and blood of Christ," Yvonne says.

Does it? It still looks like bread and wine to me.

"Well . . . it is, but it's not," she hesitates, but then she rallies. "Wait a minute!" she says. "You're not going to deny the Real Presence, are you?"

"What real presence?" Jeremy asks.

Most Christians believe that Christ is truly present in the assembly when they gather for Eucharist; some, like Roman Catholics, believe that presence to be found in the actual bread and wine.

"Do you deny that?" Yvonne asks.

No, I'm not denying the real presence of Christ in the Eucharist. But why limit our sense of the real presence of Christ to the elements of bread and wine? Think a minute. What's the point of having Christ incarnated in bread and wine? Why doesn't God transubstantiate the candles or the incense into Christ? Wouldn't it make more sense to have Christ incarnated in a statue that we could worship throughout the rest of the week?

"But you can't eat a statue," Yvonne says.

So what? Why do you have to consume the divine?

"To become one with it?" Marj asks.

Exactly. When Christians gather to worship, they don't hunker down to a festival of fond memory. They do remember, but they remember with a purpose: they recall that the body of Christ, which they are, is not a metaphor but a reality. The Eucharist is an invitation to participate in the body of Christ. Eucharist is timeless, the way a sacred text is. When we participate in it, we are not remembering the supper of the Lord. No, we're there in the upper room with Christ. "This is my body," proclaims the priest who stands in for Christ and the whole congregation, not "This *was* my body." We eat of the bread and drink of the wine, and we are one with Christ. And not merely symbolically. We *are* the body of Christ. We *are* Christ for the world. The Eucharist is food for the journey for the Christian; the Eucharist is unity with Christ, but it is also our commissioning.

We are Christ for the world. Christ for others. Christ for the common good, not just for our own. This is the absolute culmination of Bible-centered Christianity.

An Yvonnian Objection

"I don't think there are ten people in my church at home who would know what you're talking about," Yvonne says. "I certainly wouldn't have before this adventure of ours."

"I wonder," Thad says, "if it's because of their—our—primary socialization."

"How so?" Marj asks.

"Are we really that different from the status-driven freed slaves of Corinth?" Thad asks, and when I move to object, "Oh, I know," he adds.

"Two different social constructions. And we shouldn't overstate similarities between ourselves and people who lived two thousand years ago. But hear me out."

I back down and he continues.

"Our primary socialization is to succeed as individuals, a lot like theirs . . . but that's not my point. The freed men and women of Corinth resisted Paul's call to secondary socialization because they were too concerned about their own or their family's situation and not enough concerned about others."

"So how is that different from today?" Jeremy asks.

"I guess it isn't," Thad says.

"But aren't you confusing their situation with our own?" Marj says. "Two social constructions. Remember?"

"Maybe the Bible transcends social construction," Jeremy says.

Maybe we're experiencing the timelessness of sacred texts, the way they speak to every age in its own situation and in its own language.

"How's this?" Thad asks. "The situation of the Corinthians and Paul acts as a 'heads up' to us today."

"Yeah," Jeremy says. "The Bible tells us to wake up and look around at the sewer this country has become."

"That's a bit too abstract for me," Marj says, staring at her food. "And maybe a bit too colorful. But I like what Thad is saying. The text is a wake-up call for us to see ourselves . . . ."

"That's it!" Thad interrupts. "We've already seen that the Bible invites us to enter the world of the text."

"That's what I was going to propose," Marj says, "if given half a chance."

"Sorry," Thad says. "Anyone want a cold onion ring?"

Return to Paul and his articulation of the Great Reversal. He goes to Corinth and specifically to the freedpersons of the city because, as he puts it, God chose the weak. God didn't choose the weak in order to make them strong, but to give witness *to* the strong. How does he put it, Jeremy?

"'And base things of the world, and things which are despised, hath God chosen.'" He is quoting the King James version of 1 Corinthians 1:28. "'Yea, and things which are not, to bring to nought things that are.'"

God chose the lowly and the despised of the Roman world in order to, in the words of the New Revised Standard Version, "reduce to nothing things that are." Why? Why does God call forth this reversal? Look at the text.

"That no flesh shall glory in God's presence," Jeremy says.

"Paul is saying that the people who appear to be the weak and the lowly have a job to do," Marj says.

"Their job," says Jeremy, "is to give witness to the powerful. To tell them the truth, the way things really are."

"To *show* them the truth, not just talk about it," Thad says. "To live the truth."

"So what is all this truth, anyway?" Yvonne asks.

"I think I see it," Thad says. "To live the truth is to live as a member of the body of Christ, right?"

"The despised freed slaves of Corinth are to enflesh the presence of Christ for Corinth," Marj says. "You told us that."

Yes I did.

"And they're a wake-up call to us," Jeremy says. "They tell us that we have to be the body of Christ for the current age. Even if this is Catholic theology, I think I like it."

Actually, it isn't exclusively Catholic. It's Christian biblical interpretation, and that's probably why Jeremy approves. Although our circumstances are very different from those of the past, we are called no less than the freed-persons of Corinth to challenge a culture that worships status and security and denigrates those who do not measure up. We Christians must join Christ at the margins of modern society, just as Paul enjoins the Corinthians to join him at the margins of Roman society. We will find Christ among the messi-ness of the poor, in tenements, in *barrios,* in nursing homes, in the charity wards of hospitals, on rural farms, in soup kitchens and settlement houses.

"So the poor are defined economically?" Thad asks.

For the biblically Christian the poor constitute anyone who has migrated, or been shoved, to the margins of the dominant society, anyone who is op-pressed by others.

"So lesbians and gay people are the poor?" Thad asks. "Even if they don't have AIDS?"

To the degree that they are discriminated against, yes.

"But they're different," Jeremy says. "They're not the poor. They're sinners."

"They are not," Thad says.

"I think the point is irrelevant," Yvonne says, and we look at this some-what traditional matron with surprise. "Whether they're sinners or not, they *are* looked down upon in this culture, and if that's the case, then they're on the margins."

But Christ wouldn't consort with sinners, would he? I look to Jeremy and he offers a wan smile.

"Point made," he says. "Christ spent a lot of time with sinners."

A lot?

"OK, OK," he says. "He probably spent most of his time with people that his culture considered sinners."

And so must we. Paul and the Corinthians remind us that we are the body of Christ with and *for* the very people the primary cultural socializa-tion rejects.

"And for the rich, too, right?" Marj says.

And yes, for the rich. And even for those people who push people to the margins. Paul challenges us to "reduce to nothing things that are, so that no one might boast of the presence of God."

"Yeah," Thad says. "The rich? Off 'em."

"Somehow," Marj says, "I don't think that's what Paul had in mind."

We Field More Objections

"I agree with Jeremy: I like what you're saying," Yvonne says. "But what can I do in the face of all the suffering in the world?"

"I was thinking the same thing," Thad says.

"Who was it that said it's better to light one candle than curse the darkness?" Marj asks.

"I don't know," Thad says. "But anyone can do that."

"And I would hope anyone and everyone would," Marj says.

"But is Christian service different?" Thad asks her. "If so, how? And if not, how is my service going to make Christ manifest to the world?"

What is Paul's solution?

"Does he address any of this?" Thad asks.

To be honest, I don't think that Paul thinks the way you two do. He does exhort the Corinthians to pay attention to how they comport themselves as individuals, but such exhortation is usually made in the context of the behavior of the community as a whole. I could be wrong here, but I think he wants the community as a whole to be present to Corinth as the body of Christ.

"But even if we're supposed to be the body of Christ as a group," Yvonne objects, "how am I as an individual going to relate to the poor? I'm a white, female, middle-class data processor. I mean, now, let's be real. How am I going to relate to a gay guy with AIDS? I don't even know any gay people."

"Or so you think," Thad says.

"You know what I mean," she responds. "Not in a million years and with all of the best of intentions would I be able to go to a soup kitchen regularly and weed out the day-old donuts with the bugs in them."

"You saw that too," Marj says of our coffee hour after church.

"You ate a donut, though," Thad says. "I saw you."

"Of course I did," Yvonne replies. "I didn't want to be rude. But I couldn't do that every week. I couldn't live that way."

"I'll bet you could if you tried," Thad says.

"But I don't *want* to try," she says. "Does that make me a bad Christian?"

Again, look at 1 Corinthians. Each individual is a part of Christ's body and brings to the community a gift. And not all gifts are the same. Thad can work with people with AIDS, Jeremy can serve in a soup kitchen, and Yvonne can do something else, perhaps helping inner-city kids learn how to use a computer. You could do that, couldn't you?

"Yes, I suppose so," she says.

"Or you could teach them how to paint those rocks you paint for Christmas," Marj says. "You have a gift, you know."

Yvonne has many gifts. Each of us does. Paul and the Corinthians invite us to recognize our gifts and place them at the disposal of the poor and the marginalized. If we do that and we do it together as a community, then we are revealing the power of the body of Christ to and for the world.

Jeremy has been listening quietly but now he speaks up.

"My church has been doing outreach ministry for years," he says. "But we've made very little progress."

I'm not surprised. As we've said before, people in our culture have been socialized primarily in the direction of individual success here and now.

"But is it realistic to think that we can change that reality?" Jeremy asks. "How do we get a group to change its primary socialization?"

You know the answer, Jeremy: with the Bible.

Recall the words of Paul Achtemeier: Scripture "has the ability to *author* reality, that is, to create a certain identity previously nonexistent in those who hear its witness." This is the source and the effect of the Bible's authority; it has the power to create and shape a vision of reality quite different from what Achtemeier terms "the dominant ethos of the surrounding culture."

"That's the call to counterimagine the world," Thad says.

"I like that idea in theory," Marj says. "But what does it mean in practice? How would it feel for the Bible to create a new reality for me?"

Good question. To answer it, check your comfort level.

"What do you mean?" she asks.

Is the effect of your religious experience to make you feel comfortable with yourself and your life?

"Of course my religion makes me feel comfortable," Yvonne says. "That's the point, isn't it?"

Is it? Was Paul challenging the freedpersons of Corinth to inhabit their collective comfort zone?

"Wasn't that the point of reading the Song of Songs?" Yvonne asks. "To discover that we can all relax, since God is drunk with love for us?"

Yes, but that is why we also looked at 1 Corinthians. Paul's letter is a clear reminder that Scripture doesn't merely console Christians and confirm our human experience; Scripture confronts us as much as it validates us.

"So Christianity's got to hurt for it to be real?" Thad asks.

No, but to be real it has to be about more than your own comfortable, meaningful life.

The Bible is our memory, and if we remember who we are as a people we will not retire to the den in comfort. We Christians have as a Church forgotten who we are. Leander Keck puts it right out there. Amnesiac Christians—and he includes himself in this—

> turn Christianity into a pagan Jesus-cult designed to fulfill our wants; we make of God the patron of the status quo, and turn our backs on the world of nature in order to cultivate a self-serving spontaneity.

In other words, we look for the god we expect to find. We want a god that we can manage, the one *we* create and who validates us, our class, our nation, our Church. Thus, Keck claims, we have a god who "stands for what we already are or want to be" and we create an idol.

"We've talked about this before," Thad says.

Indeed we have. A number of commentators have proposed that one of the effects of Corinthian boasting as Paul saw it was to objectify and transform God into a manageable reality. That is the crux of Paul's problem in 1 Corinthians 1:22-25, in which he denounces the folly of human wisdom. Remember? Greeks seek wisdom, he says, and Jews demand signs. A number of years ago Hans Conzelmann correctly saw Paul's problem here: both Gentile and Jew expect God to submit to human scrutiny and fit into predetermined human categories. Let God be God! And if you do, God will do what God intends, not necessarily what you or I or a priest or a pastor or a pope wants. God will not be limited by our limited view of things.

Keck declares that Scripture unmasks our self-deception, speaking as it does of a God "with an identity of his own, and a freedom of his own, by which he uncovers our illusions and our idolatry." To recover a biblical vision of reality must allow God to *uncover* us. God is not accountable to us, but we to God. And as we approach this God we cannot distance ourselves from our part in the sin of the world, the injustice. But as we approach this God we are called to an encounter with Christ, the One whom we find in the poor and the marginalized.

This is significant for our journey: Keck, who is about as plain-vanilla, mainstream Protestant as you can find in a theologian, lands in the same place as the radical Roman Catholic Latin American liberationists. God, he says, "calls us to perpetual reformation so that we might share in God's own mission of liberating the world from bondage to every kind of death that robs [hu]mankind of life."

Does this help answer your question, Marjorie? Can you imagine how it would feel to be invited into this new vision of reality?

"I think so," she says. "Though I'm not sure I want to go there."

Good answer! If these guys are right, an easy-fitting, conventional, and (dare I say it?) comfortable Christianity will take us only so far on the journey to God. When we look at the Bible, when we take it down from its pedestal and open it and read it, what we find is a series of texts shot through with a challenge to imagine a new reality. Scripture provides a glimpse, an invitation, really, to participate in what J. Louis Martyn (another mainstream theologian, no radical he) termed "God's liberating invasion of the cosmos."

"The cosmic invasion of the crucified God," Thad muses. "This is not Mom and Dad's garden variety, ole-time religion you're preaching here, sir."

"That's an understatement," Yvonne says.

"I have to think about this," Jeremy says.

We all do. For now, though, it's time to wind down this journey.

"I feel like we're still in the middle of it," Thad says.

I know. We still have loose ends everywhere. The exegesis of 1 Corinthians isn't complete. We didn't even mention a number of critical tools we might have used on the letter. We never did nail down anything for sure with respect to the Song of Songs.

"And ten minutes after I leave here," Yvonne says, "you can bet I won't remember what hermeneutics or eschatology or, what was it, stigmata, means."

Schismata.

"Whatever."

I warned you that this peregrination of ours would not lead us to final answers to all your questions. Your conversations have just begun. It's the journey, not the arrival, that will matter for you in the long run.

"Peregrination," Yvonne says. "There's another one. I think if I learned anything it's that I need to keep a dictionary around the house."

Let me close with a couple of questions:

Do you believe that God loves you, warts and all? Indeed, that God's drunk with love for you as we learned from talking about the Song of Songs?

Affirmative nods all around.

"I'm trying," Yvonne adds.

Do you believe that each of you is called by God to be a member of God's holy people?

Even Yvonne nods.

Do you believe in the truth of Paul's image of the Christian community as the body of Christ? That it's not just a metaphor but an articulation of our reality?

Yes, they do.

Do you believe that the purpose of the Christian community is to be Christ's real presence to the world?

Yes, they believe.

Do you believe this mission is critically important and cannot be put off until a more convenient time in your life or the life of the Church?

They agree.

So. You believe that God loves you and calls you to be a member of the Christian community, which is the body of Christ for the world. Good.

Last question:

If you are not willing to put on Christ, if you are not willing to be Christ for the world, Christ for the poor and the marginalized, if you are not willing today to incarnate the Word of God . . . well, then, who will?

That is who we are.

Epilogue

"Die, spawn of Satan!" Jeremy swats a mosquito.

"They love you because you're so sweet," Jenn says, and she's met with the anticipated dark scowl.

They continue to push their way through the brush.

"Why couldn't we stay on the path?" Jeremy asks. "Where are we going, anyway?"

"Just follow me," Jenn says. "We're almost there."

They break through and enter a small clearing at the top of the hill. From here they view a panorama of rolling hills and green forest. They are not twenty miles from downtown Boston, but there is not a single sign of human habitation.

"I found this place a few months ago," Jenn says. "When you were away. I come here when I want to get back to a sense of the garden."

She leads him over to a large, smoothly rounded boulder and scrambles up onto it. "This is my Eden," she says as he joins her.

They sit for a moment in silence.

"You seem even grumpier than usual," she says. "Care to talk about it?"

He swats at another mosquito.

"Hey, beautiful," she coos, but he maintains radio silence; she decides to respect it.

"It's pretty," he says after a while, just as she expected he would if she let him alone. Her mother was right: men are so predictable. Now he'll open up.

"Do you think I treat our religion like an idol?" he asks her.

"What do you mean?"

"You know how I complain about the Catholics," he says. "The way they worship statues and the pope and all."

"I know how you complain about that," she says. "But I'm not sure it's true. What you say about Catholics, I mean."

Neither takes an eye off the horizon, where the late summer sun is in the process of making a fiery but somehow hazy and peaceful departure. It flattens as it approaches the horizon, as if it will bounce when it lands there.

"The prof said something that disturbed me," he says.

"He seems to have said many things that disturbed you."

Jeremy smiles for the first time this evening.

"Yeah, I know," he says. "But this was one of the last things. He quoted this guy, one of his scholar friends, I think. He said that Christians have to be careful not to turn their beliefs into a pagan cult of Jesus."

"What does *that* mean?"

"That we can turn God into an idol of our own making," Jeremy says. "That we can shape God into a god who meets our own needs."

"But God is there for our own needs," Jenn says.

"But this guy warns that some people's faith is nothing but self-serving spirituality."

Jenn takes his hand and is surprised when he doesn't resist. "I don't think your faith is self-serving, Jeremy," she says. "And it's certainly not idolatrous."

They lapse into silence again as a cool breeze comes up from the woods behind them.

"I'm reading this neat book," Jenn says. "You might like it."

"What's it called?"

"*A Big-Enough God,*" she says. "It's subtitled *A Feminist's Search for a Joyful Theology.* By Sara Maitland."

Jeremy turns to her. "Now why in hell," he says, "would you think that I would want to read a book on feminism?"

"Why in hell?" She turns and scans his eyes. His mood is lifting.

"Well, for one thing," she says, "she focuses on the joy more than on the feminism."

"A joyful feminist," he ponders. "Can there be such an animal?"

"It sounds as feasible to me as a cheerful fundamentalist," she says.

"So what does she say?"

"She says that the word *joy* comes from the Old French and Middle English word for *jewel,*" Jenn says. "And it's related to the modern French verb *jouer.*"

"Is that so, Ms. Language Major?" Jeremy says. "And what would *shoe-ay* mean?"

"J-O-U-E-R, *jouer,*" she says. "To play."

"So, joy is connected to play," he says and she nods. "But what does any of that have to do with God?"

"That's her point!" Jenn says. "She calls joy an 'ethical imperative.' It's our necessary response to the beauty of God's creation."

"Necessary response," he repeats.

"Joy is the gift of the Holy Spirit," Jenn says. "The gift the Spirit gives us to allow us into the game that God's playing."

"God is playing games?"

"He is, isn't he?" Jenn gestures to the darkening vista before them. "Look!" The evening star has glimmered into sight.

"She says that joy is the game played between God and all creation."

"Joy is a jewel and an admission ticket to the big game," Jeremy says.

"Here's how Sara Maitland puts it," Jenn says. "She says—I memorized this so I could tell you—she says, 'Joy is the game, the playing, between God and God's creation; it is the movement of delight and imagination and learning and power.'"

She squeezes his hand. "I love that quote," she says. "I love it!"

"Enough to memorize it, apparently."

"You are such a grump," she says, undaunted. "I'm getting a chill. Let's go back to the dorm."

They hop off the rock and enjoy a last look at the fire in the sky.

Joy can be a scary thing for the serious-minded, Jenn says to herself.

II

"Honey, hurry up!" Yvonne shouts. "You're gonna be late and your father's waiting."

"Commmmminnnnggg!"

The new morning sun turns a patch of one wall of the yellow kitchen into a radiant zone of light. The philodendron hanging in the corner seems to throb with color; can anything natural be that green?

Paula bursts into the kitchen like a gust of wind and stirs up the quiet. She takes the toaster tart her mother hands her.

"Paula, I wish . . ."

"Not now, Mom," her daughter says, and she gulps her orange juice. "I know you don't want me eating these things."

"That's not what I was going to say," her mother sighs.

Paula stops and Yvonne can feel her daughter center herself. It spooks her sometimes, the way Paula can focus immediately when she wants to. She envies her daughter's sheer force of will.

"Mom, I told you," Paula says. "I *will* go with you and Dad tomorrow."

"I know," Yvonne says as she wipes the counter without conviction.

"Momma, come here."

Yvonne complies and submits to an embrace from her much taller child.

"You know how happy I am now that you and Dad are spending so much time together," Paula says as she holds her. "And you know I believe in what you're doing down at the church."

"I know, honey."

"And—now hold still. I'm not done—and you know I'll help you on Sunday with the reading program now that my work schedule's changed. It sounds like it'll be a lot of fun."

"I know, honey."

"I'll bet some of those Haitian immigrants of yours can teach me something about voodoo," Paula says, but the attempt at humor does not have the intended effect.

"Oh, Momma, you know I'm still not going to Mass," Paula says with as much warmth as she can muster. "I'll meet you in the church hall afterward."

The jarring sound of a car's horn jolts them out of the moment.

"You're going to be late," Yvonne says and then adds, "I love you and I respect you, but . . ."

"I know, Mom."

"But I'm not giving up on you and the Catholic Church."

"You are *relentless*," her daughter says. She kisses her mother quickly on the forehead, takes up her bag, and heads out the door.

Yvonne doesn't move. She shrugs and savors the moment—the sun of early spring, the smell of coffee and slightly burned toast, the prospect of another day with Terri and her other friends at work.

She smiles, takes a deep breath. She checks the kitchen clock and looks over at the clutter in the sink. Suddenly she imagines the Blessed Mother here in her kitchen in twenty-first-century middle America doing the dishes. The Holy Mother of God, up to her elbows in a basin full of soapsuds, turns and gives her a broad, knowing smile. Kids, she seems to say.

"Relentless?" Yvonne murmurs to herself. "She thinks I'm relentless?"

There's still time for another cup of coffee and some quiet before she heads to the office.

"Paula, dear," she whispers, "you haven't seen anything yet."

III

Up against the wall! Yeah, that's right—you better pray. Pray to your Shotgun Jesus, baby, 'cause I'm about to take you out.

Whoof. Where'd that come from? It never ceased to surprise her, the strength of her feelings and the way doing laps seemed to force them out of her gut and into her brain.

Marjorie reaches the edge of the pool, touches it, pivots, and pushes off, resuming the butterfly.

She clears her mind and invites in a new thought, any new thought. A daydream. She's eager for something to surface so she can observe it, relish it, let it play itself out.

This is the best part of the day. Night, after work, is the best part of her day? She savors the freedom of mind and body when she's swimming. The body knows its paces so the mind can wander.

My own thing. My own body. Her body tingles with energy and fatigue; she's tired but not exhausted. It's the kind of tired that actually feels good. My own body. This is my body. This is my body of Christ.

Eating and talking together. Community. Been there. Done that. I need to do my own thing.

Tuck, pivot, push off.

She doesn't often admit it, even to herself, but she sort of misses going to church. The music, harmonizing with her sisters. The comfort of the familiar words of ritual, even if they were sexist. The feeling of being fed and feeding others. Communion.

She imagines a Eucharist she wouldn't mind attending. One that would bring her grace, not rage. Incense? Yes, incense and lots of candles. Touching. Embraces as we pray. No male priest. Zip! he's gone. Replaced by a woman in full vestments. White watered silk. The people standing around the imposingly sacred marble altar. Everyone pronouncing the holy words of the consecration together. This is my body. This is my blood. We all sing the responses in unison. A swelling of organ music and a truly great Great Amen.

Tuck, pivot, push.

The room. Too big. Zip. In a small back chapel, everyone together around a wooden altar, guided by their leader. Nah, no priest, not even a woman. Zippola. Gone.

Not in a chapel. No, they're back at John's place. The five of them together, a nucleus of a community. How would that be? Families and friends arrive with covered dishes and bottles of wine and crusty loaves. Chemise/Jane with a bowl of fruit fresh from California. All of us around that big pine square of a table. Jeremy and Jenn on the sofa with the cats. Thad and Mark on the floor, crossed legs and brawny, tanned shoulders poking out of tank tops, holding hands. John and Yvonne in the two wing-back chairs presiding. No, not presiding. They're the elders hosting the gathering.

The best part: I would finally be able to sing again.

IV

"You know, I don't normally approve of drinking with students," his professor says.

"Hey, it's my birthday," Thad says. "I'm twenty-one, this is my first legal beer, and I wanted to share it with someone special."

"The angels weep when a professor lets down his guard like this," the professor says. "Boundaries, my son. Boundaries."

They sit at a small round table before the fire at a rustic pub with upscale dinners at the southern edge of town. A dark stone hearth dominates a room lined with bookshelves and posters. The air smells of the wood smoke that foretells the coming of autumn and the approach of the cold.

"So," the professor says. "You came to me a year ago and asked me why you should care about all this religion stuff. You, a philosophy major."

"That's right," Thad says.

"Well?"

Thad deliberates for a moment. "I think," he says with customary slowness, "I still am asking that question."

A professorial eyebrow rises almost preternaturally up into the older man's generous forehead.

"It's not that I haven't learned anything," Thad says. "But I'm finding it hard to reconcile what I know, or what I think I know, philosophically and scientifically with what we talked about."

"You're a lot like me," says his elder. "The intellect gets in the way of our emotions and it short-circuits our access to the deeper realms of spiritual passion."

"I think you're right," Thad says.

"You know, you can make an honest living as a philosopher and at the same time be a disciple of the Risen Christ."

"But how?"

His teacher passes him a book. Thad turns it over in his hands.

"The Wisdom of the Desert," he reads. "By Thomas Merton."

"Turn to page fifty. There. Read paragraph seventy-two. Read it out loud."

Thad finds the page and begins.

> Abbot Lot came to Abbot Joseph and said, "Father, according as I am able, I keep my little rule, and my little fast, my prayer, meditation and contemplative silence; and according as I am able I strive to cleanse my heart of thoughts: now what more should I do? The elder rose up in reply and stretched out his hands to heaven, and his fingers became like ten lamps of fire. He said: Why not be totally changed into fire?"

He repeats the last line, "'Why not be totally changed into fire?'" and takes a sip of his Guinness.

They savor the words, and the fire sparks and crackles suddenly.

"Change into fire. I like it," Thad says. "But how?"

"Ah, my friend," his mentor says with a shake of his head. "You ask the best questions."

Notes, Citations, Suggestions for Further Reading

What follows is a listing of books and articles fit for the general reader. In the process of composition other more technical sources were consulted; however, I have only included such material when it became the object of direct citation. So, for instance, we must begin with the quotation by Annie Dillard that precedes the introduction, found in *For the Time Being* (New York: Random House, 1999) 88.

Chapter 1. The quotation from the *Boston Globe* is taken from Bill Kaczor, "Hill says he won't appeal and hopes to be executed," December 21, 1994.

Chapter 2. Sandra M. Schneiders introduces the distinction between reading the Bible for *information* and approaching it in anticipation of *transformation* in chapter one of *The Revelatory Text* (2nd ed. Collegeville: The Liturgical Press, 1999). David Robert Ord and Robert B. Coote discuss the difference between steno and tensive language on pp. 34–37 of *Is the Bible True?* (Maryknoll, N.Y.: Orbis, 1994).

Chapter 3. We made reference to Phyllis Trible's *Texts of Terror* (Minneapolis: Fortress, 1993). For more detail concerning how to begin the journey of biblical interpretation, see Gerard S. Sloyan's *So You Mean to Read the Bible!* (Collegeville: The Liturgical Press, 1992); parts one and two of *The Good Book: Reading the Bible with Mind and Heart,* by Peter Gomes (New York: William Morrow, 1996); Chapter Four in Robert R. Hann's *The Bible: An Owner's Manual* (New York: Paulist, 1983) 81–122; Gordon D. Fee and Douglas Stuart, *How to Read the Bible for All Its Worth* (Grand Rapids: Zondervan, 1982) for an evangelical Christian perspective. For the Roman

Catholic approach see Chapter Two of Raymond Brown's *The Critical Meaning of the Bible* (New York: Paulist, 1981) 23–44, and *Interpreting the Bible,* by James A. Fischer (New York: Paulist, 1996).

Chapter 4. Roland Murphy introduces the Song of Songs in his article on the book in *The Anchor Bible Dictionary* (New York: Doubleday, 1992) 6:150–55. Akiba's praise of the Song of Songs is found in *Mishnah Yadayim* 3:5, quoted here from the translation of Jacob Neusner, *The Mishnah: A New Translation* (New Haven: Yale University Press, 1988) 1127.

The Oxford Companion to the Bible (New York: Oxford University Press, 1993), edited by Bruce Metzger and Michael Coogan, is a clear and accessible reference work for our journey into the Song of Songs; consult it for more information on the Masoretic tradition, the Septuagint, or the languages of the Bible. *The Harper's Bible Commentary* (San Francisco: Harper & Row, 1988), edited by James L. Mays, is another reliable one-volume commentary on the Bible. Two important commentaries on the Song upon which we will rely throughout our journey are Marvin Pope's *The Song of Songs* (Garden City, N.Y.: Doubleday, 1977) and Roland Murphy's *The Song of Songs* (Minneapolis: Fortress, 1990).

Chapter 5. The work of Elisabeth Schüssler Fiorenza is an essential starting point when exploring the hermeneutics of suspicion. In addition to *In Memory of Her* (New York: Crossroad, 1983), see *Bread Not Stone* (Boston: Beacon, 1984) and *Discipleship of Equals* (New York: Crossroad, 1993). Two other collections of helpful essays are *Feminist Interpretation of the Bible* (Philadelphia: Westminster, 1985), edited by Letty M. Russell, and Adela Yarbro Collins's edition of *Feminist Perspectives on Biblical Scholarship* (Chico: Scholars, 1985).

Those interested in philology should consult Roland Murphy, *The Song of Songs,* 3–11 and 67–91, as well as his article on the Song in *The Interpreter's Dictionary of the Bible, Supplementary Volume* (New York: Abingdon, 1962) 836–39.

Phyllis Trible's reflections on the Song of Songs can be found in Chapter Five of her *God and the Rhetoric of Sexuality* (Philadelphia: Fortress, 1978). To learn more about the arguments concerning female authorship of the Song of Songs see *A Feminist Companion to the Song of Songs* (Sheffield: Sheffield Academic Press, 1993), edited by Athalya Brenner.

Chapter 6. The critical tools used in biblical interpretation are clearly presented in the essays found in *Hearing the New Testament: Strategies for Interpretation,* edited by Joel B. Green (Grand Rapids: Eerdmans, 1995); on pp. 197–221 James Bailey explores the role of literary criticism in his chapter on genre analysis. Also on form criticism see Edgar V. McKnight, *What Is*

Form Criticism? (Philadelphia: Fortress, 1969) and Gene M. Tucker, *Form Criticism of the Old Testament* (Philadelphia: Fortress, 1971).

Origen's thoughts on the Song may be found in the translation of R. P. Lawson's *Origen: The Song of Songs. Commentary and Homilies* (Westminster, Md.: Newman, 1957); see p. 205 for the citation in which Origen characterizes the Song as a drama. Rowan A. Greer provides a more recent but less complete translation of the prologue of the commentary in *Origen* (New York: Paulist, 1979) 217–44. Roland Murphy discusses Origen and others who suggest different genres of the Song in *The Song of Songs,* 16–21 and 57–60.

Marvin Pope discusses Arab *wasf* in *The Song of Songs,* 141–45. The nineteenth-century *wasf* we examined is found there. Marcia Falk discusses the poetry of the *wasf* in *Love Lyrics from the Bible* (Sheffield: Almond, 1982) 80–87. T. J. Meek writes about fertility cults and their resemblance to the Song in an essay, "The Song of Songs and the Fertility Cult," pp. 48–79 in *The Song of Songs. A Symposium* (Philadelphia: The [Philadelphia] Commercial Museum, 1924), edited by Wilfred H. Schoff et al. Samuel N. Kramer's thesis and the texts cited in this chapter are taken from his book *The Sacred Marriage Rite* (Bloomington, Ind.: Indiana University Press, 1969), particularly 85–106. Michael V. Fox analyzes Kramer's theories in *The Song of Songs and the Ancient Egyptian Love Songs* (Madison: University of Wisconsin Press, 1985), especially 240–43.

The quotation at the beginning of the chapter attributed to Akiba is taken from his midrash (or interpretation) of the Song, found in Murphy's *Song of Songs,* 6. The codified law and reflection of the early rabbis is available in a readable translation by Jacob Neusner, *The Mishnah.* Our reference to the rabbis' use of the Song of Songs as part of a vineyard festival may be found in *m. Taanit* 4:8 (Neusner 315–16).

Chapter 7. Those who want to dive more deeply into the questions we sidestepped in this chapter (structure and the intricacies of Hebrew poetry) can jump into the following:

On structure: Murphy, *The Song of Songs,* 62–67; Pope, *The Song of Songs,* 40–54. On Hebrew poetry the first stop must be Robert Alter's *The Art of Biblical Poetry* (New York: Basic Books, 1985), particularly 185–203. See also Francis Landy's chapter on the Song of Songs, pp. 305–19 in *The Literary Guide to the Bible* (Cambridge, Mass.: Harvard University Press, 1987), edited by Robert Alter and Frank Kermode; and Adele Berlin's "Introduction to Hebrew Poetry," pp. 301–15 in *The New Interpreter's Bible* (Nashville: Abingdon, 1996).

Ilarion's letter to Alis is found in Bernard P. Grenfell and Arthur S. Hunt, eds., *The Oxyrhynchus Papyri* (London: Egypt Exploration Fund, 1904) 4:243–44 (= *POxy* 744). For an account of Grenfell and Hunt's discovery see E. G. Turner's *Greek Papyri: An Introduction* (Oxford: Clarendon Press, 1968) 26–31.

Biblical specialists who have examined ancient social constructions include Howard Clark Kee, *Knowing the Truth* (Minneapolis: Fortress, 1989); Bengt Holmberg, *Sociology and the New Testament* (Minneapolis: Fortress, 1990); and Bruce J. Malina, *The New Testament World: Insights from Cultural Anthropology* (Atlanta: John Knox, 1981) 51–52. Malina's books can be a difficult read but they are worth the effort; see in particular his series of essays, *The Social World of Jesus and the Gospels* (London and New York: Routledge, 1996).

Chapter 8. Brian Fagan ruminates on the mistaken romantic view of the work of archaeology in his introduction to *The Oxford Companion to Archaeology* (New York: Oxford University Press, 1996). Also helpful is Fagan's *Archaeology: A Brief Introduction* (4th ed. New York: HarperCollins, 1991); Bill McMillon's *The Archaeology Handbook: A Field Manual and Resource Guide* (New York: John Wiley and Sons, 1991); and Paul Bahn's *Archaeology: A Very Short Introduction* (New York and Oxford: Oxford University Press, 1996).

Popular introductions to archaeology and the Hebrew Bible include H. Darrell Lance's *The Old Testament and the Archaeologist* (Philadelphia: Fortress, 1981); Walter E. Rast's *Through the Ages in Palestinian Archaeology* (Philadelphia: Trinity Press International, 1992); *Archaeology of the Land of the Bible, 10,000–586 B.C.E.* (New York: Doubleday, 1990), by Amihai Mazar; and Raymond E. Brown's *Recent Discoveries and the Biblical World* (Wilmington: Michael Glazier, 1985).

Concerning archaeology and the New Testament see Graydon F. Snyder, *Ante Pacem: Archaeological Evidence of Church Life Before Constantine* (Macon, Ga.: Mercer University Press, 1985); Jack Finegan, *The Archaeology of the New Testament* (rev. ed. Princeton: Princeton University Press, 1992); and William H. C. Frend, *The Archaeology of Early Christianity* (Minneapolis: Fortress, 1996). I also recommend two periodicals of the Biblical Archaeology Society: *Biblical Archaeology Review* and *Bible Review.*

For theories about the conquest of Canaan see Norman K. Gottwald, *The Tribes of Yahweh* (Maryknoll, N.Y.: Orbis, 1979), particularly 191–227; John J. McDermott's *What Are They Saying About the Formation of Israel?* (New York: Paulist, 1998); and *The Bible's First History,* by Robert Coote and David Ord (Philadelphia: Fortress, 1989), whose comments on the historicity of Joshua may be found on p. 19.

Chapter 9. Sources we consulted on Egyptian love poetry include Michael V. Fox's *The Song of Songs and the Ancient Egyptian Love Songs* (Madison: University of Wisconsin Press, 1985), upon which we relied heavily in researching this chapter and from which the poetic excerpts have been taken (see pp. 10, 14, 19, and 23), and John Bradley White's *A Study of the Language of Love in the Song of Songs and Ancient Egyptian Love Poetry* (Missoula: Scholars, 1978). Fox provides a summary of his ideas as part of his article in the *Anchor Bible Dictionary,* "Egyptian Love Songs," 2:393–95.

Chapter 10. For material on the Egyptian love songs consult the book from which Jeremy quotes at the beginning of this chapter, *The Literature of Ancient Egypt* (New Haven: Yale University Press, 1972), edited by William Kelly Simpson. The texts denounced by Jeremy are found on pp. 297–300. Other authors consulted: Roland Murphy, *The Song of Songs,* 45–48 (the quotation from Rabbi Akiba is found on p. 13); Miriam Lichtheim, *Ancient Egyptian Literature: A Book of Readings* (Berkeley: University of California Press, 1976) 180–81; and Michael Fox's *The Song of Songs and the Ancient Egyptian Love Songs,* which once again provided us with translations of the poems, as well as a solid basis for our discussion, up to and including the references to Ezekiel, Isaiah, and Akiba, which he discusses on p. 249.

Chapter 11. For mainstream discussions about Jesus see Paula Fredriksen, *From Jesus to Christ* (New Haven: Yale University Press, 1988); Jaroslav Pelikan, *Jesus Through the Centuries* (New Haven: Yale University Press, 1985); Luke Timothy Johnson, *Living Jesus* (San Francisco: HarperSanFrancisco, 1998); Bart D. Ehrman, *Jesus, Apocalyptic Prophet of the New Millennium* (New York and Oxford: Oxford University Press, 1999); John P. Meier, *A Marginal Jew: Rethinking the Historical Jesus* (3 vols. to date; New York: Doubleday, 1991, 1994, 2001). For the adventurous reader: John Dominic Crossan, *Jesus: A Revolutionary Biography* (San Francisco: HarperSanFrancisco, 1994); Elisabeth Schüssler Fiorenza, *Jesus: Miriam's Child, Sophia's Prophet* (New York: Continuum, 1994); and Robert W. Funk, *Honest to Jesus* (San Francisco: HarperSanFrancisco, 1996). For a concise comparison of mainstream and more radical positions on aspects of the life of Jesus see the dialogue between Marcus J. Borg and N. T. Wright in their work *The Meaning of Jesus. Two Visions* (San Francisco: HarperSanFrancisco, 1999).

Bart D. Ehrman provides a clear introduction to questions about the origins of Christian Scripture in *The New Testament: A Historical Introduction to the Early Christian Writings* (New York: Oxford University Press, 2000), while Richard Horsley discusses the social context of Jesus' life in *Archaeology, History, and Society in Galilee* (Valley Forge, Pa.: Trinity Press International, 1996), and Carolyn Osiek does the same for the whole of the Scriptures in *What Are They Saying About the Social Setting of the New Testament?* (New York: Paulist, 1992).

Leonard Foley discusses the nature of gospel texts in his brief article "How the Gospels Were Written," edited by Jack Wintz and published by the St. Anthony Messenger Press as part of the series *Catholic Update* (n. d.).

Chapter 12. To learn more about Paul and his letters, turn first to a basic introduction to the New Testament. I recommend several: Stephen Harris, *The New Testament: A Student's Introduction* (3rd ed. Mountain View, Calif.: Mayfield, 1999) 236–47; Bart D. Ehrman provides a series of chapters on the life and thought of Paul in *The New Testament.* Helmut Koester discusses the way Paul traveled and set up his communities in his *Introduction to the New Testament* (Philadelphia: Fortress, 1982) 2:97–112. See also Richard S. Ascough's *What Are They Saying About the Formation of the Pauline Churches?* (New York: Paulist, 1998).

For more detailed information about the letters consult Joseph A. Fitzmyer's remarks on pp. 1329–1337 of *The New Jerome Biblical Commentary* (Englewood Cliffs, N.J.: Prentice-Hall, 1990), and Hans Dieter Betz in *The Anchor Bible Dictionary,* 5:186–201.

These books offer clear introductions to Paul's life and thought: Jerome Murphy-O'Connor, *Paul the Letter-Writer* (Collegeville: The Liturgical Press, 1995), and *Paul: A Critical Life* (New York: Oxford University Press, 1996); Joseph Fitzmyer, *Paul and His Theology* (Englewood Cliffs, N.J.: Prentice-Hall, 1988); Calvin Roetzel, *Paul: The Man and the Myth* (Minneapolis: Fortress, 1999); John L. White, *The Apostle of God* (Peabody, Mass.: Hendrickson, 1999); and Virginia Wiles, *Making Sense of Paul* (Peabody, Mass.: Hendrickson, 2000).

Chapter 13. Solid commentaries on 1 Corinthians include Hans Conzelmann, *1 Corinthians* (Philadelphia: Fortress, 1975); Gordon D. Fee, *The First Epistle to the Corinthians* (Grand Rapids: Eerdmans, 1987); Richard A. Horsley, *1 Corinthians* (Nashville: Abingdon, 1998); and Raymond F. Collins, *First Corinthians* (Collegeville: The Liturgical Press, 1999). See also Helmut Koester, *Introduction to the New Testament,* 2:97–145.

Three good books on ancient letters: William G. Doty, *Letters in Primitive Christianity* (Philadelphia: Fortress, 1973); Stanley K. Stowers, *Letter Writing in Greco-Roman Antiquity* (Philadelphia: Westminster, 1986); and John L. White, *Light From Ancient Letters* (Philadelphia: Fortress, 1986).

Chapter 14. Much of the discussion of Paul's use of rhetoric is adapted from my earlier, more technical work, found in chapter 3 of *A New Temple for Corinth* (New York: Peter Lang, 1997). To learn more about rhetorical criticism see Burton Mack, *Rhetoric and the New Testament* (Minneapolis: Fortress, 1990); George A. Kennedy, *New Testament Interpretation Through Rhetorical Criticism* (Chapel Hill: University of North Carolina Press, 1984); C. Clifton Black, "Rhetorical Criticism," 256–77 in Joel B. Green, ed., *Hearing the New Testament* (Grand Rapids: Eerdmans, 1995), and Patricia K. Tull, "Rhetorical Criticism and Intertextuality," in Stephen R. Haynes and Steven L. McKenzie, eds., *To Each Its Own Meaning* (Louisville: Westminster/John Knox, 1999) 156–80.

Several exegetes have applied rhetorical analysis to 1 Corinthians as a whole: Margaret M. Mitchell, *Paul and the Rhetoric of Reconciliation* (Louisville: Westminster/John Knox, 1993); Antoinette Clark Wire, *The Corinthian Women Prophets* (Minneapolis: Fortress, 1990); and Elisabeth Schüssler Fiorenza, "Rhetorical Situation and Historical Reconstruction in 1 Corinthians," *New Testament Studies* 33 (1987) 386–403.

The English translation of Terentianus's letter is taken from pp. 174–75 of John L. White's *Light from Ancient Letters;* the parentheses in the text are White's, the brackets mine. For the Greek original see Herbert C. Youtie and John G. Winter, eds., *Papyri and Ostraca from Karanis.* Michigan Papyri 2nd ser. 8 (Ann Arbor: University of Michigan Press, 1951) 54–58.

Chapter 15. The commentaries and other sources we consulted on factions and leaders at Corinth included Johannes Munck, *Paul and the Salvation of Mankind* (Atlanta: John Knox, 1959), particularly 136–39; Raymond F. Collins, *First Corinthians* (Collegeville: The Liturgical Press, 1999) 71–73 and 79–81; John C. Hurd, *The Origin of 1 Corinthians* (new ed. Macon, Ga.: Mercer University Press, 1983) 96–107. On Apollos see the work of Richard Horsley, especially "Wisdom of Word and Words of Wisdom in Corinth," in the *Catholic Biblical Quarterly* 39 (1977) 224–39, and L. D. Hurst, "Apollos" in *The Anchor Bible Dictionary* 1:301. Hans Dieter Betz provides information on Peter and Paul at Galatia in his *Galatians* (Philadelphia: Fortress, 1979).

For a more detailed analysis of the rhetorical issues in 1 Corinthians see Elisabeth Schüssler Fiorenza, *Rhetoric and Ethic* (Minneapolis: Fortress, 1999), especially 105–28. And last, Krister Stendahl proposes his minimalist light touch in *Final Account: Paul's Letter to the Romans* (Minneapolis: Fortress, 1995) 13 and 22.

Chapter 16. To visualize the sites of ancient Corinth described throughout this journey see the slide series *Archaeological Resources for New Testament Study,* edited by Helmut Koester and Holland Hendrix (Minneapolis and Philadelphia: Fortress Press and Trinity Press International, 1987, 1994). In the first volume Steven Friesen provides detailed analysis of many aspects of the Roman city, and I add to his observations found in a section of volume two.

For the latest in archaeological finds and analysis for Corinth consult *Hesperia,* the quarterly publication of the American School of Classical Studies at Athens. For further references and discussion of the scholarly approaches to Paul as a wisdom teacher see Wayne A. Meeks, *The First Urban Christians* (New Haven: Yale University Press, 1983) 82–83; Helmut Koester, *Ancient Christian Gospels* (Philadelphia: Trinity Press International, 1990) 55–62; and the appropriate sections of Margaret Mitchell's *Paul and the Rhetoric of Reconciliation.*

Chapter 17. Information concerning the excavations at Corinth has been in the process of publication for many years. The Julian basilica, original home to the statue of Augustus at Corinth, is described most fully in Saul Weinberg, *The Southeast Building, The Twin Basilicas, the Mosaic House. Corinth Excavations* 1/5 (Princeton: American School of Classical Studies at Athens, 1960). For a description and analysis of the statue see Franklin P. Johnson's *Sculpture* (vol. 9 in the same series, 1931) 31–33. The Babbius monument was published in 1951 by Robert Scranton in vol. 1/3 of the series, *Monuments in the Lower Agora and North of the Archaic Temple* (Princeton: American School of Classical Studies at Athens, 1951) 17–32. The Babbius inscription was published by Allen Brown West in *Latin Inscriptions 1896–1926,* vol. 8/2 (Princeton: American School of Classical Studies at Athens, 1931) 107–108, while the Erastus inscription and Commodus's long genealogy can be found in John Harvey Kent's companion volume, *The Inscriptions 1926–1950,* vol. 8/3 (Princeton: American School of Classical Studies at Athens, 1966) 99–100 and 52.

Our discussion about Augustus and power relationships comes from the treatment of Simon Price in *Rituals and Power* (Cambridge and New York: Cambridge University Press, 1984) and Paul Zanker's study, *The Power of Images in the Age of Augustus* (Ann Arbor: University of Michigan Press, 1988). For further discussion of ancient patronage and social systems see Richard Saller, *Personal Patronage Under the Early Empire* (Cambridge and New York: Cambridge University Press, 1982); Bruce Malina, *The Social World of Jesus and the Gospels* (London and New York: Routledge, 1996); Geza Alföldy, *The Social History of Rome* (Baltimore: John Hopkins University Press, 1988); Ramsey MacMullen, *Roman Social Relations* (New Haven: Yale University Press, 1974); and *Patronage in Ancient Society,* edited by Andrew Wallace-Hadrill (London and New York: Routledge, 1989).

To explore how the early Christians fit into this social world of patrons and clients see *Modelling Early Christianity,* edited by Philip F. Esler (London and New York: Routledge, 1995); Bruce W. Winter, *Seek the Welfare of the City* (Grand Rapids: Eerdmans, 1994); and David A. de Silva, *The Hope of Glory* (Collegeville: The Liturgical Press, 1999).

Macrobius related the story of Octavian and the loquacious ravens in his *Saturnalia* 2.4.29.

Chapter 18. On the situations of ancient slaves and freedpersons see the recent volume of essays, *Slavery in Text and Interpretation. Semeia* 83–84 (Atlanta: Society of Biblical Literature, 1998), edited by Allen D. Callahan, et al.; Keith R. Bradley, *Slaves and Masters in the Roman Empire* (New York: Oxford University Press, 1984) and his *Slavery and Society at Rome* (Cambridge and New York: Cambridge University Press, 1994); A. M. Duff,

Freedmen in the Early Roman Empire (Oxford: Clarendon Press, 1928); Keith Hopkins, *Conquerors and Slaves* (Cambridge and New York: Cambridge University Press, 1978); Susan Treggiari, *Roman Freedmen During the Late Republic* (Oxford: Clarendon Press, 1969).

For the social world of the first Christians see Gerd Theissen, *The Social Setting of Pauline Christianity* (Philadelphia: Fortress, 1982) and *Social Reality and the Early Christians* (Minneapolis: Fortress, 1992); Wayne A. Meeks, *The First Urban Christians;* Abraham J. Malherbe, *Social Aspects of Early Christianity* (2nd. ed. Philadelphia: Fortress, 1983); Ekkehard W. Stegemann and Wolfgang Stegemann, *The Jesus Movement* (Minneapolis: Fortress, 1999); and Justin J. Meggitt, *Paul, Poverty, and Survival* (Edinburgh: T & T Clark, 1998). Dale Martin provides a detailed study of Paul's use of slavery as a metaphor in *Slavery as Salvation* (New Haven: Yale University Press, 1990). Richard Horsley's statement about the "atomization" of individuals in Roman Corinth may be found in "1 Corinthians: A Case Study of Paul's Assembly as an Alternative Society" on p. 243 of *Paul and Empire,* a book of essays he edited in 1997 for Trinity Press International.

Last, the Corinthian freedpersons' inscriptions cited in this chapter were published and translated by John Harvey Kent in *The Inscriptions: 1926–1950,* 113, 100–101, and 34–35. I have on occasion slightly modified the word order of Kent's translation to make the correspondence with the original Latin more clear.

Chapter 19. For more about ancient practices and purposes of crucifixion see Martin Hengel, *Crucifixion* (Philadelphia: Fortress, 1977) and the first chapter of *The Crucifixion of Jesus* by Gerard S. Sloyan (Minneapolis: Fortress, 1995). Hans Dieter Betz discusses the cross as a visual image in his commentary *Galatians* (Philadelphia: Fortress, 1979) 131. The citations from Victor Paul Furnish are found on p. 68 of "Theology in 1 Corinthians," taken from David M. Hay, ed., *Pauline Theology II: 1 & 2 Corinthians.* (Minneapolis: Fortress, 1993). See also Furnish's *The Theology of the First Letter to the Corinthians* (Cambridge and New York: Cambridge University Press, 1999). Jerome H. Neyrey's "map of honorable persons" is discussed in his *Paul, In Other Words* (Louisville: Westminster/John Knox, 1990) 60–61.

Other sources for this chapter include Neil Elliott, "The Anti-Imperial Message of the Cross," in Richard A. Horsley, ed., *Paul and Empire* 167–83; Raymond Pickett, *The Cross in Corinth.* JSNT Supp. Series no. 143 (Sheffield: Sheffield Academic Press, 1997), especially 37–84; Peter Berger and Thomas Luckmann, *The Social Construction of Reality* (Garden City, N.Y.: Doubleday, 1967); Peter Lampe, "Theological Wisdom and the 'Word About the Cross,'" *Interpretation* 44 (1990) 117–31; and Hans Conzelmann, *1 Corinthians,* 47.

If you ever find yourself in need of information about the minutiae of ancient history, the best place to look is *The Oxford Classical Dictionary* (3rd. ed. New York and Oxford: Oxford University Press, 1996).

Chapter 20. For information about the rise of modern science and philosophy, and their effects on the practice and study of religion, begin with André Goddu, "Science and Religion," in *The Oxford Companion to the Bible,* 681–84. For our purposes a good introduction for the popular reader is Peter Gay's two-volume work: *The Enlightenment: An Interpretation* (New York: Knopf, 1966–1969). For samples of some of the primary texts of the period (Descartes, Kant, Rousseau, Hobbes, all the usual suspects), see Crane Brinton, ed., *The Portable Age of Reason Reader* (New York: Viking, 1956).

For two prominent religionists' reactions to Enlightenment thought see Huston Smith, *Why Religion Matters* (San Francisco: HarperSanFrancisco, 2001) and Walter Brueggemann, *Texts Under Negotiation* (Minneapolis: Fortress, 1993). Thad's quotation concerning the nature of objectivity as "an agreement of everyone in the room" comes from Brueggemann, p. 8. The quotation concerning the reversal of the role of the Bible and the world in human perception is taken from Brevard S. Childs, "Interpreting the Bible Amid Cultural Change," *Theology Today* 54 (1997) 201.

We also referred to John Burgess, *Why Scripture Matters* (Louisville: Westminster/John Knox, 1998), especially p. 47, and Paul Achtemeier's *Inspiration and Authority* (Peabody, Mass.: Hendrickson, 1999) 130–39. Sandra M. Schneiders presents a detailed exposition of the three worlds of a sacred text in *The Revelatory Text.* Fernando Segovia critiques the three umbrellas in *Decolonizing Biblical Studies: A View from the Margins* (Maryknoll, N.Y.: Orbis, 2000) 3–33.

Chapter 21. For Walter Brueggemann's contribution to our discussion see *Texts Under Negotiation,* 12–18, 20. John P. Burgess's insight concerning Scripture is taken from his article "Scripture as Sacramental Word," *Interpretation* 52 (1998) 382. Wilfred Cantwell Smith's comments derive from his article, "The Study of Religion and the Study of the Bible," found in Miriam Levering, ed., *Rethinking Scripture: Essays from a Comparative Perspective* (Albany: State University of New York Press, 1989) 18–28.

Chapter 22. For Paul Achtemeier's suggestions about the authority of Scripture see his *Inspiration and Authority,* 146–52. The thoughts of Wilfred Cantwell Smith can be found in his book *What Is Scripture?* (Minneapolis: Fortress, 1993) 17, 19, and 231. The quotations from Vatican II come from its *Dogmatic Constitution on Divine Revelation,* nos. 8 and 21, and the *Constitution on the Sacred Liturgy,* no. 7. These documents are available in a number of editions; see, for instance, Austin Flannery, ed., *Vatican Council*

II: The Conciliar and Post Conciliar Documents (Northport, N.Y.: Costello, 1975). The insights from the *Catechism of the Catholic Church* (New York: Doubleday, 1994) concerning the liveliness of Scripture may be found in section 108, also in several editions.

For a more detailed analysis of the allegorical approaches to the Song of Songs see Roland Murphy, *The Song of Songs,* 12–41. Diane Bergant discusses Song 8:6 in *Israel's Wisdom Literature: A Liberation-Critical Reading* (Minneapolis: Fortress, 1997) 139. The citation from Teresa of Avila is taken from *The Collected Works of St. Teresa of Avila,* translated by Kieran Kavanaugh and Otilio Rodriguez. 3 vols. (Washington: Institute of Carmelite Studies, 1980) 2:242, while John of the Cross's poem "Spiritual Canticle" is found in *The Poems of St. John of the Cross,* translated by John Frederick Nims (3rd ed. Chicago: University of Chicago Press, 1979) 3–17. For John's commentary on his poem see his *Spiritual Canticle,* translated and edited by E. Allison Peers (Garden City, N.Y.: Doubleday Image, 1961).

Michael Casey, a Cistercian monk, introduces the ways of Christian prayer in *Toward God: The Ancient Wisdom of Western Prayer* (Liguori, Mo.: Triumph Books, 1996). He focuses on the *lectio divina* in *Sacred Reading* (Liguori, Mo.: Triumph Books, 1996). Other introductions to this form of prayer include M. Basil Pennington's *Lectio Divina* (New York: Crossroad, 1998) and various works of Thomas Keating, particularly *Intimacy with God* (New York: Crossroad, 1994). For reflections on spiritual formation in Protestant traditions see M. Robert Mulholland, *Shaped by the Word* (Nashville: The Upper Room, 1985).

Chapter 23. Stanley Hauerwas's views are taken from *Unleashing the Scripture: Freeing the Bible from Captivity to America* (Nashville: Abingdon, 1993) 9, 15, 23, and 26; the citation from biblical scholar G. E. Wright (about the individual's need for peace, rest, and joy) is found on p. 26.

For more detailed discussion of the image of the community as the body of Christ see John A. T. Robinson, *The Body: A Study in Pauline Theology* (London: S.C.M. Press, 1952); on the "crudity" of the image, as he puts it, see p. 51. See also Robert Gundry, *Sōma in Biblical Theology* (Grand Rapids: Zondervan, 1987) 223–44, and Jerome Murphy-O'Connor, *Paul: A Critical Life* (New York: Oxford University Press, 1997) 203–205. Gustavo Gutiérrez discusses the metaphor (if we can still call it that) in *We Drink from Our Own Wells* (Maryknoll, N.Y.: Orbis, 1984), particularly 68–71. On the centrality of the issue of bodies and bodily control for the early Christians see Jerome H. Neyrey's *Paul, In Other Words,* 102–46, and Dale B. Martin's *The Corinthian Body* (New Haven: Yale University Press, 1995).

Chapter 24. Theological assistance in this chapter was found in the following: Paul J. Achtemeier, *Inspiration and Authority,* 144–52; Leander

Keck, "The Presence of God Through Scripture," *Lexington Theological Quarterly* 10.3 (1975) 10–18; Hans Conzelmann, *1 Corinthians,* 47; and J. Louis Martyn, "The Apocalyptic Gospel in Galatians," *Interpretation* 54 (2000) 255.

The theology of Eucharist played a big part in this chapter, and our conversation may have raised more questions than it answered. For a history of the Christian understanding of Eucharist see Josef Jungmann's *The Mass* (Collegeville: The Liturgical Press, 1976) and Edward J. Kilmartin, *The Eucharist in the West* (Collegeville: The Liturgical Press, 1998). For eucharistic theology turn to Tad Guzie, *Jesus and the Eucharist* (New York: Paulist, 1974); Nathan Mitchell, *Real Presence: The Work of Eucharist* (Chicago: Liturgy Training Publications, 1998); Robert Fabing, *Real Food: A Spirituality of the Eucharist* (New York: Paulist, 1994); and just about anything you can find by the very witty and wise Benedictine Aidan Kavanagh, particularly *Elements of Rite* (New York: Pueblo, 1982) and *On Liturgical Theology* (Collegeville: The Liturgical Press, 1987). For a third-world approach to Eucharist (one that is not too popular in the Vatican of late), see Tissa Balasuriya, *The Eucharist and Human Liberation* (Maryknoll, N.Y.: Orbis, 1977).

Epilogue. Sara Maitland's meditation on joy can be found in *A Big-Enough God* (New York: Henry Holt, 1995) 149–91. Abbott Joseph's fiery advice is taken from Thomas Merton's *Wisdom of the Desert* (New York: New Directions, 1960) 50.

Index

Jesus, 20, 21, 72, 107, 108, 109, 110, 111, 113, 119, 120, 121, 157, 173, 191, 201, 202, 206
John of the Cross, 236, 285
Josephus, 108
Joshua, 71, 72
Judaizers, 153, 155, 159
Julius Caesar, 164, 173
Junia, 4, 131

Keck, Leander, 213, 265, 285–86
klētos, 149
Koester, Helmut, 124, 280, 281
Kramer, Samuel N., 50, 51, 52, 54, 277

Lampe, Peter, 213, 283
lectio divina, 242–46, 248, 285
liberti/ae. See freedpersons
Lichtheim, Miriam, 99, 279
"Lillian", 136–37, 166
Luke, Gospel of, 118, 243–44

Macrobius, 173, 282
Maitland, Sarah, 270–71, 286
Malina, Bruce, 181, 278
Martyn, J. Louis, 266, 286
Meek, T. J., 50, 277
Merton, Thomas, 274, 286
Munck, Johannes, 154, 281
Murphy, Roland, 47, 86–87, 96, 236, 276, 277, 279, 285
Murphy-O'Connor, Jerome, 254, 280, 285
mystērion, 167, 168
myth, 12–14, 229–31

Nero, 69, 117, 147, 196
Neyrey, Jerome, 181, 211, 283, 285
Norris, Kathleen, 242

objectivity, 217–18, 248
Octavian, 173, 174, 282
Old Corinth, 105, 135, 157, 159, 167, 182, 187, 207
Ord, David R., 9, 71, 275, 278
ordination, of women, 65

Origen of Alexandria, 46, 47, 235–36, 277
Oxyrhynchus, 61, 66

pagan worship in Bible, 50
Palestine, 71, 86
Papyrus Beatty I, 78, 79
Papyrus Harris 500, 78, 80, 82, 85
patronage, 179–82, 188, 195
Paul, vii, 20, 38, 64, 106, 112–13, 117–25, 127–38, 141–46, 149–59, 167–71, 174, 179, 184–86, 196–98, 203–208, 209–14, 260
Peter, 196–98
Philippi, 44, 124, 142, 164
Philo, 207
Phoebe, 30, 131, 167
Pickett, Raymond, 213, 283
Pontius Pilate, 108, 109
Pope, Marvin, 49, 276, 277
positivism, 228
power, 174–79, 207
prayer, 241–46
primary socialization, 182, 208, 213, 231, 254, 260–61, 262, 264
Psalms, 15, 239–40

Ramesseum, 78
Ramses V, 79
rationality. *See* Enlightenment
redaction criticism, 58
Regilla, 181
rhetoric, 139–44, 167, 280–81
Robertson, Pat, 2
Robinson, John A. T., 253, 285
Romans, Letter to, 117, 124, 131, 167, 186, 254

Salinger, J. D., 224
Samuel, 15
schismata (dissension), 149, 152, 154, 254
Schneiders, Sandra, 224, 275, 284
Schüssler Fiorenza, Elisabeth, 39, 153, 158, 159, 276, 279, 281
Scorsese, Martin, 201